FUTSAL

FUTSAL

THE INDOOR GAME
THAT IS REVOLUTIONIZING
WORLD SOCCER

JAMIE FAHEY

MELVILLE HOUSE
BROOKLYN • LONDON

FUTSAL

First published in Great Britain in 2021 by Melville House UK
Copyright © 2021 Jamie Fahey

Melville House Publishing
46 John Street
Brooklyn, NY 11201

and

Melville House UK
Suite 2000
16/18 Woodford Road
London E7 0HA

mhpbooks.com @melvillehouse

ISBN: 978-1-61219-980-1
ISBN: 978-1-61219-981-8 (eBook)

Typesetting by Roland Codd

Printed in the United States of America

1 3 5 7 9 10 8 6 4 2

CONTENTS

FOREWORD

BY ROBERTO MARTÍNEZ

FUTSAL IS ESSENTIAL. I think it should be part of football development everywhere. I always had the influence of futsal due to my experiences growing up in Balaguer in Spain. As well as playing it as a boy on the street and in school, I used to follow the Liga Nacional de Fútbol Sala (LNFS) – a very competitive league in Spain, a fantastic sport in its own right. We all liked to follow it. While at Real Zaragoza, I used to go to watch games in packed stadiums with 10,000 people watching. It's an amazing game. I've always had this influence.

In any football programme in any country, players should be playing futsal, because you get to a point where the coach cannot make you any better technically. It's about repetition. There's no better game which gives you the amount of action and practice that futsal does. It's almost a micro-programme within football, to develop the player so quickly.

How? First, because the ball is smaller, it doesn't bounce, meaning the ball is always under your feet. You constantly have to adjust both feet, resulting in improved balance. Futsal gives you the opportunity to have many more touches, it's four-v-four plus the two keepers.

You learn very quickly the importance of the tactical understanding of playing with others and the synchronisation involved as a partnership in a two-v-two. It shows the importance of everything starting with the keeper. The keeper is the one who starts the first pass and the number four in futsal is the first defender. So it brings concepts like these from the modern game, and then even further – as it shows the goalkeeper can easily be the one in possession, making the extra player – there are many exercises where the keeper can become an extra player and you play a five v four. All players are forced to be able to make decisions and know how to defend and attack in one-v-one situations.

In Spain, I played futsal in school – like everyone does. Then, we would train three days a week with the football team and play a match on Saturday. For a young player, there is never too much football: it was Monday eleven-a-side, Tuesday futsal, Wednesday eleven-a-side, Thursday nothing, Friday a futsal match, Saturday eleven-a-side, Sunday a recovery day. This is THE best way of developing. Because it's competition. Because it's practice. Because you're testing yourself. And it's about the understanding of bringing aspects from the small court into big football. That makes a big difference. It's not a surprise why we've seen so many number tens from Spain coming to the British game since around 2007. You have had Santi Cazorla, Juan Mata, David Silva – footballers that weren't necessarily physically strong enough to win the 50-50 ball when young players, but who are exceptional at controlling the ball, finding a pass, in the timing of their play, the appreciation of space, when to receive the ball and turn.

This is something that gave Spain the trademark of possession football when they became the most successful squad, winning the three major tournaments in 2008, 2010 and 2012. It's not just about winning. It's about knowing how to win.

PREFACE TO NORTH AMERICAN EDITION

Kick-off is minutes away. The persistent breeze is no more than a decoy, the steady bluster of warm air proving every bit as deceptive as the artistic magicians about to adorn the glistening green canvas on a searing summer's day in Texas.

Vivid memories of the cooling rain shower outside the Dallas Cotton Bowl an hour ago have long since faded.

Inside the stadium, the temperature is on the rise.

It's Brazil versus the Netherlands. The samba elegance of Pelé against the totaalvoetbal of Cruyff. Rivellino versus Neeskens. Mário Zagallo versus Rinus Michels. This afternoon, in July 1994, it's Romário versus Bergkamp. A World Cup quarterfinal in front of 63,500 giddy souls, nakedly exposed in the roofless arena, and countless millions glued to televisions around the world.

"There he is," points Paddy O'Brien. "That's him…" My friend and fellow street footballing urchin from Liverpool stares excitedly beyond the two starting 11s emerging into the sunshine from the arena's innards.

It certainly looks like him, trailing along behind, with the substitutes. Ronaldo, we think he's called. We've read the stories, seen the pictures in the papers. He's the coming man—or gawky teenage boy—of Brazilian soccer.

In truth, we'd been hoping to see Ireland play Brazil. Our Liverpudlian-Irish roots run deep. But the Dutch made it instead. We're not complaining. Just desperate to witness the latest Brazilian prodigy take to the immaculate Cotton Bowl turf freshly laid for the first-ever FIFA men's football World Cup staged outside Europe or South America.

Brazil didn't need him. They triumphed 3–2. Romário stole the show, grabbing the opening goal then later joining Bebeto for the famous baby-cradling celebration in the corner of the ground from where we were fortunate enough to be applauding. The tournament climaxed eight days later with Brazil taking a historic fourth title.

But what's all this got to do with futsal?

It's about the story.

About a time, 1994, and a place—the United States—that capture the essential spirit of this book.

The Ronaldo moment is a personal snapshot.

A time-stamped sporting illustration of many details explored in these chapters: the surging influence on eleven-a-side soccer of futsal, freshly anointed as FIFA's small-sided game of choice in the early 1990s; the role of Brazil in the evolution of both sports; my reflections as a touring street soccer refugee from Liverpool; and of course, the vast potential for growth of futsal in the United States and elsewhere. Then and now.

Not only did Paddy and I watch the peak of one generation of futsal-formed Brazilians, the Romário era, give way to the awkward teenage embodiment of the next.

We also witnessed the second coming of US soccer, a decade after the North American Soccer League's top-dollar roller-coaster juggernaut—with the likes of Pelé, George Best, and Franz Beckenbauer on board—came to a juddering halt.

USA 94 gave birth to Major League Soccer, the league kicking off in 1996 after being a key plank of US Soccer's World Cup bid.

The US women's game was already on top of the world, the culmination of a quiet revolution by a charismatic coach called Anson Dorrance.

Born in Mumbai, India, Dorrance led the US national team to glory in the first women's World Cup in 1991, just six years after combining the role with his day job as resident talent-whisperer for the North Carolina college team, the Tar Heels.

Firing the players' motivation in what he calls his "competitive cauldron," Dorrance bred a generation schooled in the arts of high-pressing and robust one-versus-one excellence.

There was more to it though. "I've had my players play futsal forever," he told soccertoday.com in 2020, citing 1990s stars, such as Mia Hamm and Kristine Lilly, and their 21st-century counterparts Crystal Dunn and Tobin Heath, as players who became "masters of the ball" with the aid of regular jousts in the small-sided game. Another of Dorrance's Tar Heels stars, midfielder Allie Long, hails the calmness and creativity honed in futsal as her "secret weapon" in 11-a-side.

It's the key to the US women maintaining a "dynastic dominance" in global soccer, Dorrance says.

The men's game reached its own significant milestone just four years after my Dallas day in the sun.

September 18, 1998 was the day Ronaldo Fenômeno came of age, celebrating his 22nd birthday in Italy while shining at Inter Milan after tracing Romário's pathway from PSV in the Netherlands to Barcelona.

It's also the day the future of US soccer was born.

The day Mark and Kelley Pulisic—two former soccer stars at George Mason college in Virginia—bequeathed to the nation the boy hailed as "Captain America" two decades later for leading the US national team to the Qatar World Cup finals in 2022.

Christian Pulisic and Ronaldo share more than a birthday, however.

The story goes that Mark Pulisic, a prolific goal-scoring midfielder for Harrisburg Heat in the six-a-side indoor National Professional

Soccer League throughout the 1990s, vowed to expose young Christian to futsal while coaching the Detroit Ignition men's indoor team, such was his regard for the futsal-formed Brazilian ball masters in his squad.

The problem was there were no youth futsal leagues. So coach Pulisic set one up, giving seven-year-old Christian vital exposure to the sport renowned as an incubator—or a "competitive cauldron" perhaps—for creative high-speed wizardry.

Pulisic Jnr is not the only US soccer icon with a futsal story. As will be seen later, Landon Donovan recognises the value of the sport as a "game changer."

The United States boasts a long history of indoor soccer, dating back to the 19th century, when a New Jersey outfit hosted the visiting Western Ontario FA team in a six-a-side joust at Newark Skating Rink hailed by the Toronto Globe on December 7, 1885 as "one of the fastest, most exciting, as well as most novel games in the history of football." The peak came in the era of "human pinball"—with hockey-style side boards—of the six-a-side Major Indoor Soccer League from 1978 onwards, which eventually gave way to the NPSL, where Pulisic Snr shone.

The United States is far from alone in courting the more artistic five-a-side pursuit of futsal as a mass participation game to revive a lost culture of inclusive, child-led "pick-up" games to counter the corrosive rise of exclusive, over-coached "pay to play" models. US Soccer's bold mini-pitch initiative to build 1,000 outdoor courts by 2026 bears testimony to this fact.

But futsal is also a bona fide professional sport in its own right.

And nowhere is this more apparent than in Portugal, whose men's futsal team continued their startling progress (covered in a later chapter) to claim a first World Cup title in 2021 just a few months before retaining their UEFA Euros title in the Netherlands.

In retiring captain Ricardinho's swan-song tournament—"I have written a beautiful page of futsal history," he said later—Portugal deposed reigning champions Argentina in Lithuania.

Head coach Jorge Braz celebrated the rise "to the top of the mountain" by restating his pride in "creating our own players" after triumphing in the first futsal World Cup final without a single Brazil-born player involved.

The latest of those home-grown Portuguese stars, 20-year-old Zicky Té, served notice of his stark potential with a poacher's strike to equalize against Spain in a dramatic quarterfinal comeback. One of a powerful cohort from UEFA Champions League 2020/21 winners Sporting, Zicky moved to Lisbon from Guinea-Bissau aged six before rising through the futsal ranks after learning his game nous in the renowned Bafatá rink, a street playground named after a city in his birth country.

Ricardinho, another boy from the streets of Gondomar, near Porto, claimed the golden ball as MVP. Brazil's Ferrão topped the scoring charts, edging out Portugal's prolific winger Pany. The powerful Kazakhstan team, fired by Leo Higuita and the rest of their Brazil-born contingent, lost out on penalties in the semifinals to Portugal.

Other notable stories include the presence of the US national team, led by Serbian coach Dusan Jakica and former US national futsal team goalkeeper Otto Orf, after making the finals for the first time since 2008. Quarterfinalists Morocco and impressive first-timers Angola, two of Africa's three qualifiers along with Egypt, showed the bewitching potential for futsal in a continent of 1.2 billion people.

With Lionel Messi watching from afar, charting the Albiceleste's progress for his 315 million followers on Instagram, the matches burst open a pressure valve imposed on the indoor sport during 18 months of Covid-19 disruption.

Futsal was back. But what about its legacy?

The biggest stars in the women's game used the tournament to launch a campaign calling on FIFA to finally launch a women's futsal World Cup.

Zicky Té's ascent continued three months later, helping Portugal retain the UEFA Euros title—without Ricardinho, of course—this time scoring twice against Spain in yet another stirring comeback in the semi-finals in Amsterdam. The youngster also picked up the MVP accolade.

"It has been a work of many years," Braz told me in the aftermath of the final victory over Russia. The Portuguese federation set out to make futsal "the game of the schools" in a nation obsessed with 11-a-side football, he said, pursuing a "vision and mission" to grow futsal from youth level to the adult professional Liga Placard.

It's a mission other countries could do well to follow.

Canada-born Braz is well aware of the potential for futsal in North America. "The US is a country with a lot of population, sporting passion, excellent facilities, high sport development in so many sports, and most of all, connection between school, university and clubs," he explained. The huge challenge for the US Soccer federation is managing to "organize all the practice of futsal in such a huge country" with a long history of diverse forms of indoor soccer. "In Portugal, we took that step in 1997," he said, when the Portuguese federation included all variants of five-a-side under one set of rules as FIFA-sanctioned futsal.

The final World Cup legacy strand is futsal's influence on the eleven-a-side game.

The Technical Study Group—led by FIFA instructors Graeme Dell and Miguel Rodrigo—was unequivocal. Comparing data from all 52 games with football matches at the Arab Cup 2021, they analyzed every pass, dribble, interception, and goalkeeper involvement in and out of possession to conclude: "Futsal can contribute in a unique way to wider player development across the football family."

Although clearly a standalone sport in its own right, the report went on, the significant "transferable" skills from futsal to football—due to the much greater repetition of key technical actions and smaller playing area—were notable and in need of greater understanding.

That particular quest begins here.

INTRODUCTION

I BLAME A blurry vision of Pelé toying with a piece of fruit. Head, shoulders, knees and toes. Both feet. Relentless and repetitive. The memory stems from sepia-tinted footage of the great man himself – sporting the immaculate white Santos kit, performing keepy-uppies with a grapefruit as the voiceover on an early colour documentary lauds the dedicated artistry of Brazilian footballing finesse. A cinematic version came years later, in 1981, when the man who started life as a boy called Edson Arantes do Nascimento, growing up in poverty in São Paulo, also appeared in *Escape to Victory*, the hit Second World War movie starring Sylvester Stallone and a host of football legends. While effortlessly juggling a football in the dusty prisoner-of-war camp, Corporal Luis Fernandez (Pelé) responds to the fascinated English Captain John Colby (Michael Caine) by confiding in him how he learned his skills as a boy 'in Trinidad, in the streets, with the oranges'. That was it for me. Although Pelé had long since retired, Zico, Eder and Sócrates filled the void at the 1982 World Cup, sealing in the mind of football-mad kids like me a sense of wonder and mystique about the Brazilian way of mastering a ball. This was what the Brazilians did: dancing about entranced in a never-ending juggle-fest using up scraps of food – when they were not casually flicking balls about on the sun-drenched beaches of Rio de Janeiro, of course.

Many years later I discovered the words of Emilio Miranda, São Paulo University's esteemed professor of soccer, who described the true 'laboratory of improvisation' in Brazil. The *real* story was *futebol de salão*, it turns out. Or futsal, as it later became known. 'No time plus no space equals better skills,' explained the professor. *Futebol de salão* (Portuguese for hall/indoor football) originated in South America. Futsal is the contraction of the phrase and its equivalent European name, *fútbol sala* or *fútbol de salón* (Spanish for hall football).

This book came about after my own voyage of discovery in the five-a-side game. At first glance, futsal seems to be a shrunken version of football – but in fact it boasts many more layers, creativity-inducing restrictions and tactical complexities. It's a thinking player's game, originating as a sport heavily influenced by various other games, including basketball and handball. The book assesses the state of play within the sport, delving into its politics, history and global reach. I'll also attempt to discover the soul of the game via the thoughts of its biggest characters – including professional footballers with a futsal background. I've dedicated two chapters to figures who had a vital impact both on Everton (the club I support), and on my own thinking about sport: Wayne Rooney and Roberto Martínez. I also analyse the biggest skill transfers to the eleven-a-side game, and shed light on the intricacies of a small-sided sport that many football fans may have heard of, but precious few understand.

First, the basics: futsal is played with five players on each side, on a hard surface, usually indoors, and measuring anywhere from the size of a basketball court (twenty-eight metres by fifteen metres) to that of a handball court (forty metres by twenty metres). Traditionally there are four on-court players and one goalkeeper, using a small, dense ball, hockey-size goals (three metres by two metres), sidelines and end lines, with no restrictions on the height to which the ball can be played. There is no offside rule. Futsal is a bona fide professional sport in its own right, as well as a renowned 'laboratory' for intense, focused fun – fuelling the skill sets of the best eleven-a-side footballers the world has ever seen. But it's far from simply a reduced, micro version of eleven-a-side football.[1]

In 2021, futsal is governed by the overseer of eleven-a-side football, the Fédération Internationale de Football Association (FIFA), and is played by at least sixty million people worldwide, according to the most recent count in 2016, making up 20 per cent of the 300 million total for all forms of football. In the decade and a half after 2001, futsal's 100 per cent rise in participation – up from thirty million – made up more than half of the overall increase from 250 million. Brazil and the big Asian nations lead the way: an estimated sixteen million adults and children play the game in Iran, nearly 20 per cent of the eighty-four million population; in Brazil, where more people play futsal than football, the figure is thought to be ten to twelve million, or 5 per cent of the population. In England, where conventional five-a-side has dominated – with the bouncy football, wide letterbox goals and side boards instead of lines – participation in futsal has never gone beyond the levels of a passionate cult. Its reputation is growing, but more than a decade after starting its national league, the English FA recorded a little over 17,000 official players, with a generous estimate of those unaffiliated but dabbling in it thought to take the figure closer to 50,000. The eleven-a-side game's grip on England shows no sign of loosening.

Globally, the FIFA statistics reveal a different story entirely: in 2018 two-thirds of its 211 nations – 140 countries – had a male futsal team and fifty-five had a women's national side too. But FIFA's

---

1. Watching the sport at the highest level can help our appreciation of the skills and sheer intensity inherent in the game. There's an abundance of footage available to watch online – I recommend the 2016 World Cup final between Russia and Argentina as a fine starting point.

version is not the only form of futsal played. A rival global governing body, the Asociación Mundial de Futsal (AMF), acts as a successor organisation to the original governor of futsal, the Federación Internacional de Fútbol de Salón (FIFUSA), and makes bold claims about being more faithful to the original rules that evolved in South America in the decades before FIFA got involved in the 1980s. FIFA's game is massively more popular than the AMF version, but the failure to establish futsal as an Olympic sport by 2020 is seen as a barrier to further growth.

So what does futsal look like for its sixty million-plus players in 2021? It's a bit like football on amphetamines – an intense, juddering high fuelled by the game's potent cocktail of constraints. Five-v-five on a forty metre by twenty metre court equates to the same population density as 37-a-side on a standard-size adult football pitch (defined as one hundred and five metre by sixty-eight metre in the English Premier League). The ball is hugely important. Originally in South America it measured somewhere between a conventional size 2 and 3 football, whereas FIFA uses a slightly bigger size 4; all futsal balls are filled with foam, which kills the bounce (60 per cent less than a football), giving it a dense, heavy, tactile feel. Squad sizes are limited to fourteen in the adult game. Unlimited substitutions are allowed at any time. The use of sidelines rather than walls, as is common in some five- or six-a-side competitions around the world, is credited with honing the ball-retention and protection skills of the best players in the world.

The other factors driving futsal's skill development include the 'four-second rule', meaning that players taking set pieces – free kicks, kick-ins (instead of throw-ins) and corners – are limited to four seconds, a referee's countdown beginning when the player sets the ball down stationary,[2] while goalkeepers are also restricted to four seconds in possession when in their own half. They must also refrain from touching the ball after releasing it, unless in the opposition half, or if an opponent has made contact with it. At the competitive level, the clock stops when the ball – as in basketball – goes out of play, each game consisting of two twenty-minute halves with one timeout for each team per half. A five-foul limit applies to each team in a single half, meaning that every foul over and above the limit gives the opposition a ten metre spot kick, known as a 'long penalty' because it's taken from four metres further out than the standard penalty. This punishment acts as an effective deterrent to persistent brutality or tactical fouls. Futsal also has its own positions. While all on-court players defend and attack together, a little like basketball, the roles are clearly defined. Sitting in front of the goalkeeper is the main defender, the *fixo* (Portuguese) or *cierre* (Spanish for 'closer/ stopper'). In a conventional 3-1 formation, this player defaults to the centre of the back line. An *ala* (winger) occupies either side and a *pivô* (Portuguese) or *pivot* (Spanish) fills the role of primary attacker.[3] A versatile player is known in Spanish and Portuguese as a *universal*.

The signature technique of a futsal player, one of the many imported into eleven-a-side football by the biggest stars of the world game, is impeccable control of a rolling ball with the sole of the foot, an action as natural as breathing in futsal due to the game's high speed. Xavi Hernández, the exemplary Spain and Barcelona midfielder who grew up playing futsal in Catalonia, spoke for a twenty-first century generation of futsal-formed football stars around the world when he declared: 'In futsal, you see whether a player is really

---

2. In the AMF game, the limit is five seconds. Throw-ins are used instead of kick-ins. And teams are restricted to fifteen seconds to get the ball forward into the attacking half once possession is regained.

3. See diagram on p.285

talented. In normal football you don't necessarily identify talent as easily because it's so much more physical. But with futsal, you notice the small details in quality, class and tactical understanding.' The roll call of footballers eulogising about futsal is extensive, with the words of the twenty-first century's offering to the Greatest of All Time debate, Portugal's Cristiano Ronaldo and Argentina's Lionel Messi, the most often recited by futsal advocates pushing the creative impact of the sport.

The sheer intensity of the game became apparent once I dipped my toe in the water as a curious grassroots football coach in Reading, Berkshire, in 2008. With a bag of size 2 futsal balls and a court, I soon discovered futsal was, in many ways, the missing link in the English sporting and societal landscape – a void made ever more conspicuous by the increasing absence of street football in the twenty-first century. The UK is one of the many nations where the young generation's preference for playing FIFA on screen rather than on a pitch is compounded by the dearth of accessible areas to physically play.

The futsal story is set against the backdrop of my own journey from street footballer in the poverty-stricken streets of Liverpool in the 1970s and 80s, to semi-professional footballer and aspiring youth coach. A look back at my own childhood environment in Liverpool – at a time when both the city's clubs were at the top of their game – reveals strong links to five-a-side and informal street play. Liverpool FC's five-a-side obsession (credited with propelling them to European glory in the late 1970s) is the stuff of legend. Perhaps less well known is Everton's penchant for Brazilian-style head tennis under Howard Kendall, which I saw first-hand as a teenager at the Everton school of excellence. At 'grassroots' level in Liverpool, five-a-side was everywhere: on the streets, in youth clubs and parks – due especially to the unrivalled annual youth competition run by Merseyside Police throughout the era. As well as taking coaching qualifications in futsal (to complement my football UEFA B award) and coach mentoring (for the English FA) in football, my decade of exploration involved starting to play competitive amateur futsal at the age of forty. Quite simply, futsal offers the closest experience to my childhood street football buzz that I've ever encountered.

This informal street culture is more important in the twenty-first century than ever. Futsal is certainly one of the answers, but the question of how to provide a vital self-directed active experience for children is far from a novel one – and it is more psychological than might be expected. Back in 1961, the lifelong researchers into the culture of childhood, Peter and Iona Opie, could have been issuing a cry for futsal to be made compulsory when they bemoaned the loss of 'the art of self-entertainment' in England. In an article in the *Observer* newspaper, the married couple – who devoted their lives to chronicling the rhymes, rhythms and folklore of childhood – pined for the return of a bygone age when children lived free from adults dictating and supervising their street games. Whether futsal is a separate sport in its own right, or a footballing development tool (spoiler alert: it can be both), it's essentially a game of the streets that moved indoors. It deserves more attention as a sport of global significance simply because it's a hothouse of excitement, allowing players – from youngsters in the *favelas* of Rio de Janeiro to adult professionals in leagues from Murcia to Moscow – to do more of what acts as a siren call for millions of futsal fanatics: playing with a ball at their feet.

CHAPTER 1
MERSEY PARADISE

THE CITY OF Liverpool, a once-mighty port of global significance, was fast becoming a byword for economic and social decay by the time the new prime minister, Margaret Thatcher, took up residence in Downing Street on 4 May 1979. The Conservative leader eulogised about her mission to replace 'discord' with 'harmony', 'error' with 'truth' and 'despair' with 'hope'. For Liverpool, the despair, error and discord would only grow, in tune with the chaotic surge in unemployment and social stasis that came to define the city in the period between 1972 and 1982, during which it lost a staggering 80,000 jobs.[4] Unemployment soared, in keeping with the national picture, but throughout the 1970s and 1980s, Liverpool's male jobless rate veered between double and treble the national percentage. For youngsters, the prospects were worse. In parts of the city in 1980, one in two sixteen- to twenty-year-olds were on the dole.[5] By 1985, six years into what was later revealed by Thatcher's chancellor,

---

4. BBC News, 'The English City That Wanted to "Break Away" from the UK' by Helen Grady, 8 November 2014.
5. Figures cited by David Alton in the House of Commons, 4 July 1983: https://hansard. parliament.uk/commons/1983-07-04/debates/7669d4e2-68b0-4afc-a18b-09d87be34054/ Liverpool(Unemployment)

Geoffrey Howe, to be the 'managed decline' of the city, things had deteriorated. Only one in twenty youngsters aged sixteen managed to become gainfully employed once leaving school in 1985. As the economic storm clouds darkened, Liverpool's image as the most significant port in Europe (with all the associated wealth and vibrancy) transformed into one with an altogether less flattering reputation for handouts. The city adopted a new status as a chief recipient of the scheme devised by the European Economic Community to prop up its very poorest regions. Qualification for Objective One grants and funding required the area's per capita GDP to be at or below 75 per cent of the EEC average. An impoverished Liverpool clearly sunk beneath the threshold, and began receiving the handouts from the early 1990s, when I was in my twenties.

Speaking two years after the 1981 flare-up of Liverpool's racial and socio-economic troubles in the deprived inner-city district of Toxteth, the MP for Liverpool Mossley Hill issued a plea for help in the House of Commons. David Alton cited mass joblessness as one of the causes of the riots and declared unemployment in Liverpool was worse than ever. 'The picture is bleak and depressing,' he told the Commons. 'Imagine life in a city where one in five people are on the dole, where half the people in some districts are without a job and where young people face a lifetime without employment.' He broke down the stark figures in various districts of the city, including Everton, where I lived: there were '3,795 people unemployed and only thirty-two jobs are available', he said. In 1983, this corrosive social and economic decay, exacerbated by Thatcher's free-market fundamentalism – complete with conscious neglect of struggling communities – provided fertile territory for the seeds of left-wing radicalism to germinate and flourish. The result was a socialist Labour-run city council, whose leader, John Hamilton, and deputy, Derek Hatton, took up the fight against the Tory government. Many in the city craved the sense of defiance and ambition shown by the group; others saw them as renegade infiltrators operating as a 'militant tendency' wing of the Labour party. Democracy prevailed, and a big swing towards Labour in the city's elections put Militant in control – on the promise of opposing the huge financial hardship inflicted from Whitehall. I spent my youth amid the turmoil of this era.

I grew up on the streets of the city. We had a council house, yet the city's streets – and the freedom they brought – were where I truly flourished. In the district of Everton, where Alton noted there were more than a hundred unemployed people for every job vacancy, things were on the up in one significant way: football. Liverpool FC's dominance from the mid-1970s onwards was complemented by Everton's purple patch in the mid-1980s. Throughout this time, the city's streets were the place to be – if you loved football, that is. Kicking a ball about offered a simple and effective remedy for the stresses of the day. So too did watching our heroes. The author David Goldblatt sums up its relevance in the city in *The Game of Our Lives: The Meaning and Making of English Football*, his book deconstructing the social and sporting context of football in England: 'Football offered a parallel universe of success alongside the otherwise vertiginous urban decline of the city.'

My family was typical. Both parents boasted Irish ancestry, like almost everyone else in the city. My dad, Lenny, was jobless, like almost everyone else in the city. My mum, Kathleen, busied herself as a mum. Meanwhile, my older brother, Tony, played football with me whenever and wherever we could. It was our release, our freedom, our mode of expression. In 1971, the year I was born, my dad was laid off from the city's sprawling docks. He never again had a legitimate job. In and out of 'work', sometimes as a mechanic, usually a labourer of some sort. Brickie, plasterer, joiner, roofer, digger of holes, knocker down of walls. A master of all trades. A labourer touting his skills for a pittance in the shadow economy – seemingly the only jobs available to many people in a city whose industries were being hollowed out before their very eyes. I recall many days in the late 1970s, me and my brother trawling along with my dad while he 'went on a message'. Always walking, sometimes with my younger sisters, Kathy and Carla. Days off school were devoted to football in the street or walking with my dad. Generally in the rain. It rains a lot in Liverpool. Head down, busy with unstated intent, Dad skittled along a touch faster than our comfortable half-jog, but too slow for us to run steadily to keep up. Flushed and with furrowed brows, we'd try to keep pace, slightly out of breath, pausing only occasionally when he stopped to light up a cigarette or 'let on' briefly to someone he knew. As for buses? Never. 'Do you think I'm made of money? It'll only take us half an hour . . .' was the usual response.

Our solution was simple: we took a ball. Dribbling it along the streets and pavements, dodging the obstacles thrown up by daily urban life: stationary bins, bollards, bus stops and lamp posts, barking dogs, distracted and shuffling pedestrians with 'messages' on their minds. One-twos and passing games gave way to an occasional one-v-one when we spied a 'goal' ahead. Approaching bus stops triggered a fight to keep possession until we got close enough to hammer a shot at the vertical screens – often of glass, usually mixed concrete slabs or metal – surrounding the gaggle of uninterested faces sheltering patiently from the drizzle while awaiting a number seventy-five bus to Huyton or an eighteen to Croxteth. Usually my dad was on a mission to see his erstwhile employer – a tall, gangly, awkward-looking fella known simply as 'The Shiteman', with a forced, rictus grin. If Shitey had any work for him, we would then loiter for a few hours, generally at a semi-derelict garage in Everton, a windy and rainswept renovation project at one of the grandly down-at-heel Edwardian mansions surrounding Newsham Park, or the shell of a terraced house anywhere in the Anfield or Kensington areas. Going 'cards in' with a reputable employer never seemed a viable option, when I look back now. It was about survival, about 'getting by'; sometimes he signed on, often he didn't. It was consistently turbulent, usually chaotic. Money and hope were in short supply, a bit like the sunshine over the drizzly Mersey.

Despite these material hardships, we didn't feel poor. Far from it. We were suffused with commonality, brimming with solidarity, sharing a steely confidence in knowing who we were and what we did. The two postcodes we lived in while growing up (we moved a quarter of a mile closer to Anfield and Goodison Park when I was seventeen) have been firmly entrenched in the most deprived 0.1 per cent of England since the official Indices of Multiple Deprivation were first mapped in England in the early 2000s.[6] Back in the 1970s and 1980s – when relative deprivation wasn't deemed worthy of measurement – it was exactly the same, but it hardly occupied my mind. I've long wondered whether this is me peering through rose-tinted glasses. Yet we were all in the same boat; if others had more money than us, we didn't know it. So how could we feel deprived? Why in that case would we feel second-class? The flipside of this sociological coin, however, was that we didn't appreciate how rich we were either. The wealth of opportunities to play was striking, on reflection – because the licence to do so is something too many children in subsequent UK generations no longer enjoy.

Playing has long been linked to happiness. A Children's Society report in 2015 found that children in England were among the least happy in the world. Focusing on 53,000 children aged between eight and twelve in fifteen diverse countries, it concluded that English children were outdone in the unhappiness stakes only by South Korea. In twenty-first century England the inner cities are filled

---

6. Per the OpenDataCommunities.org Indices of Deprivation 2015 explorer, available to view at http://dclgapps.communities.gov.uk/imd/idmap.html

with children playing indoors, not out. The streets are thronged with cars, the slivers of recreational land long since seized upon by cash-strapped local councils desperate to boost their coffers by flogging space to the developers with the deepest pockets. Then there are the distractions to modern children: 'teaching to the test' in education; and outside the school walls, smartphone and video games gobble up the time and mental energy of a generation of kids who know no different. The rise of the sedentary child presents huge health implications. Its primary causes – lack of opportunity to play and the distractions of the online age (plus the rise of cheap junk food) – are not confined to England or the UK. But the change over a few decades is striking. Obesity is a rising scourge. A study in 2016 by the NCD Risk Factor Collaboration revealed that in the UK obesity among boys was up from 2.4 per cent in 1975 to 10.9 per cent in 2016. Among girls it rose to 9.4 per cent from 3 per cent. The UK ranks seventy-third among 200 countries when it comes to the prevalence of childhood obesity. To put that into context, the study also found that in total 124 million children aged five to nineteen were obese worldwide. The majority, seventy-four million, are boys. The global figures for obesity mirror the UK surge: worldwide the figure for girls was 0.7 per cent in 1975 and 5.6 per cent in 2016; for boys it was 7.8 per cent, up from 0.9 per cent. Meanwhile, in some low-income countries, mainly in Africa and Asia, the main problem is still undernourishment. There are still an estimated 192 million children severely or moderately underweight worldwide.

Previous generations were not without distractions. Television, early video games and schoolwork existed in my day. But a massive priority was just getting out to play. It was the way we lived. Children being children, playing, competing and thriving in games we designed ourselves. My subsequent two decades of experience as a football and futsal coach and mentor has rammed home just how important the power of play is to the enjoyment and fulfilment of any endeavour. It was a naturally fertile environment for talent to prosper. Unlike the city's rapidly dying docks, the streets were very much alive with the hope, expectation and innate creativity of children playing. The only indicator of the stifling role adults can inflict on kids was the obligatory 'Ball games prohibited' sign hanging high on a wall, a target for shooting at rather than an effective deterrent. It could be a case study for the principle of 10,000 hours' practice – disputed and nuanced since being espoused by the psychologist and author Malcolm Gladwell in his book *Outliers* (citing research on skill acquisition by Professor Anders Ericsson from the University of Colorado). The street: a perfect environment for constant, challenging 'deliberate practice' when it comes to football.

Street gamers were not choosy. Any car park, pavement, alleyway, road or patch of grass (an 'oller' in Scouse parlance) could be utilised to get a game of footy going. The ball didn't matter either. Hard balls, 'flyaways', burst balls, small balls, tennis balls, we really weren't picky. That's not to say that if we managed to procure a 'casey' (a leather football known as a case ball), or the king of street footballs – the regal ball of orange gold, the Wembley Trophy – we would simply revel in the luxury. The volume and intensity of live commentary from the kid – there was always one, often several – who talked us all through every move often ratcheted up a notch. 'Great touch by Fahey, he glides past Sudbury, a one-two with the shopping trolley. Skips past the dogshit . . . and he's through on goal. Just Titch and the kerb to beat. And it's there . . . 1–0. What a finish!' Thrilling stuff. Especially the mandatory sign-off at the end of a move: 'Clive Tyldesley, Radio City, the Goldstone Ground.' Why it was always the Goldstone Ground I'll never know. None of us had ever been to Brighton.

The council estate where I lived in Everton, less than a mile north of Liverpool city centre, was essentially a car park without cars. We were in good company in Kilshaw Street as a family who never owned a car. It gave us a clear advantage when it came to playing opportunities: a car park with no cars was perfect. The estate sat snugly between the city's biggest maternity hospital, Mill Road, and a huge tobacco factory, Ogdens. At one end of the street was the famous Grafton Ballroom, by the 1970s a notorious nightclub but once a venue for a host of famous names, from the Beatles to Duke Ellington. In between these three landmarks, our street football games took many forms – other than the massed scrambles with kids of all ages, battling to seize the ball and become the hero. One of my favourites was 'shooties'. Usually one-v-one, it involved two goals, one ball and each player taking turns trying to score past the other. Shooting, risk, reward and goalkeeping prowess all in one. I played it a lot with my good mate, Anthony Scott, because he had a perfect pitch near his house. His goal was always a big, ornate green gate guarding a side entrance to the maternity hospital. My goal was painted on the side of a house.

Away from the streets, primary school offered another, albeit limited, opportunity to play. Unfortunately, in the infants' section of St Michael's, balls were banned. We were not easily beaten though: every day, the labours of a detailed smuggling operation would bear fruit. Kevin Beckett, Stuart Carrington, Nicholas 'Nicko' Hughes, Tony Maher, Brendan O'Brien and I took turns to sneak in one of an assortment of small objects to covertly use as a 'ball' in the playground. Most days, it was a piece of robust plastic (Lego figures did the job). In the autumn, nature called. We switched to conkers, which offered a true test of our nascent ability to read the direction of a barely visible object skittling across the ground – ricocheting off the shins of skipping and screeching girls – after being propelled by a mighty toe-end and summoning up a guttural roar of 'Rivelllllliiiinooo' or 'Riiiioccchhhhhh'. The 'Rioch' shout greeted a brutish, unstoppable power drive. A 'Rivellino' goal also screamed power. But it had more. Maybe swerve, or bend, usually left-footed, often a hint of something extra, something exotic.

Something Brazilian. Either way, these contrasting 1970s stars were on the tips of our tongues when celebrating a wonder goal.[7] I didn't know it at the time, but only one of these footballing super Rs was synonymous with futsal – a game with uncanny links to the very street football we were living, breathing and playing in Liverpool's chaotic urban landscape.

---

7. The Bruce Rioch thing was an odd one. He only played thirty games for Everton in the mid-1970s, sandwiched between spells at Derby County, where he won the league championship first time round. But the boy born in Aldershot, who became the first person without a Scottish birthplace to captain Scotland, clearly made an impression at Goodison Park with the fans. Rivellino was different. He was seen as the embodiment of exotic Brazilian flair. Not as obvious as Pelé. More left-field, literally and metaphorically speaking. The moustache, the fearless dribbling and the fearsome cannon of a shot. We all knew who he was, without ever having seen him play.

CHAPTER 2
THE BIRTH OF FUTSAL, RIVELLINO AND THE 1970S

THE SON OF Italian immigrants who moved to Brazil, Roberto Rivellino was described by Pelé in 1970 as 'simply one of the greatest midfielders ever to play for Brazil . . . unbelievably skilful. An incredibly intelligent footballer.' Rivellino endowed the *seleção* ('selection', a popular nickname for the Brazil national squad) with one of the most unmistakable profiles in world sport. Renowned for his bending, swerving free kicks, the stocky left-footed powerhouse boasted a repertoire of mazy dribbles, improvised passes and a restless invention that would have commanded a long list of high-profile European suitors had he been playing thirty years later.

The *elastico*, or 'flip flap', became his calling card. Translating as 'rubber band' in Portuguese, it is often called *la culebrita* (little snake) in Spanish. Regardless of the name, it is an audaciously fleet-footed move that has been copied, adapted and followed by footballing greats over subsequent decades. Rivellino's first use of it came in the 1960s, wearing number ten for Corinthians. He copied the move from a former youth teammate called Sergio Echigo. Usually from a standing start, the attacker's micro-shuffle of the hips precedes a near-simultaneous double-touch of the ball. In Rivellino's case, he first feigned to dart left, then followed up with a rapid swish of the

27

left instep which shunted the ball to the right, as the defender rocked backwards, bemused. Both the original Ronaldo '*O Fenômeno*' (the Phenomenon) and his Portuguese namesake, Cristiano, became arch exponents too. The great Brazilian Ronaldinho Gaúcho also bamboozled defenders with it.[8] In Rivellino's case, the art of deception practised so frequently at Corinthians came from his formative years jousting on *futebol de salão* courts. The sport that would eventually be renamed futsal was young Roberto's game. Not eleven-a-side football. Not on grass. Outside, yes – but on smaller courts, streets or scraps of land before progressing to indoor halls with wooden or tiled surfaces. Rivellino's unique artistry was shaped on the anvil of informal play and the emerging force of organised *futebol de salão*.

It's easy to see why, in the early 1970s, the exploits of Rivellino, Pelé and co. were still freshly ingrained on the minds of youngsters thousands of miles away. The 1970 World Cup was the first to be televised in colour. The symbolism is profound. Brazil's passion and flair suddenly appeared more detailed, visual and vivid as live footage confronted viewers with a sporting excellence unprecedented in its lavish, arresting technicolour. It was a feast of excitement born on the *futebol de salão* court. Both Pelé and Rivellino testify to their grounding in the game. 'Futsal requires you to think and play fast,' declared Pelé. 'It makes everything easier when you later switch to football.' Rivellino's autobiography *Get off the Street, Roberto!* says it all, the young Roberto often playing in the dirt and dust until his bones ached and shoeless feet bled. He also often played without a ball although, as with the street hustlers in Liverpool two decades

---

8. More recently, France's Paul Pogba got the *elastico* trending in the world of football again when playing for Juventus against Inter Milan in 2015. He used it to skip past two Inter defenders on the eighteen-yard line, danced into the box and, being the enigma that he is, promptly fluffed his chance to score. Samir Handanović parried his tame effort and the ball spun up, over the crossbar and out for a corner.

later, the definition of 'ball' was an extremely loose one. If it was kickable, it was desirable. Rivellino's first formal *futebol de salão* club was São Paulo's Clube Atlético Barcelona, which later merged with a basketball club, Clube Atlético Sorocaba, and Estrada de Ferro Sorocabana Futebol Clube to become Atlético Sorocaba football club, a participant in the top flight of São Paulo state football, the Campeonato Paulista, in 2020.

Back in 1971, with Pelé's and Rivellino's technicolour exploits fresh in the minds of football fans worldwide, there was more than just 'big football' samba flair in the air. Just a couple of months before I entered the world (in the maternity hospital yards from where I would kick a ball about incessantly a few years later), the Federación Internacional de Fútbol de Salón (FIFUSA) was born. Fittingly, it was in Rivellino's home city, São Paulo, where a series of meetings at the headquarters of the São Paulo football federation led to a deal on 25 July to form a governing body to unify the game's laws and bring order to the burgeoning small-sided game. This landmark day for *futebol de salão* paved the way for a host of controversial changes that reshaped a game now enjoyed by millions all over the globe.

Initially comprising just seven countries – Argentina, Bolivia, Brazil, Paraguay, Peru, Portugal and Uruguay – FIFUSA came under the auspices of the parochial Brazilian Confederation of Sports (CBD) and the Confederation Sudamericana de Futsal (CSFS). But the goal was to go global. João Havelange, who led from the front as president of the CBD from 1958, took up the leadership role. In truth, he achieved little, as he was somewhat preoccupied with the small matter of pursuing the biggest job in world football. But *futebol de salão* now had a man, Havelange; a plan, to unify the rules and introduce a world championship to spread the gospel of the sport to other continents; and a base from which to grow the game, Rio de Janeiro. FIFUSA ushered in an era of international tournaments as the growth and recognition of the game exploded at grassroots level, heralding a decade-long power struggle for the ownership of *futebol de salão* – and a simultaneous tug-of-war over the name. Although the sport was eventually renamed futsal, the change was a long time coming.

* * *

The sport had not always looked as it did in the 1970s, let alone the way it does in 2021, after three decades of FIFA rule. A little over forty years before the formation of FIFUSA in 1971, the game was but a twinkle in the eye of an inspirational Argentinian professor called Juan Carlos Ceriani Gravier. The birthplace was not his native Argentina, though; nor Brazil. It was Uruguay. The indoor gymnasium of Montevideo YMCA to be precise, on Colonia 1065, at the corner of Rio Negro in the heart of the city centre.

Why Uruguay? It was simple economics: a case of supply rising to meet growing demand. The global financial crash of 1929 heralded a fresh surge of immigration from countries such as France, Italy and Spain as economic turmoil engulfed Europe. Swelling the ranks of football-loving foreigners resident in the long-established enclaves dotted around Uruguay's biggest cities, the new arrivals joined a nation on the rise in footballing terms. The 4–2 victory over rivals Argentina in Montevideo's Estadio Centenario to secure the first ever World Cup in 1930 intensified the craving for the game, an appetite already fuelled by the men's Olympic team taking successive gold medals in the 1924 and 1928 Olympics. Uruguay's largest city, with about one-third of its 300,000 or so population born overseas, heaved with pent-up demand from football-crazy citizens desperate to play.

The clamour in Montevideo led naturally to the YMCA, or Christian Youth Association as it was known in Latin America at the time. The association's role in developing and promoting world sport is unparalleled. A few decades before Ceriani started working his magic in Montevideo, the sports of basketball and volleyball were also invented in YMCAs in the United States, by James Naismith and William Morgan respectively. Necessity is said to be the mother of invention, and in Ceriani's case, it was strikingly apposite. He set out to overcome two huge hurdles to meet the surging demand for football in Montevideo. Both space and opportunity to play were at a premium in a city where most fields were privately owned; when youngsters *did* find a field, the high annual rainfall often proved a washout for outdoor games. The professor turned this twin adversity to his advantage. He saw youngsters shunning the YMCA staples of basketball and volleyball in favour of kicking balls about randomly in the halls. Such renegade exploits extended to dance halls, which were being increasingly used by footballers smashing balls about in a manner that broke many windows – but also propelled Ceriani to shatter the uneasy status quo.

He decided a new sport was required, one that recognised the new trend for using basketball courts as football pitches. Using the English name 'Indoor-Foot-Ball', the professor brought sport-crazy children indoors to play a hybrid sport he hoped would 'civilise' the eleven-a-side game, which he saw as dangerous and violent. His invention was soon dubbed 'foot-ball-room', which translates as *futebol de salão* in Portuguese. The rules were an amalgam of four different sports: football, water polo, basketball and handball. The essence of the game – a directional team 'invasion game' with a ball being moved towards a goal with all parts of the body bar the hands – clearly derived from football. Water polo provided restrictions on the goalkeepers' movements and actions. Handball lent the limits applied to the on-court players, particularly where they could shoot from. Basketball was perhaps the biggest influence – the court size and markings, the number of players in a team, the duration of the game (forty minutes became the norm) and the manner of substitutions. Although becoming unlimited as the adult game evolved, in the informal infancy of the sport, when it applied only to children, instead of substitutions more players simply entered the fray, resulting in six- or seven-a-side contests.[9] In the early days, the goals were either benches, or were marked out on walls (those chalked-up goals yet another striking similarity to the street football I experienced four decades later in Liverpool). The ball was vital. In early games a volleyball was used, but Ceriani soon dismissed it as too light and bouncy. It needed to stay on court (if only to avoid breaking windows). A period of starkly unscientific experimentation ensued, involving prototypes made of cork, rags, horsehair and sawdust.

The sport took off in Montevideo. By 1933, the loosely codified rules were documented by Ceriani and handed out to educators at a specially convened training course in the city by the Technical Institute of the Latin American Confederation of the YMCA. The 'coaching the coaches' gathering mirrors the sort of course I've been involved in as an FA coach mentor, with a vision to engage more people in futsal at the grassroots in England. The 1933 Montevideo gathering inspired many missionaries to spread the gospel of *futebol de salão*, most notably João Lotufo (an inspirational basketball coach) and Julián Haranczyk from São Paulo, and José Rothier and Aníbal Monteiro from Rio de Janeiro. American YMCA veteran James Summers, the YMCA institute's director, was another vital convert. A graduate of the famous Springfield College, Massachusetts – where James Naismith invented basketball at the YMCA training school gym – Summers successfully spread word of

---

9. Incidentally, basketball's contribution grew as futsal evolved. A common denominator in the two sports is the intentional block, a physical act of stopping an opponent used regularly to unpick a rival's defensive plan and steal a moment's freedom for a teammate to seal a potentially game-changing advantage.

the game back to the New York headquarters and then on to YMCAs around the world.

Within a decade the sport boasted a six-page document of rules, written by Ceriani, and was a fully fledged adults' game, particularly in Brazil, as well as a refuge for bored children in YMCA halls. In 1936 an article in the sixth edition of *Physical Education Magazine* outlined the rules of the sport. By 1949 the Latin American Confederation of the YMCA had a committee devoted solely to *futebol de salão*.

By the 1950s, when Pelé and Rivellino were cutting their teeth in *esporte da bola pesada* (the sport of the heavy ball), as it became known due to the dense, low-bounce ball, the game was thriving in Uruguay and the Brazilian hotbeds of São Paulo and Rio de Janeiro, where it was played outside as much as in the halls. Rio de Janeiro is where a man seen as the true pioneer of the sport in Brazil came to prominence, forming the world's first ever futsal federation. The Metropolitan Football Federation of Salon (later the Futsal Federation of Rio de Janeiro) was founded in July 1954, a move led by twenty five year-old player Newton Zarani, who was later nicknamed the 'Charles Miller of *futebol de salão*' after the founder of football in Brazil. Zarani pioneered futsal at América FC and lays claim to being the first officially federated player in history. 'Futsal arose out of a need,' the Carioca later explained, according to the Brazilian news site *O Globo*. 'We had nowhere to play in América, so we decided to create football that could be played in a smaller space.' As well as playing until his seventies, Zarani went on to coach at América and at Club Municipal before becoming a sports journalist at *Jornal dos Sports*.

Meanwhile, back in 1954, about 250 miles from Rio – close to the dusty streets where a young Roberto Rivellino was falling in love with the game – the São Paulo YMCA played its part by starting the first league, with games played on indoor basketball courts. In 1955, the São Paulo Federation of Futsal was established. As if to emphasise the sport's links to basketball, the meeting to thrash out the federation's founding charter took place in a room kindly provided by the Paulista Basketball Federation. About thirty clubs were in attendance, including the prominent football giants São Paulo FC, SE Palmeiras and SC Corinthians Paulista, the club where Rivellino would shoot to fame in the eleven-a-side game, earning the nickname *O Rei do Parque* (King of the Park). It was here in São Paulo where two key names in the history of the sport came to the fore. Habib Maphuz, a professor at the city's YMCA, took on the federation presidency. He was later replaced by Luiz Gonzaga de Oliveira Fernandes, who helped spread the sport into Europe and assumed the role of secretary general at FIFUSA in 1971, at the right hand of the increasingly influential João Havelange. Maphuz and Gonzaga rationalised futsal's rules and injected uniformity into the sport at a time when myriad forms of the game still existed.

Gonzaga's 1956 futsal rule book – building on Maphuz's work – enhanced Ceriani's admirable efforts two decades earlier. Until that point, the game's oddities had thrown up extraordinary shenanigans. According to the author Alex Bellos in his excellent book *Futebol: the Brazilian Way of Life* – which describes futsal as 'an incubator of the Brazilian soul' – one of the most bizarre rules involved a ban on speaking in games, an edict that even extended to fans at times. Perhaps the most unusual rule prior to the mid-1950s was one that led to the sight of stumbling, falling players performing bodily contortions trying to land on the floor using anything but their hands, an oddity caused by a ban on touching the ball with any body part while a player's hands were in contact with the ground. The (presumably) unintended consequence was that futsal became the most dangerous sport in Brazil – no mean feat in a country obsessed with death-defying motor racing. The law was reportedly scrapped once researchers highlighted the number of broken arms and shoulder injuries sustained. Gonzaga's redefinition of the game formed the basis of the laws eventually adopted by FIFUSA in 1971 and was broadly accepted by FIFA when it took over the sport. The new rules also coincided with the end of experimentation over the ball. Gonzaga's endeavours settled on the idea of manufacturing balls using foam rubber for the first time.

Off the court, the 1950s saw further progress in Brazil's internal organisation. In 1957 Sylvio Pacheco, president of the CBD, created the Salon Football Technical Council to bring unity of purpose to the growing band of federated states in the country. Within months João Havelange, a close ally of Pacheco's, had taken control of the CBD, immediately recognised futsal and brought the sport in-house. Then in 1959, meaningful competition was added to the futsal landscape when the first Brazilian championships kicked off, involving ten clubs. Fluminense emerged victorious. The final act in establishing Brazil as the fully functioning heart of the game was not straightforward. Initial attempts to create a national futsal-specific federation were frustrated in 1957, and it was not until 1979, with the FIFUSA bandwagon fully rolling, that the Brazilian Futsal Confederation (CBFS) was founded at a meeting in Rio de Janeiro. Appropriately, the venue was the city's João Havelange Building. The reconfiguration of national sports governance renamed the longstanding CBD the Brazilian Football Federation (CBF) – concerned with football alone – and created separate federations to look after specific sports, including futsal's CBFS. Fortaleza, in the state of Ceara, was chosen as the headquarters – a decision seen as a compromise to avoid the potentially distracting turf war between São Paulo and Rio de Janeiro over futsal governance.

Havelange's role in the history of futsal is difficult to overstate. Although his legacy will forever be tainted by the stain of corruption at FIFA that seemed to envelop him in the years before he died at the age of one hundred in 2016, his ascent in the world of sports administration was dizzying and impactful. A fierce competitor who represented Brazil in two Olympic Games – swimming in Berlin 1936 and water polo in Helsinki 1952 – Havelange was a man on a mission. In *Global Sport Leaders: A Biographical Analysis of International Sports Management*, authors Emmanuel Bayle and Patrick Clastres explain how no sooner had he become vice-president of the CBD than his eyes were fixed on the presidency – and replacing his big ally, Pacheco:

> His triumphant election in 1958, where he won 158 of the 177 votes cast, shows both his popularity within Brazilian sport and the extent of the network he had built up. His rise through the echelons of sports administration was so spectacular that just five years later, in 1963, he was co-opted as a member of the IOC [International Olympic Commission]. Immediately after his election as president of the CBD, Havelange began implementing an ambitious policy that he would later apply to FIFA … the people Havelange gathered around him at the CBD showed his acute political sense.

By the time he felt ready to pursue the position of FIFA president, Havelange had presided over three football World Cup victories for Brazil (1958, 1962 and 1970). He called on his old friend, Pacheco, to help him compile a 'glossy, four page brochure' outlining his suitability for the role. This strident self-promotion exercise worked a treat, as the head of FIFUSA swapped *futebol de salão* for the lucrative world of football. It was only a matter of time before he would again covet his first love. Despite Havelange's swift departure, FIFUSA brought much-needed order and structure to the game. Its cause was helped by the end to a battle over the historical narrative and ownership of the game. It was a straight fight between Brazil and Uruguay.

The belief among Brazilian observers, researchers and writers at the time was that *futebol de salão* was being practised informally in the metropolises of Rio de Janeiro and São Paulo at the time when Ceriani 'invented' the game. In Uruguay, the narrative was straight-forward. Ceriani's complex and messy amalgamation of four sports into one was the starting point. His first stab at the sport's rules in 1933 were the literal proof of his invention. Brazil's case to be the father of the game is undone slightly by the lack of documentation. Crucial archived documents of the CBD, held at the temple of football in Rio that is the Maracanã, are said to have been lost to flood damage at the Estádio Jornalista Mário Filho. The claim, while difficult to confirm, adds to the narrative and intrigue surrounding the game, the idea that flooding may have literally muddied the waters when it comes to a definitive history of its origins. From Montevideo to Manchester, the indoor game has long been seen as a solution to inclement weather, a sanctuary from the torrential rain that floods precious outdoor pitches around the world.

The battle was finally resolved in 1967 thanks to a breakthrough at a specially convened summit in Rio de Janeiro. The São Paulo YMCA's Luiz Gonzaga joined forces with Havelange at the CBD to summon representatives from YMCAs all over Brazil and Uruguay. The agenda was simple: to decide once and for all the true origins of *futebol de salão*. According to the French futsal analyst Jérôme Brachet, who wrote the research paper 'The Amazing Story of Futsal from 1930 to Today', the conclusion was clear: *futebol de salão* was born in Uruguay 'but acquires the nationality when it becomes adult Brazilian'. The Brazilians accepted Ceriani had invented the game in Montevideo. In turn, the Uruguayans acknowledged it was raised and nourished into adulthood in Brazil. *Futebol de salão* had become a naturalised Brazilian citizen – a striking parallel, as we shall see, with the coming era of Brazilian players. The 1956 rule book laid down in São Paulo by Gonzaga and Maphuz was accepted as the 'passport' of proof allowing the game to travel the world on an odyssey of influence. The subsequent calm brought the order needed to create the sport's first governing body, FIFUSA, four years later.

So in 1971, Brazil was firmly at the centre of the wider footballing world. The Pelé and Rivellino-inspired *seleção*'s eleven-a-side World Cup victory, coupled with its confirmed prominence in the 'sport of the heavy ball', added a sporting lustre to the country's newfound economic and social confidence. Seven years after a brutal military coup ousted the left-wing president, João Goulart, the country's dictatorship had coined a phrase to sum up a nation's burgeoning self-belief: '*Brasil, ame-o ou deixe-o*' (Brazil, love it or leave it). A so-called 'economic miracle' was in full swing. But the 1973 oil crisis halted the near double-digit growth, and the rest of the decade bequeathed an enormous debt burden to the nation, paving the way for a return to democracy in 1985.

The *futebol de salão* boom proved far more sustainable. Among the seven founding nations of FIFUSA experimenting with mass participation in the game, Portugal played a pivotal role in its importation to Europe. The game's early adoption and the common language with Brazil proved instrumental in its development on the Iberian Peninsula and beyond. The name 'futsal' was increasingly visible too. José Antônio Inglêz, a journalist at the São Paulo-based sports newspaper *A Gazeta Esportiva*, broke new ground by using the novel term while writing about the sport. By 1980, the vast majority of Brazilian states had established futsal federations and the country's dominance in South American competitions remained strong. Despite losing the inaugural South American national championship in 1965, a four-team tournament also involving Uruguay, Argentina and the hosts and winners, Paraguay, Brazil recovered their poise to remain unbeaten in a match until 1979, winning the nine subsequent South American tournaments until Paraguay triumphed again in 1989. The nation that nurtured the sport of the heavy ball had established a pattern of relentless dominance in the smaller game.

* * *

In Europe, Belgium was a surprise early adopter of the game, beating FIFUSA founding member Portugal to the punch by setting up a national futsal association in 1968. In the same year, the Netherlands started a national futsal league and soon had an estimated 100,000 people playing the game it calls *zaalvoetbal* (room football). Portugal's neighbours, Spain, arrived on the scene in the early 1970s, when a version of the game was played at the YMCA in Madrid before spreading around the country, with competitions and tournaments contested fiercely at adult level.

FIFUSA's early momentum faded as the organisation struggled financially. According to Francisco Javier Plana Segura, a Spanish researcher of the game, the main source of income was the $250 annual payment from each affiliated federation. In his chronicle of the sport, titled *Furor Sala* (Fury Room), Segura says the end of the 1970s signalled a marked change of approach at FIFUSA. Again, it was a citizen of São Paulo who led the way. Januário D'Alessio Neto, an insurance tycoon and secretary of the football giants SE Palmeiras, was elected president in 1980. According to Segura, D'Alessio Neto's handover gift comprised a shoe box filled with bundles of notes. Unfortunately, none of it was cash: the FIFUSA coffers were empty. D'Alessio Neto's financial largesse breathed new life into the federation, as the 1980s heralded a period of tumultuous change and the game extended its reach further beyond South America. D'Alessio Neto's first act was to condense and unify the rules of the game, just like Ceriani and Gonzaga had before him. He also commissioned the sports manufacturers Penalty, founded in São Paulo in 1970, to print thousands of copies of a new futsal rule book to be distributed in Portuguese, Spanish, French and English. Within months, the first pan-American futsal championship was held in Mexico, with Brazil triumphing in a tournament contested by seven countries.

D'Alessio Neto didn't stop there. The game's global breakthrough came two years later with the first futsal world championship, a seminal staging post on the sport's journey from the streets, via the dusty YMCA indoor halls of South America, to arrive as a bona fide indoor spectacle attracting huge crowds. Fittingly, São Paulo hosted the event. Naturally, Brazil won it, defeating long-time rivals Paraguay 1–0 in a tightly contested final in front of 15,000 spectators at the Ginásio do Ibirapuera. An estimated 5,000 fans were locked out of the arena, a sight that would no doubt have brought a smile to the face of the man who gambled on the future of the game with his own savings, Januário D'Alessio Neto. Live television and radio coverage vindicated his decision to invest. Coming just twenty-four hours after the majestic Sócrates and Zico kicked off the Brazilian football team's tilt at the 1982 World Cup with a 2–1 victory over the Soviet Union, the indoor world championship flagged up *futebol de salão* as the primary source of samba flair.

The diverse group of nations in São Paulo offered a tantalising glimpse of the indoor game's potential reach. Japan's participation, and the presence of three countries from Europe – Czechoslovakia, the Netherlands and Italy – presaged the rapid geographical spread. Not all were fully paid up futsal-playing countries, of course, with many of the players schooled in the amorphous indoor football leagues dotted around the world. The rich variety of influences presented the South American contingent – Colombia, Argentina, Brazil, Costa Rica, Paraguay and Uruguay – with 'new' opponents, ideas and tactical approaches, adding extra colour and flavour to the game. Although the Brazilian playing and coaching methodologies still retained authority decades later, the culture clash on court was a fact of life the dominant South Americans would have to get used to.

The wildly differing formats of small-sided football variants meant not all countries were playing by anything close to the FIFUSA rule book. In the United States, a nation obsessed with indoor sports, the Major Indoor Soccer League (MISL) kicked off in 1978 and flourished for fourteen seasons, with matches attracting average attendances of over 7,000. It might have been played on artificial turf, with boards instead of sidelines, and a bouncy football instead of the *futebol de salão* 'heavy ball', but it was still a huge draw.

Back in Europe, a version of indoor football was also firmly established in many countries. As far back as 1959, the Latvian Football Federation had begun putting on indoor six-a-side tournaments for eleven-a-side teams to try. The growing appetite for the game there spread to other nations in the former Soviet Union, particularly Yugoslavia. Further west, the vision of the former joint coach of the Austrian national football team came to fruition in 1959 too when the first Wiener Stadthalle indoor football tournament was held in Vienna. Josef 'Pepi' Argauer returned from the 1958 World Cup in Sweden inspired after stumbling across the beguiling sight of Pelé and the Brazil football team training indoors with *futebol de salão* vim and vigour. Running for fifty years until 2009, the Wiener Stadthalle tournament attracted the biggest professional football teams. By the start of the 1970s, an indoor game similar in character to the coming MISL was prospering in parts of Europe.

Such was the pull of the Vienna tournament, even Germany's mighty Bayern Munich entered in 1971, lifting the prize with Franz Beckenbauer and Gerd Müller in the team. That same year, the year FIFUSA was founded, Europe's most prestigious and long-lasting European indoor tournament kicked off in Yugoslavia. Still attracting Croatia's best professional footballers and futsal stars in its fiftieth year in 2020, the annual *kutija šibica* (matchbox) event is an indoor six-a-side competition with big cash prizes for the winning teams. In its golden era – in 1985 nearly 700 teams took part – the *kutija šibica* helped fuel the growth of futsal too, with the Yugoslav futsal team making its debut in 1987. *Kutija šibica* boasts an extensive roll call of the finest football stars, including the former Dinamo Zagreb and Real Madrid striker Davor Šuker – president of the Croatian FA in 2020 – the former Red Star Belgrade, Real Madrid and Barcelona midfielder Robert Prosinečki and, more recently, Croatian internationals such as Vedran Ćorluka and the 2018 Ballon d'Or winner, Luka Modrić. While not quite futsal – it's six-a-side played with a size 5 football – it shows the depth of attraction to the indoor game across the whole age profile, in a nation that also boasts a vibrant street football culture.

Germany's version of Yugoslavia's *kutija šibica* and Austria's Hallenmasters (indoor masters) came in the late 1980s after the indoor game, plus occasional professional tournaments, grew in popularity in the 1970s. Backed by the German FA (Deutscher Fussball-Bund), the Hallenpokal (indoor cup) attracted eleven-a-side players during the winter break for more than a decade, spawning a more durable female version in 1994 that ran for two decades. While futsal took off in the former Yugoslav nations along-side its bespoke *kutija šibica* culture, the presence of a viable indoor game in Austria, Germany and other places in this era sated any appetite to follow Spain, Portugal, Italy, Russia and other parts of the former Soviet Union in making futsal the small-sided game of choice. Handball's popularity was a big factor in Germany. Along with the Nordic nations of Denmark, Norway and Sweden, it was among the first to develop the sport, with the modern rules formed in Berlin in 1919. Primarily a women's sport offering a more civilised alternative to football, the game's early rule book was swiftly updated to accommodate male players by one of the three architects of the laws, the sports educator and former athlete Karl Schelenz. The hugely successful professional handball Bundesliga was founded in 1966. It was FIFA's growing pressure on the German FA to fall into line by replacing its six-a-side football competitions with futsal – with all the associated changes in size of teams, goals, pitches and ball – that spelled the end for the last redoubt of its traditional indoor football culture: the female Hallenpokal in 2015. The demise of elite-level six-a-side left Germany free to join the rest of the world by finally embracing futsal.[10.]

The smörgåsbord of formats on the indoor menu throughout Europe in the 1970s – including the FIFUSA-backed *futebol de salão* – triggered a bout of indigestion among the power-brokers, leading UEFA to try to simplify the menu by unifying the recipe for the South American delicacy. Not for the first time, the thriving, fast-growing baby brother of football defied strenuous attempts to restrict, restrain or define its limitations. It wanted to remain free from the interference of a federation responsible for overseeing what was seen as a different sport: eleven-a-side football. UEFA stopped short of imposing strict conformity and opted instead for recommendations in 1977 rather than hard and fast rules. The continuing variety of and court sizes and game laws within the single *futebol de salão* format wedged open a fissure in the sport's governance that was to burst apart in the next decade of acrimony. It also revealed how different culturally-determined game constraints directly affected skill development. While the South American countries had grown up playing *futebol de salão* indoors and out on basketball courts, in Europe significantly larger handball courts were generally used. The extra constraint imposed by

---

10. In 2015, the sustained popularity of non-futsal indoor football, particularly in the United States, Canada and Mexico, was confirmed when its governing body, the World Minifootball Federation (successor to the International Fast Football Federation) hosted its first World Cup in the United States.

the tighter court, intensified by the commitment to the smaller, less bouncy size 3 *bola pesada*, is seen as a factor in fuelling the greater South American ball mastery, particularly among the Brazilians. At the other end of the practice spectrum, the six-a-side MISL indoor soccer craze, with expansive pitches sixty metres long and twenty-five to thirty metres wide, challenged players much less with far fewer confines of time and space.

A UEFA conference for national associations in 1980 exposed a degree of fear and mistrust over the South American game, with the ever-traditional English FA dead set against international futsal. Elsewhere, just like in Germany, handball proved an obstacle. The story of the game's evolution after it was first codified by Schelenz in 1919 clouded the thinking of some UEFA decision makers. Originally outdoors and eleven-a-side when it first appeared at the 1936 Berlin Olympics, handball had morphed into a seven-a-side indoor game by the time it returned to world prominence in the 1972 Munich Olympics. Furthermore, the indoor, shrunken version was much more exciting. Alarm bells sounded in the rarefied meeting rooms at some football federation headquarters amid fears the beautiful game could suffer the same fate. Austria made a strident case for banning futsal to eliminate all risks, a sentiment that may have retained some support in Vienna, given that the country didn't launch a national team until 2018.

Notwithstanding this considerable hostility towards the game, the 1982 FIFUSA *Campeonato Mundial de futebol de salão* (futsal world championships) marked a pivotal moment in the sport, proving the game of the streets and YMCAs was now a player on the global stage. An intrigued João Havelange, by now stationed in Zurich drawing a handsome salary from world football's governing body, FIFA, was looking back admiringly at one of his first loves. History showed that as a consummate political operator, he tended to get what he wanted. The coming battle over the game of futsal was to prove no different.

CHAPTER 3

THE 1980S: THE DECADE OF THE STREETS

'Everything for me started in the street. From as early as I can
remember, we played football everywhere we could . . . from
then on the Ajax stadium became my second home.'

JOHAN CRUYFF

LIVERPOOL'S PLACE IN the world is an odd one. Frank Cottrell-Boyce,
author and resident Scouse socio-literary commentator, observed it
neatly in a *Guardian* article offering up a collective paean to Europe,
days before the unmet Brexit deadline of 31 October 2019. He
recalled how Liverpool's away leg of the UEFA Cup final at Borussia
Mönchengladbach in the 1970s turned the focus of many in the city
towards the continent:

> That night was the start of our love affair with Europe. Until
> then, Liverpool's gaze was fixed the other way – over the sea to
> Ireland, New York, Valparaíso – the old sea routes our fathers
> had travelled. It was football that bounced Europe into our lives.
> Liverpool often felt disconnected from the rest of England, but
> football connected us to Europe like a perfectly weighted pass.

As the 1970s gave way to the 1980s, this fetish with Europe became
entrenched along with Liverpool FC's seemingly endless glory days.
The reality on the ground in the city was unchanged too. Street
football still ruled. Grass pitches were bumpy, muddy patches of
greeny-brown dirt, scattered with broken bottles and stained with

shit, whether it was an oller next to a 'bombdy' (one of the thousands of bomb-damaged homes littering the streets thirty years after the end of the Second World War) or an actual field with goals. The nearest 'proper' pitch to my street was in a gated field, connected to a primary school, where my first grassroots football team, White Rock, played our games.

Maybe it was the cold and rain-soaked fields. Maybe it was just the guarantee of playability elsewhere. Either way, hard floors were the overwhelming favourite for most kids. The subway tunnels under nearby West Derby Road were prime venues offering a hard surface and, crucially, weather protection. The entrance at either end of the tunnel formed a ready-made goal – the height and width made them almost identical in size to futsal goals. The exceptional hazard in these games was caused by the camber of the subway floor, the pitch dipping downhill from either entrance to a halfway line marked by two big drains. When the drains got blocked – a frequent occurrence – a massive puddle of rain and drain water appeared. It had to be leapt over, waded through or just missed out by a long raking pass into the attacking half, or a ricochet off the graffiti-laden side walls. It was a unique environment of adventure, strategy and game understanding with a ball.

Elsewhere on the Kilshaw Street estate was the main car park pitch. This was the place where a boy called Sonny Phillips stunned us all one day with an outlandish piece of skill no one had ever seen before. Stepping on a half-flat casey and pirouetting past another kid like a street-urchin ballerina, Sonny danced into our consciousness that balmy summer's day. It turned out he'd learned the manoeuvre from his cousins, Stephen and Alan, who lived in the Netherlands. On that day in the car park he revealed to us the 'Maradona', several years before Diego Armando Maradona spun away gracefully from Peter Reid and the whole England midfield at the Azteca Stadium on his way to one of the best goals the World Cup has ever seen.

The 'Maradona', the 'Zidane', the 'Marseille turn', '*la roulette*', it has since been given many names. But in Kilshaw Street it was known as the 'Sonny Phillips', in honour of this daring splash of artistic beauty – learned on the same street canvas as the ultimate Dutch master, Johan Cruyff.

The same carless car park was the scene of an array of competitive street games: knockout doubles and singles (up against one keeper), three and in (score three to go in goal), headers and volleys (shooting past a single keeper) and its timed equivalent, sixty seconds. Then there was kerby, a one-v-one game involving hitting the opposite pavement kerb with the ball. A scruffy ungrassed oller permitted another great combination play: football and minding cars – both peculiarly Scouse passions. 'Mind yer car, mate?' is a phrase inextricably linked to the city due to the long tradition of lads and girls patrolling the streets near Anfield and Goodison on matchday offering a bespoke junior security service for an unnamed price. In our case it was the visitors to the Grafton nightclub invited to pay for our reassuring presence, while we kicked a ball about nearby.

The next step up on the competitive ladder in Liverpool in the early 1980s was the annual Merseyside Police five-a-side tournament, a high point of the city's football calendar, with finals at either Goodison or Anfield. From the age of nine upwards my White Rock team was alive and well playing eleven-a-side football on massive muddy pitches in the Scotland Road league, a stark contrast to the surfaces used in our winter training regime – a floodlit supermarket car park (with trolleys for goal posts and no cars to be seen). Our team – managed by a guy called Pat Laffey and his son, Alan – comprised mainly my primary school Lego brigade, plus new boy Ian Byrne, an immigrant from Cantril Farm (known as 'Canny farm'), an overspill area on the outskirts of the city built to house people removed during the slum clearances in and around Everton in the 1960s. Young Ian's early displays of solidarity on the pitch led naturally to his role as a trade unionist as an adult – who was then elected as Labour MP for the city's West Derby constituency in the 2019 general election. As well as the kids from St Michael's in our team, we had mates from nearby estates who went to other schools. Some went to 'Proddy' (Protestant) schools – and a few were even Kopites (aka Liverpool fans). But we got on. We were a team, and we had some great tussles on the Flinders Street fields on Sundays, mainly against opponents from the Scotland Road area called Four Swallows, and another outfit named Scottie Club, whose manager, Joe Murphy, spent ages trying to poach one or two of us to join his squad of stars assembled from all over the city. A skinny kid called Steven McManaman was the subject of Murphy's attentions too.

McManaman was an interesting character. A nice, quiet boy from nearby Kirkdale, he attended St John's primary school, our arch-rivals. We only lost once in the whole season – and it was to them. I remember the cruel 4–3 defeat like it was yesterday. Not because it was our only loss, or because of McManaman's prodigious dribbling ability (he scored four second-half goals to overturn a 3–0 half-time deficit). It was because it was a small-sided game – seven a side. The pitch was smaller, naturally, and the lower numbers meant that as a central midfielder I was constantly involved. I recall our teacher, Mr Doyle, praising the quality of the game. He knew. We knew. And I'm sure McManaman's team knew: this was what football should be about at this age. The scouting network that unearthed McManaman for Liverpool was huge in the city in the 1980s. Speaking shortly after Wayne Rooney's explosive entrance on to the world stage in 2004, McManaman told *FourFourTwo* magazine why he signed for the Reds not the Blues. 'Liverpool's youth policy was much better. When I was younger I was desperate to sign for Everton but they weren't as forthcoming.' The long line of Evertonians who broke through at Liverpool is testament to this assertion. From Ian Rush to Robbie Fowler, Michael Owen and Jamie Carragher, they all ended up wearing red after being snapped up from under Everton's noses. McManaman went up further in my estimation years later when he revealed he used to celebrate headed goals in training at Liverpool by wheeling away roaring 'Latchford!' in honour of Everton's legendary late-1970s number nine Bob Latchford.

A few rungs below the pro clubs, another scouting network was operating in north Liverpool, led single-handed by Ronnie Brown, a sprightly refuse collector known as 'running Ronnie' because of the mileage he clocked up daily shuffling around the city; sometimes running for fitness, but usually on a mission – or 'a message' – to recruit players. Ronnie didn't coach at a grassroots football club. It wasn't even eleven-a-side. Running Ronnie knitted together teams of boys and girls to enter five-a-side tournaments in the city and beyond. He would no doubt have lapped up futsal in all its small-sided glory. Playing for Ronnie was a dream; there was no coaching as such. He simply put us on a pitch and reminded us to work hard, be brave and play as a team. And to never stop running. As well as our big Friday nights at the Rock – an indoor hall at a church youth club that became a mecca for five-a-side clashes between player-led teams from rival estates – many of us would get a call from Ronnie in midweek, saying he'd got the Rock for an hour or two. It was usually late afternoon, not long after getting home from school. Not that any of us would ever say no, but his presence at your front door, smiling through the exertion of bombing round the streets snaring players, always felt like a massive confidence boost. He's putting in the effort, so we should too, I thought.

When I caught up with Stuart Carrington, who now works for Liverpool FA and mentors FA grassroots coaches like I do, he told me he felt exactly the same. 'Ronnie was amazing,' recalls Carrington. 'Yeah, he'd give you a knock and if we weren't in school we'd go to the Rock for about an hour. It was constant one-v-ones. You'd come off the pitch exhausted.' The one-v-one sessions in the Rock were the epitome of simple, effective coaching in perfect conditions: a hard surface, indoors, goals, games and competition. Ronnie's calling card wasn't only an invitation to the Rock. Sometimes he'd just get us out running with him. Carrington recalls another visit when Ronnie lured him on a run to deliver a letter. Only once they got running did Ronnie reveal the destination. 'It was Canny Farm . . . the round trip was about twenty miles in all,' recalls Carrington. 'It was crazy. When we got there, Ronnie knocks at the door, hands the letter to this woman. She gives us two glasses of water. We just swigged them – and then ran back!' Ronnie's passion for running was matched by his desire to recruit players. 'He wasn't really a coach,' explains Carrington. 'He was a scout. Always on the lookout for players, putting them in teams. Teams that won loads. Scouse street footballers. Adults and kids. Always small-sided tournaments, and usually five a side.' When he died in 2016, aged eighty-eight, Ronnie was described as 'a legend' in the *Liverpool Echo* for his work in north Liverpool. For me, he was the man who sowed the seed of the small-sided game in us at a young age. We knew the game offered something different.

* * *

São Paulo FC had reached the big stage. The main stand was packed. An iconic name of Brazilian football was back on the hallowed turf of Goodison Park, less than two decades after Pelé's Brazil had graced it with their presence in the 1966 World Cup. It was a crisp September evening in 1984. The towering floodlights illuminated the Grand Old Lady as clouds of foggy air clung close to the head of each player storming around the pitch. With ten seconds remaining, an explosion of sound and energy greeted the fierce scream of the referee's whistle. He pointed to the penalty spot. A São Paulo defender's desperate lunge had crudely taken out the marauding opponent heading for goal with just the keeper to beat. The penalty was converted to level the game at 3–3, a dramatic conclusion to the contest. Now it was penalties. São Paulo's jubilant and relieved opponents celebrated as though they'd won.

I remember it clearly. The small and spindly counter-attacker upended in the dying seconds? That was me. The offender? Stuart Carrington, my friend, teammate and, for several weeks that late summer and early autumn, a fierce and uncontactable rival. His move to São Paulo caused a sensation in our north Liverpool world. He didn't have to go too far. They were not actually from Brazil. They were from West Derby, a mile or so down the road. Their choice of name, a nod to one of the most famous football clubs in Brazilian football, bears testimony to the regard with which all things samba were held in a football-mad city such as Liverpool. The fact that they actually called themselves 'San Paulo' was a nice Scouse touch. 'Spell it like you say it' is a Scouse tradition I'm all in favour of. They were a big attraction. Run by the father of one of their players, Michael Jeffrey (who went on to play for Newcastle United and for Fortuna Sittard in the Netherlands), everything about them screamed professional. The footage of the game – which I've watched more than a few times since – was captured by one of their parents on a device most of us had never seen before: a video camera. I was playing for Ronnie Brown's all-stars that night, for a team named after a police officer who had died. It was the under-14s clash between San Paulo and Bill Green in the highlight of the footballing calendar for many of us: the finals of the Merseyside Police five-a-side tournament.

Started in 1976, the annual multi-round battle to reach finals day involved an estimated 10,000 boys in well over 1,000 teams competing in under-12, under-14 and under-16 categories. The event assumed a more important role in a city whose social fabric was torn and fraying amid the economic hardship and ill-feeling towards the police that exploded in violence in Toxteth in 1981. We knew the finals were a big deal. Ronnie Brown wore a suit and a tie. He looked like a different fella without his baggy, homemade-looking blood-red trackie bottoms and loose-fitting grey sweatshirt, a fag hanging from his mouth at all times when not pounding the streets. He sat nervously, edgily, but proudly in the Everton home dugout, the one from where Howard Kendall would punch the air in delight a few months later when Everton upended mighty Bayern Munich in the European Cup Winners' Cup semi-final (a game at which I was a ballboy) on the way to clinching a league and European trophy double.

Within ten seconds of kick-off, Stuey had given San Paulo the lead. The tinder-box was ablaze. We scrapped like dogs, fighting for control of the ball in a relentless first few minutes. It was the intensity, looking back now, that I realise I've rediscovered since falling for futsal. The rules were as close to futsal as we could get back then, with side lines, not walls, and underarm roll-ins. But the classic British five-a-side no-over-head-height and penalty area restrictions applied. The game itself was a rollercoaster. We equalised five minutes into the ten-minute first half and took the lead shortly after the restart. Then Stuey struck again. A corner on their right was played invitingly across the penalty area, the no-man's-land where no player could venture. As it ran harmlessly out of play, all of us successfully blocking the San Paulo players' runs, the ref peeped his whistle and pointed at Nicko. He was standing two yards inside the penalty area, hands outstretched, looking back at Stuey. 'He pushed him in the area, ref,' we all shouted. Nicko was furious. Stuey was quietly ecstatic. Michael Jeffrey stepped up and dumped the ball past our goalie, Gerry O'Leary. It was 2–2. After another goal each, we went to penalties. They won, 4–3. Despite most of us being a year younger than our opponents, we had gone toe to toe with the team with the fancy trackies and Brazilian finesse.

Stuey told me years later that it wasn't the jazzy kit that encouraged him to switch to San Paulo. 'It was the sweets, mate. When we won, we'd get a load of sweets. We were just kids. That was the big attraction.' He got the sweets, we just got bitter. But all was forgotten soon enough. When Nicko tragically died of a heart attack in 2014, Stuey helped carry his coffin. Nicko's younger brother, Anthony (a former professional footballer at Crewe Alexandra who shone for England under-20s before retiring through injury), delivered a moving eulogy to his big brother at the Anfield crematorium, a short goal-kick from Stanley Park. When he got round to thanking those who'd helped carry the coffin, he shattered the pall of mourning hanging over the crowds gathered inside and out by recalling the penalty-area dark arts that Stuey had inflicted on his brother two decades earlier. The gallows humour raised warm smiles, inviting us to note that this was not the first time Stuey had held his big mate Nicko in a box.

The clue was in the name. De La Salle, my secondary school in Croxteth, Liverpool, offered a sign that futsal was in my education – at least implicitly. Although the school's name derives from the Lasallian Christian brothers, its literal translation from French is 'in the room', strikingly similar to the origins of the term 'futsal'. And it's fair to say we lived up to our name in De La Salle. As well as one of the strongest eleven-a-side footballing schools in the city, we also boasted a passion for playing informally, whether outside in crazy multi-game playground mayhem, or indoors in incessant games of bench ball, fast and frantic games with benches turned on their side as goals in the tiny, cramped gymnasium. The competitiveness was full-on in an all-boys school with a reputation for turning out top players and winning teams. The roll call starts with Mick Lyons, the Everton captain in the late 1970s, and includes Paul Jewell, the ex-striker who never quite made it at Liverpool but played hundreds of

Football League games – and later, as a manager, guided Bradford City into the Premier League – while the more recent breed of De La Salle products includes most notably England's record goalscorer and ex-Everton and Manchester United striker, Wayne Rooney.

Rooney formed one half of a strike partnership that made sporting history for the school in February 2003, when he was a seventeen-year-old prodigy making waves in the Premier League – just eighteen months after leaving the classroom behind. Rooney made his first of 120 England appearances at half-time in a friendly against Australia at West Ham's Upton Park ground. He walked on the pitch with another former pupil, Francis Jeffers, also making his international debut after leaving Everton to sign for Arsenal as Arsène Wenger's much-heralded 'fox in the box'. Jeffers and Rooney led the line together. Two kids from the same Croxteth school. Jeffers scored the goal in a 3–1 defeat. But it's fair to say their career paths proved far less symmetrical from that day onwards. For Jeffers, it was his one and only cap.

There were many other strong sportsmen in my school. A prolific athlete in the year below me, Steve Smith, eventually soared to world prominence by winning a bronze medal in the high jump at the 1996 Olympics. Back on the football pitch, a boy called Ian Horrigan stood out in Smith's year, signing for Liverpool as an apprentice midfielder – only for his path to the first team to be thwarted when manager Kenny Dalglish signed a seventeen-year-old prodigy from Bournemouth named Jamie Redknapp. In the year below Ian at De La Salle, another central midfield dynamo, Darran Connor, forced his way into our under-18s first XI team alongside me despite being two years younger. In my year, by this time John McGreal, my earlier central midfield partner for school and Sunday team, had signed for Tranmere Rovers after evolving into a ball-playing central defender. He played two seasons in the Premier League for Ipswich Town and went on to manage Colchester United. Another teammate, Joey

Murray, starred for England under-15s – keeping a young Andy Cole (later of Newcastle and Manchester United fame) out of the team – and was widely tipped as the player most likely to make it big at Liverpool ahead of McManaman. Joey was a rapid, ruthless goal-scoring sensation in his teenage years – a hybrid version of Rooney with a hint of Liverpool's Ian Rush – but he ended up playing against me in non-league football after a spell as a pro at Wrexham, having been released by Liverpool at the age of eighteen for suddenly being 'too small'. Much of our secondary school footballing experience was defined by small-sided, simplified and intensely enjoyable games on hard floors. No real coaching instruction. It was a case study in the phrase that became trendy in the FA's coaching parlance from the early 2000s: 'Let the game be the teacher.'

The opening of the luxurious Croxteth Sports Centre ready for the start of term in September 1985 was a game-changer for me. One of five brand new sports centres sanctioned by the Militant city council, honouring its commitment to give people what they needed despite the austerity imposed on the city from central government, it was a huge hit in Croxteth, opening our eyes us to all kinds of indoor court sports including squash, basketball and volleyball. Exposure to new court sports coincided with my year at Everton's school of excellence in 1985–6, where I trained every Monday night at the club's Bellefield training ground a couple of miles from my home. The focus in training was overwhelmingly on two games that could have been designed on the streets of the city or in the favelas of Brazil: five-a-side and head tennis, or *futevôlei* as it's known in Brazil, where the game was founded in 1965. At Everton, the philosophy was about touch and tenacity, speed and silk; no deep tactical analysis or overcomplicated insight. Just play, like on the streets – but with eagle-eyed Everton coaches looking on. We were urged to master the basics first, then go into battle with the will and desire to succeed. This was the sort of football I craved: the sort of intensity of focus, with nowhere to hide, that I would later discover in futsal. It was a passion that was demanded from us by the coaches. Colin Harvey, one of the club's famous holy trinity of midfielders – along with Howard Kendall and the 1966 World Cup winner Alan Ball – was Kendall's assistant in the all-conquering first team at the time. But he also found time to coach kids like me in the school of excellence. Harvey's commitment to fiercely energetic pressing out of possession, as well as for developing a sure touch and strength in possession, proved inspirational. It was the perfect environment to complement the voluntary, child-led festival of street football I was lucky enough to be living through.

The Glasgow-born winger Alan Irvine starred in the Everton first team for its first Wembley appearance in the run of startling success from 1984 onwards. He witnessed the love of five-a-side and head tennis first hand. When I spoke to him in 2019, he told me he continued to use five-a-side games in training as a coach at Premier League clubs. They're 'always a winner' with the players, he says. The dedication to head tennis at Everton was equally firm. 'Howard took it extremely seriously,' he recalls. 'It was fiercely competitive and could be anything from one-v-one up to lots of players on each side.' For me, the combination of games felt like the streets, with every player immersed in games of touch, precision and enjoyment. Exactly what formative experiences with a ball should be for children.

The golden age for the city's two football clubs also marked the start of the big council land sell-off as hard-pressed local authorities cashed in on public space and community facilities. The book *Played in Liverpool: Charting the Heritage of a City at Play*, by Ray Physick, notes how the 'dramatic decline' of fortunes in 1980s Merseyside brought the 'golden era' of public provision to a screeching halt. Since the 1930s, cities such as Liverpool had been vying to meet the 'Six Acre Standard' – the minimum ratio of outdoor space for recreation for every 1,000 people, as decreed by the National Playing Fields Association. While some land was sold, the city's marked population decline from the 1980s onwards – by 2001 it was down to 440,000, its lowest since the middle of the nineteenth century – resulted in a paradox. The city returned close to the coveted 'Six Acre Standard' (equivalent to between two and three eleven-a-side football pitches). So even despite the marked increase in land sold to cope with the central government-imposed austerity from 2010 onwards, the space to play in cities like Liverpool was actually growing. Whether the space is indoors or out, futsal offers a ready-made solution. If the thousands of school halls, gyms and outdoor playground pitches up and down the country can be opened to the masses at reasonable cost, the void of play-free zones can be filled instantly. With a sport that was born out of a scarcity of space to play. It's also a sport that was undergoing its very own revolution of global governance, structure and participation in the 1980s – just as I was falling in love with the small-sided version of football in my home city.

CHAPTER 4
INTO THE 1990S: IT TAKES TWO TO TANGO

IT WAS NOT a pretty sight. The revered Adidas ball, stroked around so lovingly on the sun-baked grass surfaces in sultry Mexico a year earlier in the football World Cup, had been brought indoors. It was the ball itself that defined the mid-1980s as much as Diego Maradona's maverick genius: the fully synthetic and polyurethane-coated Azteca version of the Adidas Tango, first introduced in Argentina 1978, redesigned as the Tango España in 1982, then freshly adorned with distinctive Aztec-inspired imprints for Mexico 86. It was a natural evolution. But over a forty-minute indoor match in Brazil the following year, the iconic ball was simply not itself. It looked lost, marooned in unfamiliar environs. Not deflated as such; in fact, it seemed too pumped up, too responsive to every slight contact, deflection and attempt to calm its fury as it bobbled frantically around.

This was no sneak preview of the age of tiki-taka. Nor was it an addendum to the textbook on possession-based total football, by the Dutch master Rinus Michels. Hell, it wasn't even the carefully choreographed intensity of fut-sal, as *futebol de salão* had become known briefly in the early 1980s. It is best described as vaguely foot-ballish: a peculiar hybrid form of the game of association football in name only, appearing to the naked eye as though the eleven-a-side game had been scooped up and shoehorned on to a small indoor court, like a teenager's oversize foot squeezed into a dainty shoe by an over-eager parent. The game was the latest experimental incursion led by FIFA in its attempts to turn the South American obsession into a game of its own. The United States, led by the Poland-born coach John Kowalski, were playing Paraguay – and the Americans seemed less wary from the off, the ball not so much of a frustration to their strategic intent as it was for the Paraguayans. 'Thriving' would be too strong a word, but it's fair to say the pinball wizards of the US indoor game were more at home, despite being in Brazil, and without the comforting presence of the side boards traditional in indoor soccer. The South Americans tried in vain to play something resembling the cultured artistry of *futebol de salão*. But it takes two to tango, and in this case, the Adidas Tango simply didn't play ball. An ugly spectacle of unforced errors and wasted transitions ensued; a symbolic vision of the state of futsal in the mid-1980s. The South American *esporte da bola pesada* had been punted unthinkingly into a figurative limbo, fizzing about aimlessly before settling under the guidance of a caress sufficiently loving to create a new, bespoke version of the sport.

It was a game caught between two eras, a confusing stage of transition personified by the teams on show: the footballers from the country with the biggest history of indoor soccer, the US, up against the *futebol de salão* veterans of a generation or more, proudly flying the flag for Professor Ceriani's game in the continent where it was born. Every bobbling ball, mistimed control or wayward shot cried mismatch, the fumbling advances of a necessary evolutionary stage, as the old sport met the new thinking of the entryists. The US team's tactics could be said to reflect FIFA's blunt approach; the savvy and streetwise Paraguayans, on the other hand, carried the graceful air of a delicately balanced boxer, their artistic intent eventually delivering a 2-0 win. It was a metaphor for the times. But in the mid-1980s there was no guarantee the graceful pugilist of *futebol de salão* would win out against the big-hitting heavyweight with the unrivalled financial clout.

'Remember that FIFA had jumped into futsal with both feet,' says Steve Harris, a futsal journalist and veteran analyst of the game, whose testimony takes in the long journey from FIFUSA-run *futebol de sālao* to FIFA-orchestrated futsal. A straight-talking Californian who has lived in Japan since 1980, Harris explains how he jumped straight in himself after discovering the game in Tokyo, taking up key roles in FIFUSA as part of the Japan delegation easing the nation through its tentative baby steps in the game then known in his new homeland simply as 'salon'. Harris speaks proudly about working alongside the 'father of futsal' in Japan, Takao Sakae, in the FIFUSA-affiliated Japan Mini-Soccer Federation. Takao led Japan as one of the first nations to switch to FIFA by the end of the decade. Speaking in 2019, Harris recalls a flurry of experimental tournaments between 1985 and 1987 when FIFA was trying to make sense of what its own version of FIFUSA's game might look like. 'FIFA didn't know what they were doing, but they wanted nothing to do with what FIFUSA had done up to that point.' FIFA sought control of the sport that its president, João Havelange, knew only too well from his days at the heart of the very organisation it was now trying to eclipse.

A few months before the Paraguay–USA match in Brazil, FIFA invited thirteen nations to what is believed to be its first meaningful incursion into the FIFUSA-run game. The tournament gave four teams their maiden appearance under the auspices of football's governing body: the hosts, Hungary, the serial FIFUSA winners, Brazil, plus Peru and the USA. This experiment had been several years in the making. Havelange's gaze as FIFA supremo locked on the small-sided game in 1982, when FIFUSA held its first world championship. Although the word 'futsal' had been used since the 1960s by José

Antônio Inglêz at *A Gazeta Esportiva*, its growth in name recognition was somewhat stunted – unlike participation in the game itself, which spread like a feral weed. In some sections of the FIFUSA community, the abbreviation strayed too far from the original Spanish and Portuguese terms for the game, a concern borne out in the name of the second FIFUSA world championships in Spain in 1985, where the official literature made clear the tournament was called 'Fut-sal España'. Along with the mascot, Futsy the Zorro (fox), it was an unsubtle attempt to emphasise the sport's South American origins. Havelange's manoeuvring triggered a rearguard offensive from the FIFUSA bigwigs. 'They could see FIFA wanted control of the sport,' explains Harris. 'They were trying to hold on to their interests . . . and that's why they tried to hold on to the name futsal. FIFA was going to call it Football Five . . . this led to FIFUSA calling it in their documentation at the time "the wicked FIFA and its Football Five". They used the word futsal as a flag to go into battle with.'

Alexander Para was at the heart of FIFUSA as executive vice-president of the United States Futsal Federation from its inception in 1981 as the US Mini-Soccer Federation. The Argentina-born football referee responded to the pressure placed on FIFUSA members in the run-up to the 1985 tournament by seizing control of the name. The man described by the former US futsal team player and coach Keith Tozer as 'the godfather of futsal in the US' succeeded in trademarking the name 'futsal', the legacy of which is visible in Para's website for his US Futsal organisation, www.futsal.com. The Mini-Soccer Federation became US Futsal, affiliating to FIFA to become the first futsal member of US Soccer. Speaking on Tozer's hugely successfully World of Futsal podcast in 2019, Para explains the importance of the change. At the time, schools and colleges with halls for hire blanched at the name 'Mini-Soccer', fearful of a riot of flying indoor footballs smashing lights galore – a 1980s version of the identity problem Ceriani encountered at the outset of the sport in

1930s Montevideo. A change of name, with an emphasis on the new game with a smaller, less bouncy ball, would do the trick, Para hoped. And he was right: the hyphen was lost and a new, official name for the FIFUSA-led game was gained in the eyes of the law. The restrictions on its use didn't last, unlike the name itself. Within a few years the trademark lapsed, and FIFA was free to do what it wished with the sport. Para and most of the other leading figures in FIFUSA jumped ship to Havelange and Sepp Blatter's well-upholstered and alluring FIFA lifeboat. Para took up a place on FIFA's first futsal committee, a position he held until 2000, and is effusive in his praise of Havelange's sheer will and endeavour in promoting the sport he had grown up with throughout his long tenure as FIFA chief.

* * *

The Brazilian Raul's glorious title-clinching strike offered a fitting tribute to the state of the game. Rotterdam's Ahoy Sportpaleis arena was replete with 6,000 thrilled spectators sheltering indoors from the mid-January chill in 1989. The goal sealed Brazil's 2–1 triumph over the hosts, the Netherlands – a victory that yielded a magnanimous response from the crowd. Raul's moment of calm sophistication stood out. The early incarnation of futsal is often likened to a game of chess in its strategic and almost meditative state of play, and the final of the first FIFA world championship – while a little easier on the eye than the USA–Paraguay culture clash a couple of years earlier – still resembled one. Yet that opening goal showed glimpses of a greater futsal finesse to come. Of the total of seventeen nations invited to the first FIFA world championship in the Netherlands three years after its experiment in Hungary, seven more were making their debut: Algeria, Zimbabwe, Denmark, Japan, Saudi Arabia, Canada and Australia. The other six nations making up the roll call of the inaugural FIFA five-a-side football world championship, as it was officially called, had all begun playing internationals in the 1970s or 1980s in their own bespoke national versions of the game, affiliated to their national football associations. One or two, mainly the South Americans, ran teams in both FIFUSA and FIFA five-a-side during the period of transition. While FIFA's new offering was still a distance from becoming the only game in town, the presence in the Netherlands of nations from every continent was testament to its growing power and appeal. Coming a year after the Dutch masters Ruud Gullit and Marco van Basten secured a first European football title in West Germany, it marked the Netherlands out as the coming force in all aspects of football. Its long and proud history of five-a-side *zaalvoetbal* made it the obvious choice for FIFA. Clearly, it wasn't only my street kickabout mate Sonny Phillips who was inspired; an entire football-crazy country was still high on the fix of total football injected into its bloodstream.

The strong thread of footballing excellence was not confined to the host nation. Whereas the Dutch team was made up of experienced *zaalvoetbal* players, many of the nations making debuts as FIFA-affiliated teams turned to professional footballers as a quick-fix guarantee of a certain level of quality on the ball in a tournament they clearly wanted to take seriously. About half of the Algeria squad were professional footballers, as were the Danes. Japan, Canada and Australia called up players almost exclusively from the eleven-a-side game. But one man stood out as a beacon of the seriousness with which Denmark viewed the competition. Brian Laudrup donned his trainers and sparkled, the nineteen-year-old prodigy notching a hat-trick against Algeria in the group stages alongside Lars Olsen, the veteran of the 1988 European championships who went on to captain the Danish eleven-a-side team to their shock first European championship victory in 1992. The young Laudrup's futsal exploits came in the same year his older brother, Michael, signed for Barcelona, forming a formidable creative presence in Johan

Cruyff's 'dream team' as one of three overseas players alongside the Netherlands captain, Ronald Koeman, and the maverick Bulgarian Hristo Stoichkov.

The younger Laudrup holds a place in an elite band of three male players to have scored in both football and futsal World Cups. The others, Algeria's Lakhdar Belloumi and the USA's Bruce Murray, also competed in the 1989 tournament, Murray alongside German-born defender Michael Windischmann, who captained the eleven-a-side football team at Italia 90 after the USA qualified for a first World Cup in forty years. Unsurprisingly, it was the *futebol de salão* veterans of Brazil who triumphed, swiftly mastering the unusual ball in their familiar terrain of the forty metre by twenty metre court. Reflecting on the 1989 experience many years later, Laudrup – who went on to star for Bayern Munich and Glasgow Rangers – said the presence of eleven-a-side professionals was a necessary feature of the game's innovative early stages. The evolution of twenty-first century futsal means that particularly in Brazil, where some of the players are 'absolutely phenomenal', playing in both codes at the elite level is now an impossibility. 'It's a different ball game,' insists Laudrup.[11] The statistics support the Dane's observations. Only one player since the new millennium has emulated Laudrup et al. by competing in both world championships: Rolando Fonseca Jiménez, the all-time highest goalscorer for Costa Rica's football team, graced the court in the Guatemala futsal world championships two years before playing in the 2002 football World Cup, held in Korea and Japan.

The critical need for FIFA's historic 1989 tournament to make a splash cannot be overstated. So when Álvaro Melo Filho, the esteemed lawyer and president of the CBFS, accepted an invitation to talks in Rio de Janeiro in late 1988, he knew what was coming.

---

11. FIFA.com, 'Star-studded Memories of the First Futsal World Cup', 6 September 2016.

João Havelange was in town with his eventual successor as FIFA president, Joseph 'Sepp' Blatter. Melo Filho knew they meant business. As general secretary of FIFA, the Swiss administrator Blatter was Havelange's right-hand man during the displacement of FIFUSA until he took over from the Brazilian as president in 1998. Brazil wasn't the only country targeted by FIFA at the time. Australia's enormously successful National Indoor League, sponsored by the building giant James Hardie, kicked off to great fanfare in 1987. With games screened by the government-owned television network SBS, and big crowds flocking to the arenas, it was arguably the most high-profile futsal league in the world – an almighty achievement in a country dominated by rugby, Australian rules football and cricket. In the run-up to the FIFUSA world championships – held in Australia in 1988 – the battle between FIFA and FIFUSA flared up. In a report headlined 'FIFA blitz on indoor game', the Sydney-based *Daily Telegraph* newspaper told how the FIFUSA-affiliated Australian Indoor Soccer Federation (AISF), organiser of the indoor league, was coming under sustained pressure from FIFA, as it urged the Australian Soccer Federation to threaten any player appearing in the indoor league with a ban from FIFA-affiliated eleven-a-side football. The AISF fought back. One of the confrontations played out in the courts. The *Sydney Morning Herald* reported how an attempted 'show of strength' in the run-up to the FIFUSA tournament backfired when the federal court in Brisbane handed FIFA 'a bloody nose' by ruling that it could not enforce the ban.

Against this backdrop, the 1988 summit in Brazil invoked a striking echo of the 1967 meeting, also in Rio de Janeiro, called by Havelange to hammer out a deal with the YMCA to unite the game's devotees and fix a narrative about its origins, rules and identity. Havelange succeeded in getting the key players around a table, just as he had two decades earlier as head of the CBD. The difference was that in the late 1960s his powers of persuasion ultimately set the ball rolling on the eventual creation of FIFUSA in 1971. The 1988 summit arranged by the ultra-competitive former Olympian sounded the death knell for that very same organisation. The content of the conversations may well remain private, but the public impact was profound. A couple of months later, Álvaro Melo Filho willingly sanctioned the Brazil team to represent the country in the FIFA tournament, signalling a glorious victory for Havelange in his long pursuit of the biggest star in the futsal firmament. With Brazil on board, FIFA had won. Melo Filho saw it as a victory for Brazilian sport and took up a place on the FIFA futsal committee to oversee the sport's development. Fittingly, Brazil triumphed on the court too, regaining the world crown after losing it to Paraguay in the recent FIFUSA World Cup.

While the political jousting yielded a clear outcome for the steward-ship of the sport, the uneasy compromise on the amalgamation of the old and the new, the eleven-a-side veterans and the *futebol de salão* artists, ushered in an era defined by incompatible rules, clashing philosophies and a staccato, unedifying spectacle on court. Just as in those experimental mid-80s matches, the ball was a massive problem. FIFA started with rules more like the outdoor-friendly version of the game popular in the Netherlands, ditching the size 3 *bola pesada*. 'When used outside it just died,' recalls Steve Harris. 'For outdoor players it was too hard to handle. So FIFA used the size 5 bouncing ball. And they thought "while we're at it let's get rid of the stopping clock". So if you're leading . . . just kick it out, and continue winning the game.

'This is critical,' Harris states. 'You've got a size 5 ball, bouncy as hell . . . it's gonna make for really shitty futsal. And it did. They scrapped the five-foul rule. So there was as much fouling as you want.' The country of Harris's birth was the one to profit most from the rule changes. In the United States, an ultra-physical indoor soccer, with ice hockey-style side boards inviting meaty physical confrontations, was the game *du jour*. 'That's why they did so well,' says Harris, laughing. 'They were very physical. It caught the Brazilians off guard. They had guys openly body checking them off the ball. Also the clock wasn't stopping. The USA were in their element.' The United States finished in a shock third place, beating Belgium 3–2 in the play-off after losing to the Netherlands in the semi-final.

The 1990s began with FIFA in the driving seat, its new futsal committee helping propel the game into new territories. The next FIFUSA World Cup took place in Italy in 1991 with the remnants of the organisation reeling from the mass defections. As if to emphasise the scale of the change, Brazil – where the FIFA game was fast displacing the old ways of *futebol de salão* – entered a team but failed to reach the final. It was their former colonial rulers, Portugal, who flexed their developing small-sided muscle to win it, beating Brazil's conquerors in 1988, Paraguay, in the final. Brazil's status as top dog in the FIFUSA game was gone for good, its energies suddenly transferred to the FIFA code. It was a switch with huge consequences for both the original and the newly minted, evolving form of the small-sided game. The FIFUSA nations reacted by reforming under the banner of Confederação Pan-Americana de Futebol de Salão (known as PANAFUTSAL), to continue the original form of the game as a rival to FIFA's version. A flirtation with compromise raised the spectre of a grand merger of the codes in 2000, only for old divisions to resurface. This prompted the former FIFUSA nations to restate their independence with a whole new identity: the Asociación Mundial de Futsal (AMF).

The scale of the schism between FIFA and FIFUSA is evident in the official names of the first two FIFA world championships, in 1989 and 1992. The word 'futsal' was conspicuously absent. The first was called 'five-a-side football', the second 'indoor football', with 'five-a-side' relegated to brackets in the official literature.[12] The name of the game fought over so passionately for the best part of a decade was not mentioned once in the technical report after the 1989 tournament. Evidently, links with the FIFUSA version of the game were too politically sensitive to revisit. FIFA wanted it both ways: to adopt the game as its own, and at the same time to reject its history. Signs of a *détente* emerged in 1992, at the second tournament in Hong Kong. The technical report at least acknowledged that 'the official title of this type of football was again the subject of discussion'. Continuing that 'Whereas in Spanish-speaking countries the expression "futsal" (short for *fútbol sala*) is used in reference to this game of football, in English-speaking countries it is known as indoor or five-a-side football', it went on to point out that in the USA, 'where it is played with six players and perimeter boards, it is called indoor'.

On the court, the significant change was the return of the stopping clock that marked out the FIFUSA game. It was a tacit, if solitary, acceptance of the valid critique from all those recent converts from FIFUSA – that FIFA's first incarnation of the game was very much a work in progress. The baby had not quite been thrown out with the bath water – but it was hardly being cuddled, nurtured and cosseted in a warm blanket either. The gratuitous time-wasting of 1989 was eradicated at a stroke: the number of goals soared from 221 in forty matches in the Netherlands to 307 in Hong Kong, as Brazil retained their crown with a thumping 4–1 victory against the United States.

The third FIFA world championship in Spain in 1996 was when reality hit home for the FIFA futsal committee. It was an indication perhaps that the dwindling band of FIFUSA refuseniks pursuing their own PANAFUTSAL path while clinging on to their purist

---

12. FIFA's first five tournaments were called 'world championship'. The 2008 tournament in Brazil was the first to be officially called 'futsal World Cup'.

version no longer posed a threat to the sustainability of the new game – one increasingly taken up by nations with a proud history of pre-FIFA *futebol de salão*. Para told the World of Futsal podcast the battle to persuade FIFA to use the name futsal for the world championship 'took a lot of lobbying'. The critical turning point had come two years earlier, when calls for greater FIFA boldness from futsal advocates such as Para and Harris grew too loud to be ignored. The venue was Milan, which played host to what is commonly seen as the first glimpse of the second generation of FIFA futsal.

'It was a coming-out party,' says Harris, who attended the invitation-only tournament with the Japanese squad to watch teams feel their way into the experimental new laws of the game. Spain, Poland, Hungary, Croatia and Japan were invited to the tournament, officially called Calcio a 5 in accordance with the Italian hosts' name for futsal. It was the first tournament in a regular event that became known as Futsal Mundialito, held on average once every two years until 2008. The hosts, Italy, edged out Croatia in the inaugural event, with Spain taking third place. The Milan showcase was an undoubted triumph, with coming luminaries of the game on court such as Javi Rodríguez, a future double World Cup winner for Spain and star winger for Barcelona futsal team. Also in attendance was a young Mićo Martić, captaining the Croatia team during the illustrious playing days that preceded his storied career as a coach. The success of the tournament acted as a safety valve to reduce the pressure on FIFA's emerging game and offered confirmation, if any were needed, of its validity as a sport in its own right.

The reintroduction of the stopping clock brought this short era of crude experimentation to an end, with the Milan 'test tournament' confirming the growing consensus that three significant changes to the game should be adopted for the 1996 world championship. 'It was phenomenal,' recalls Harris. 'It was the birth of the modern game. The first two FIFA tournaments were just rough and tumble, a messy experiment that didn't quite work.' So what were the other two 'critically important' changes? After the clock, the second and third major rule changes involved the ball and the goalkeeper. The new law for goalkeepers mirrored the shift in direction in the eleven-a-side game from 1992 onwards. Abuse of the back-pass law allowing goalkeepers to pick up the ball from a teammate's pass slowed the game up dramatically. 'It would happen a million times in a futsal game,' says Harris. In eleven-a-side football, the new Law 12, section 2 abruptly stopped teams abusing the goalkeeper's freedom to hold on to the ball repeatedly in order to waste time.

Many football fans in England, most of them disdainful Everton supporters like me, it has to be said, readily attribute Liverpool's long spell without a league title between 1990 and 2020 to this momentous change. Their era of unprecedented success domestically and in Europe was built from the back: the sight of Ray Clemence, and later Bruce Grobbelaar, hogging the ball in neat, repetitive triangles with Alan Hansen and Phil Neal was as familiarly frustrating to many football fans as a moment of Kenny Dalglish-inspired genius at the other end was beguiling. Once Liverpool took the lead, which they did – often – they were world-beaters at the dark arts of closing out games – and the goalkeeper's freedom to persistently pick up the ball from passes precluded the need to resort to the modern equivalent of such tactical chicanery: the obligatory ninetieth-minute dash to an opposition corner flag to shield, preen and provoke as the clock ticks down relentlessly.

FIFA futsal followed the eleven-a-side game in outlawing the back-pass pick-up, making the game quicker and more creative, while encouraging higher pressing on court. This built on the law change freeing up the goalkeeper to leave the goal area – an early winner for FIFA rules – before they went one step further than the FIFUSA game by changing Law 16 of the FIFA rule book, a stipulation still applied in the FIFUSA successor AMF's game decades later, that prohibited goalkeepers from launching the ball into the opposition half without it touching the ground first. Up until the 1996 FIFA world championship in Spain, referees were obliged to blow up for an indirect free kick to the defending team if an opposition keeper went long. The rule remains a frequent cause of fierce debates in futsal, with opponents of this largesse towards keepers maintaining that the ability to go long militates against the development of creative build-up play. But one thing is clear: in a game of transitions with goalkeepers so prominent in and out of possession, the speed, directness and capacity for end-to-end attacks can only be assisted by allowing keepers to go direct. The writing was on the wall after the 1992 world championship. 'An indirect free kick never gives the same impetus of surprise as the immediate possession of the ball and direct play towards the opponents' goal,' was the sage conclusion of the tournament technical report. The change was due.[13] The most profound modification for the 1996 tournament was to the ball, the object fought over most vigorously over the decades. The flyaway, bouncing size 5 Adidas Azteca that FIFA had foisted on unsuspecting players from the 1986 Hungary experiment onwards was replaced by a size 4 futsal ball with reduced bounce – closer in diameter to a size 3 football but with the weight of a size 5. The decision was a clear sop to the growing clamour for the smaller, less bouncy *bola pesada* to return. It is the ball that defines the game, of course, the object that has long been credited with facilitating the acute technical mastery that marks out futsal players as different.

The same divergence exists in 2020: the maximum size FIFA futsal ball is a size 4 but its circumference is between 62.5cm and 63.5cm, the weight between 410g and 430g – and, crucially, the rebound

---

13. Acrobatic volleyed goals from a goalkeeper's long throw were common in beach soccer, which held its first World Cup in 1995, and played a part in influencing the thinking on changing the law to allow them to take place in futsal too.

when the bespoke foam-filled ball is dropped from a height of 2m should be between 55cm and 65cm. On average, this 'first rebound height' is about 44 per cent of an equivalent-sized eleven-a-side ball, which should bounce back to about 135cm after being dropped. In Brazil, the country where the game was played most, the early-90s switch from FIFUSA to FIFA – and the subsequent agreement on using the compromise size 4 ball – spelled the end for the traditional size 3 micro *bola pesada* that millions of young *futebol de salão* stars had grown up mastering.

The impact of the ball change was immediate. The post-tournament report recognised two apparently novel technical features on court, both involving using the toe to manoeuvre the smaller, denser ball. The skills developed in the age of the size 3 *bola pesada* had returned with the arrival of the size 4 futsal ball. 'Although most of the play indoors is on the ground,' it stated, 'the lob has proved valuable in both attack and defence.' The lob, or scooped pass, has come to typify the subtleties of the sport – a skill born out of necessity in an arena not too dissimilar to the street, playing with a half-pumped ball on a tiny pitch littered with obstacles. It's a futsal fundamental, often employed instinctively as a flicked parallel (down-the-line) pass, floating tantalisingly through the waist-height 'dead zone' – just above a straining defender's leg or thigh – or as a loftier diagonal pass over an opponent's head to find a free teammate. The second technique suddenly more prevalent in 1996 was also clear, according to the report: 'Shooting: in addition to the many hard and well-placed shots taken with the instep or the inside of the foot, there were also a lot struck with the toe. Above all, the Brazilians used this technique.' The first real Brazilian superstar of futsal, Manoel Tobias, was among those who swiftly adapted to the new size 4 version of the customary *bola pesada*, voted player of the tournament in 1996 as he shot his team to victory. He was lauded as the 'Ronaldo of futsal' in honour of his compatriot, *O Fenômeno*, who picked up the FIFA world footballer of the year accolade in that same year.

In just over a decade, Spain had played host to two tournaments that spanned the era of crude experimentation. If the second FIFUSA tournament in 1985, with Havelange and Blatter busily pursuing the game, marked the start of the organisation's crisis of conviction about its future, the third FIFA iteration of the world championship in 1996 heralds the end of any uncertainty. The veritable festival of action played out in Murcia, Segovia, Castellon and Barcelona was undoubtedly FIFA's game now. Futsal 2.0 had arrived.

Around the world, leagues of increasing competitiveness and quality were established as FIFA-sanctioned entities. The Liga Nacional de Fútbol Sala in Spain (LNFS), formed in 1989, was fast growing a reputation as the best league in the world. Elsewhere in Europe professionalism was growing in leagues in Russia and Ukraine. Meanwhile, in Brazil, the autonomous Confederação Brasileira de Futebol de Salão (CBFS) founded the Liga Nacional de Futsal (LNF) in 1996 with a franchise model inspired by the American NBA basketball league, a bold response to the new era of harmony over the game's past, present and future. Both the Spanish and Brazilian leagues, along with the Russian national futsal Super League, founded in 1991, were operated from the outset at arm's length from their national football associations, a vital separation that cannot be overlooked in any analysis of the reasons why the leagues have led the way in world futsal. Soon all the major leagues worldwide were operating with futsal as it looks in 2020: with kick-ins, the four-second limit on goalkeepers retaining possession and for set pieces, and a power-play involving the use of the fly-goalkeeper (where a player vacates the goal to join a five-versus-four attacking overload) all inspiring a new generation of coaches to enhance the look, feel and enjoyment inherent in the game. So it was no surprise when the remnants of

FIFUSA, operating under the remit of PANAFUTSAL, finally gave up the ghost.

Alex Astorgas, a Catalan former FIFA futsal referee and long-time AMF advocate, tells me Bolivia 2000 turned out to be the final championship held under the loose banner of the marginalised FIFUSA. 'The conflicts inside FIFUSA became more and more obvious,' he explains. More nations left to join FIFA. 'The solution was to create a new brand with fresh air, and to force all FIFUSA members to start from zero with the AMF.' Astorgas, whose father, Carlos, was a referee and leading light on the futsal committee in the Spanish football federation, the Real Federación Española de Fútbol (RFEF), switched attention to pushing the growth of non-FIFA futsal in Catalonia, eventually taking on the role of secretary of the AMF-affiliated Futsal European Federation in 2017. He tells me the AMF's bold ambition is to give every country 'a structure independent from football to develop futsal' as a sport in its own right. Back in the 2000s, however, with a clear delineation between what was FIFA futsal and what was not, the clarity gave rise to landmark changes. In 2008, FIFA finally wrapped up an era of wrangling over names, hyphens, rules, balls and the very ownership of the game by officially declaring the global tournament in Brazil 'the 2008 futsal World Cup', marking an end of a twenty-year journey from the tentatively named 'five-a-side football world championships' held in the Netherlands in 1989.

CHAPTER 5
THE WATFORD GAP

'SORRY SCOUSE, THERE are thousands like you . . .'

That was the end for me. I wasn't surprised, and I didn't need to sit down to compose myself. I was already sitting – a touch uncomfortably, it has to be said, as the Watford FC reserve team bus wove through a crisp, autumnal north London evening, the traffic flushing us out of town towards the notoriously chaotic junction with the North Circular, on the short trip home to Vicarage Road. The bearer of bad news was Stuart Murdoch, the reserve team manager who went on to manage Wimbledon through their painful, angst-ridden switch to Milton Keynes a decade later in 2003. He knew his stuff. And he'd seen enough of me after just a few days of a one-week trial training with the first team to know I wasn't up to it. Today was simply confirmation. I'd set off to Highbury with my boots and shin pads, all ready to pit my wits against Arsenal's new generation, after being told I might get a run-out as a triallist in the Neville Ovenden Football Combination reserve team. I didn't make the squad. They were protecting me – and themselves – from embarrassment, I guess. The following day I trained again, and for the rest of the week, found the weight of expectation lifted from my shoulders. I realised eleven-a-side football at anything approaching elite level wasn't for me.

During the match, I even enjoyed kicking my heels in the stands. As the action unfolded, I chatted about tactics, coaching and life in general with one of Watford's young strikers who was my age – twenty-one – and recovering from injury. Alex Inglethorpe went on play more than one hundred games in lower-league football, before establishing a reputation as a promising young coach. Brendan Rodgers snapped him up from Tottenham Hotspur in 2012 to manage Liverpool FC's under-21s, then swiftly promoted him to academy director, where he oversaw the next generation of young stars – and continues to do so under Rodgers' successor, Jürgen Klopp. As for the training at Watford, my most vivid memory is chasing the shadow of Luther Blissett, keeping fit with the first team after his contract had expired, who still boasted a ghostly, balletic presence a full decade after moving to AC Milan for £1m. My hopes of incessant five-a-sides in training didn't quite materialise. Watford's victory in the London *Evening Standard* five-a-side football tournament earlier that year had skewed my expectations. Held at the London Arena, the five-a-side tournament was in its third decade, and was the closest event England got to futsal at the pro level back then. The 1967 edition was famously won by West Ham United, with a hat-trick from Geoff Hurst in the final handing Bobby Moore the pleasure of lifting the trophy as captain, a year after the same combination led Alf Ramsey's England to glory in the World Cup final at the stadium around the corner.

The Watford experience put paid to my residual hopes of a football career. It was 1993, the second year of the all-new FA Carling Premiership, the hype-fuelled Sky Sports monster of commercial footballing extravagance that became known as the Premier League from 2007. As well as the shiny new name and the promise of a monopoly of riches for the biggest clubs, and the challenging new back-pass law, there was a momentous cultural shift in football tactics that heralded an age of appreciation in England for a different type of player – one whose core skills could be honed naturally on a futsal court. Eric Cantona's arrival at Manchester United shifted the tectonic plates of English football. 'The purchase of a player in Cantona's mould revolutionised United's tactical approach overnight,' says Michael Cox in his chronicle of tactics in the Premier League era, *The Mixer*. Five months after arriving from the reigning champions, Leeds, Cantona's exotic bravura led Manchester United to their first title in twenty-six years. The French maverick was unstoppable. His forte was simply going where no other forward tended to go, picking up the ball in 'the hole', 'between the lines', playing the number ten role, all phrases that would become basic entries in the football lexicographer's compendium.

The league's top scorer that season was Teddy Sheringham, who would eventually replace Cantona at United, but was busy scoring for Nottingham Forest before a mid-season switch to Tottenham. Cantona excelled with sixteen assists and was one of only two non-English players in the top ten goalscorers' list for the season, the other being United's Welsh striker Mark Hughes. Meanwhile, the following season at Kevin Keegan's newly promoted Newcastle United, Andy Cole – the boy kept out of the England under-15s team by my old school teammate Joe Murray – romped to the top of the goalscoring charts with thirty-four, assisted in no small measure by arguably the best number ten English football has ever seen: Peter Beardsley. The Newcastle-born forward, who acted as chief creator to Gary Lineker on international duty for years, grabbed twenty-one on top of Cole's haul. Suddenly everyone was looking for a number ten, a search that eventually unearthed gems such as Dennis Bergkamp at Arsenal, and later Chelsea's Gianfranco Zola. 'A wave of talented, mercurial but often inconsistent number tens joined the Premier League during the mid-90s, with mixed success,' says Cox.

After my own brief exposure to this alternative role a few years earlier, playing for my school team aged seventeen – at the height of the inimitable Beardsley's prominence at Liverpool – the elite of English football were discovering the delights of the withdrawn forward. I returned from my brief foray south of the Watford Gap knowing a career in the professional game was not for me. I'd discovered a gulf of my own: between the desire to actually touch the ball and play, and the harsh pragmatism of eleven-a-side football. After three seasons at St Helens Town, the Watford experience proved a lightbulb moment illuminating my need to play, to be at the centre of the action, to try to make things happen. I vowed to go where I would get most touches of the ball – just like on the streets – while trying to establish a day-job career as a journalist. I opted to follow the St Helens manager, Mick Holgate, who departed for Bolton-based Horwich Railway Mechanics Institute, leaving his assistant Jimmy McBride to take over at Saints. Horwich RMI were two divisions higher up the English football pyramid, and famous for being one of two clubs founded at Lancashire and Yorkshire railway depots in the late nineteenth century. (The other was Newton Heath, who later became Manchester United.) Though Horwich's pitch was among the worst in the northern non-league game, we tried to play decent football.[14] When Horwich controversially upped sticks, sold Grundy Hill and bought Leigh Rugby League Club, ten miles away on the edge of rival town Wigan, there was uproar. The club's final game was the last day of the 1994–95 season, the year I got an unexpected run in the side in the increasingly popular number ten role, starting with a 3–2

---

14. Our left-back Stu Phoenix was at the heart of it all. A former professional at Wigan Athletic, Phoenix moved from St Helens to Horwich with me and Ged Nolan, an elegantly robust centre-back from Liverpool who had been at Halifax Town. Phoenix dominated home games. For a full half, at least. The Grundy Hill pitch sloped lengthways from one end to the other. But it also fell away steeply across the pitch too, declining from the main stand behind the dugouts down. The peculiar double incline meant the corner on the highest side of the pitch became the prime target area for attacks. Phoenix would touch the ball more than any other player when attacking uphill towards the corner summit. Any free-kick or corner driven in along the ground from there would soar into the box at crossbar height. It proved crudely effective.

Boxing Day victory away at arch-rivals Chorley. The final game as Horwich RMI ended in defeat away at the newly crowned Northern Premier League champions Marine FC, a loss that relegated us from the sixth to the seventh tier of English football.

I stayed for two more seasons at the renamed, and resurgent, Leigh RMI before moving briefly to Caernarfon Town in the League of Wales, where games often felt more like rugby than football, but my pay doubled to £120 a game. Next was Vauxhall Motors, the club based at the car plant in Ellesmere Port, near Liverpool. It was here that I enjoyed non-league football most. The pitch was pristine. We played the game the right way, with the spine of the team comprising excellent lads recently released from pro clubs, including defender Carl Spellman (from Everton), ball-playing midfielder Carl Nesbitt (Liverpool) and fleet-footed striker Gregg Blundell (Tranmere Rovers and, later, Doncaster Rovers). It was joyful, intense and successful, with lightweight central midfielders like me actually involved in build-up play rather than getting a stiff neck watching the ball soar over our heads from one end to the other. After my time, Vauxhall went on to achieve successive promotions to the sixth tier of the English game. I left it behind when Emily, my then girlfriend, got a job in Newcastle in 1998 and I moved with her, switching from my job as a journalist at the *Liverpool Echo* to work at the *Sunday Sun* newspaper in the north-east. I turned out a few times for my colleague Martin Hardy's Sunday league side, the North Shields-based FC Formica, where I found the blend of passion and industrial flair I'd been used to (and actually enjoyed weekly five-a-side jousts in Gateshead and at Newcastle University much more). Having departed for London to work on national newspapers, I got married before settling in Reading. It was here that I returned to coaching – having dabbled at US summer camps in my university years – after Emily gave birth to our two sons, Conor and Dominic. By 2004, with the boys aged three and one, the world of football had moved on – and I was desperate to engage as a coach as soon as my boys could walk. It was at this time that I realised my nagging desire for an alternative form of football, something more vibrant, more engaging; something that was more me.

* * *

Matt Higginbottom's departure from the windswept pitch in the seventy-seventh minute of a Northern Counties East League Division One match against Tadcaster Albion at Wheatley Park, on the outskirts of Leeds, triggered an ovation like no other he'd experienced. 'Substitution for Garforth Town, ladies and gentlemen,' boomed the giddy stadium announcer, 'is number six, Sócrates!'

One of the giants of Brazilian football strode into the fray wearing the yellow shirt of Garforth Town, complete with the logos of Lego and Socatots. The famously laid-back, beer-swilling, chain-smoking fulcrum of the 1982 World Cup squad, nicknamed 'Doctor Sócrates' on account of his medical degree, warmed the keeper's hands with a sweetly struck first touch. The crowd, who had been snapping up £5 Sócrates T-shirts, delighted in his substantial presence, having spent the previous hour imploring the Garforth coach, Simon Clifford, to put him on. When he did appear, minus the three coats he'd been blanketed in, he lugged his bulky 1.95 metre frame on to the bobbly English pitch, conspicuous by the absence of the trademark sleek physique and Björn Borg-style headband of yesteryear. The shot and a few delicate flicks and neat passes aside, this was the sum total of his attempt to roll back the years, wearing thick black gloves, the physio's boots and lumbering around like a shadow of his former self. 'The English game is very fast,' he explained later, complaining of an 'incredible headache' due to the cold. 'And I am a fifty-year-old man.'[15] His single appearance at Garforth in November 2004 marked

---

15. *Guardian*, 'Former Brazil Captain Breaks the Ice' by Alex Bellos, 22 November 2004.

the high point of several years of outlandish escapades by Clifford, a Middlesbrough-born Leeds primary school teacher with a passion for developing football skills in the mould of the Brazilian's native *futebol de salâo*. The 1,300-plus crowd didn't care that Sócrates hardly touched the ball. The shivering superstar was mobbed after the referee, David Midgley from Huddersfield, blew the whistle to end the game at 2–2. Yorkshire had been handed a glimpse of the man described by the author Jonathan Wilson as the 'brain of Brazil' in arguably the *seleção's* most creative team ever. 'He might not quite have had the flair of Zico, but he was the central intelligence,' says Wilson.

Clifford's emergence at Garforth Town – which he bought in 2003 with ambitions to turn it into a Premier League club – came after the best part of a decade developing Brazilian soccer schools in the UK and around the world. The man who became close friends with the first true Brazilian star of the English game, Middlesbrough's silken-footed dribbler Juninho, was on a mission. Naturally Juninho grew up playing *futebol de salão* in his school in São Paulo, Oratoria Avenue Primary School in the Italian district, and was happy to share his thoughts on the skill development inherent in the game. Juninho had been snapped up by Bryan Robson, the Middlesbrough manager, after seeing him destroy England in an Umbro Cup match at Wembley in 1995. The Brazilian scored a classic *folha seca* (falling leaf) free kick, then set up another youngster, Ronaldo, for his first international goal. 'Juninho wore Brazil's number 10, the most iconic shirt in world football,' writes Michael Cox in *The Mixer*. 'It was the first of Ronaldo's sixty-two international goals, and yet everyone was talking about Juninho.' Cox says Juninho's introduction to English football completed a quartet of outstanding number tens – the others being Cantona, Bergkamp and Zola – who would change the English game for ever.

Clifford's missionary zeal on the back of the Juninho mania sweeping the nation was only intensified on a summer trip to Brazil, funded by a £5,000 loan from the teachers' union. Clifford, twenty-seven at the time, used his links with the young Brazilian to secure time observing the great Zico and Rivellino coaching, soaking up the wonders of *futebol de salão* before returning inspired and determined to revolutionise English youth football development. The trip came a year after Brazil's professional LNF had kicked off, and the 1996 world championships in Spain had settled the debate on how the FIFA indoor game should look and feel. With Clifford very much espousing the purist nature of traditional *futebol de salão*, emphasising the need for a small ball, he was soon running a company with 500 soccer schools worldwide. He also launched the groundbreaking pre-school Socatots skill development programme and was hailed as 'an absolute genius' by Keira Knightley, star of the 2002 hit film *Bend It Like Beckham*, after he was recruited to coach her and co-star, Parminder Nagra, during filming for football-playing scenes.

As a non-league footballer in Liverpool at the time, I heard Clifford's name crop up repeatedly. His appearances on Liverpool and England striker Michael Owen's BBC *Soccer Skills* series in 1999 thrust Clifford fully into the public consciousness as a one-man alternative to the win-at-all-costs culture. In the event, Garforth Town never reached the Premier League. And Clifford's shot at the big time as a coach in the professional game was short-lived too. Recruited by Clive Woodward, the former England rugby coach who was Southampton FC's performance director, Clifford was handed the chance to work with the club's second string while Harry Redknapp was first-team manager in 2004. The appointment incited a clash of cultures that led to Clifford's departure just two months later.

Clifford is not without fans of his methods among professional footballers. Micah Richards, the former England and Manchester City full-back responsible for the assist for his Argentinian teammate Sergio Aguero's first Premier League goal, is perhaps the most famous former pupil of the Brazilian Soccer Schools (BSS). At Garforth, the huffing and puffing Sócrates was restricted to a one-game cameo.

But the celebrity signings continued. The majestic Brazilian forward Careca played one game in pre-season and the former Manchester United winger Lee Sharpe added his own sprinkle of stardust for a season. Other Brazilian legends were also linked speculatively with the club. In a comment piece in the *Daily Telegraph* at the time, Clifford eulogised about his newfound collaborators in the active spread of futsal's gospel. He quoted Zico as saying: 'Playing in the court, you think faster, play faster, and when you come to play eleven-a-side you have a head start. Because of the tight spaces and smaller ball, which doesn't leave the ground, control and technique become natural elements.' Clifford continued: 'Rivellino, meanwhile, believes that in England "footballers don't train with the ball enough. All physical and technical training should be done with the ball. In England, the ball is in the air too much".' This was manna from heaven to many people in English football desperate for an alternative approach to youth development, in an era of failure that reached a nadir when the England team missed out on qualifying for the 1994 World Cup.

Nine seasons in non-league football had left me crying out for something different. As a novice coach too, the FA's Preliminary Coaching Badge, completed in 1991, offered me nothing new or different to what had gone before. On the course, we didn't even play a game. It was all basic technique and moderately opposed skill drills. Likewise, when I embarked on the all-new FA Coaching Licence – the new UEFA B qualification – in my final year as a semi-pro player in 1998 it was all very predictable. More game-based and informative, covering principles and tactics in different stop-start phases of play, but still essentially 'my way or the highway' coaching, with very little by way of debate on how to help youngsters fall in love with mastering the ball in a realistic game environment. Despite the new course structure in the FA and the imminent arrival in 2001 of the association's Charter Standard programme – a kitemark of quality for grassroots clubs and coaching introduced in changes overseen by the former Leeds United manager Howard Wilkinson – the common cry for a radical departure at the grassroots and among those playing and coaching youngsters in the game went unheeded.

One man, above all, stands widely condemned as the figurehead of this age of darkness in English football. Charles Hughes has been routinely blamed for the unenlightened approach to football in England. His book *Soccer Tactics and Skills* was seen as the coaching bible at the English FA. Its biggest failing was not persuading enough coaches to reject a fixation with rigid, formulaic command-style coaching delivered from the comfort of a snug-fitting tactical straitjacket. Hughes's obsession with exploiting the Position of Maximum Opportunity (nicknamed POMO) by getting the ball in the box, minimising risky play in defensive areas and a focus on set plays came across louder than the more nuanced messages implicit in the underappreciated tome. And there were plenty of these. While not quite a full-blown advocate for futsal, Hughes offered coded encouragement to progressive coaches with chapters on the principles of learning ('an open and enquiring mind' was seen as vital for players and coaches), and a call for 'schoolmasters' to eschew the obsession with eleven-a-side in younger age groups and engage children in 'simple progressive practices' and 'small-sided games'. But Hughes's methods ultimately harked back to his 1950s equivalent, the one-man football analyst/statistician and 'long ball' influencer in English football, RAF Wing Commander Charles Reep, and eclipsed those of more progressive voices at the FA, such as the youth coach John Cartwright (who wrote a book called *Football for the Brave*, appealing for greater focus on creativity and individual skills). In the event, too many coaches cherry-picked Hughes's POMO messages and hopped on board the regressive and short-termist win-at-all-costs bandwagon. Simon Clifford was busy pointing another way. One that involved skills honed with a smaller ball, fewer players and big dose of purposeful, game-based practice.

CHAPTER 6
BABY (FUTEBOL) STEPS: COACHING AND PLAYING

THERE'S ONE MINUTE and forty-one seconds remaining. White-knights Toffees are 2–1 up and it's getting frantic. Goring Robins have set their goalkeeper free out on court. It's five against four. But they can't get the ball. Harjot Singh Brar, an orange-turbaned ten-year-old boy from Reading, is hogging it. He's under huge pressure, the ball glued to the sole of his right foot as he dances, sways and feints just a couple of metres outside his own penalty area, his goal-keeper, Stephen Walker Boyd, lurking near him just in case he loses it. It's the last game of the south-east regional final of the English FA Futsal Youth Cup at the University of Surrey in Guildford. My under-10s team are just over a minute from making the national finals. After another ninety seconds of pinball, and a last-ditch save, the buzzer goes to signal the end of the game. The boys had made it to the national finals in their first fix of competitive futsal, and they loved every minute. It helped that the Sky Sports cameras were in Guildford, filming for a feature on futsal. When three of the players – Davis Lupindu, Benedict Bradley and Dominic (my younger son) – were interviewed by Sky for their thoughts on futsal's innate attraction, their feeling of samba stardom was complete. They all came across very well, young professionals at home in front of the cameras. I was interviewed too, but being a media amateur, my remarks were promptly edited out of the five-minute film. Aged between seven and nine, the Whiteknights FC players I coached – made up of my sons, Conor and Dominic, and their friends – were exposed to futsal alongside grassroots football. This was the start of my futsal dalliance.

It wasn't just Simon Clifford and Juninho on my mind. The moment futsal landed on the elite stage of world football with one almighty strike was also still vivid in my memory. In 2005, an audacious toe-poke from the Barcelona number ten Ronaldinho (aka Ronaldinho Gaúcho) rocketed past a helpless Petr Cech in the Chelsea goal, bringing Brazilian futsal flair to an astounded Champions League audience. The buzz around the goal intensified months later, when a Nike Joga Bonito (Play Beautifully) advert – one of a series, narrated by Eric Cantona, that included similar paeans to France's Thierry Henry, Portugal's rising star Cristiano Ronaldo and the Brazilian futsal-formed superstar Ronaldo – revealed the secrets of the young Ronaldo de Assis Moreira's powers of precision, showing footage of him dazzling as a child on a futsal court.

Ronaldinho was not the first to import the toe-poke to the eleven-a-side game. Two other famously futsal-formed Brazil and Barcelona superstars beat him to it: Ronaldo Luís Nazário de Lima, known as Ronaldo '*O Fenômeno*', and Romário de Souza Faria, known simply as Romário. For a period in the early 1990s, the exploits of the devilishly smart Romário – nicknamed *O Baixinho* (the Little One) – seemed to be a constant talking point. He was different. He was a futsal predator. 'His technique was outstanding, and he scored goals from every possible position, most of them with his toe,' noted Johan Cruyff. Later, Ronaldo did his bit for futsal, and the *seleção*'s World Cup chances, in 2002 against Turkey by blazing a toe-poked shot past the stunned goalkeeper Rüştü to send Brazil on their way to victory in the semi-final. Ronaldo later told *FourFourTwo* magazine the toe-poke finish was 'the most famous' of the many skills he had learned on a futsal court.

Inspired by these indelible images, I ran sessions with the kids using some size 2 Mitre *futebol de salão* balls – a key requirement, according to the Simon Clifford approach – alongside more regular size 4 futsal balls and footballs. My version was more random. But the kids got a feel for coping with different balls and surfaces. It was never a case of futsal purism, insisting on only a hard indoor surface. Outdoors on 3G artificial turf, on a sandy old astroturf surface, or in a school car park, they all have their uses. The futsal ball is the single most important piece of equipment. In terms of 'coaching', it was the same approach I used in football: lots of two-a-side and three-a-side games, be brave on the ball, try to win on effort and attack and defend as a team. It's your game, make your own decisions. But if you simply kick the ball away, I'm going to ask why. The only difference in futsal was the urge for players to experiment with the sole of the foot to control and manipulate the ball – and of course to embrace the toe-poke. They didn't need a second invitation.

Our indoor venue was a church hall called the Warehouse in Cemetery Junction, Reading, with a tiny court, less than one-third the size of FIFA's maximum forty-two metre by twenty-five metre futsal court. The need to use the sole to protect the ball in such confined space was vividly apparent. The goals were dinky too: a metre and a half wide and a similar height. It was not textbook futsal. On top of the equipment – the space, the ball and the smaller goals – the environment created by the game is crucial. My stated desire for kids to try multiple positions within the game – including goalkeeper – and to avoid simply kicking the ball away clearly aligned with the innate traits of futsal. Even in the elite game, specialists in one position must be comfortable elsewhere on the court.

While helping other coaches, first informally with fellow club coaches, then as part of the FA's official grassroots coach mentoring programme, I've used futsal as my go-to solution for a coach looking to inculcate in their kids the bravery to play. 'Have you tried futsal?' is one of my first questions to a new coach. To the open-minded, it feeds a desire to try a different approach. One such exemplar is the twinkle-toed Harjot's dad, Sati Singh Brar. As coach of his younger son Dilraj's Whiteknights FC football team, he picked up the futsal baton and ran with it. The players – a diverse multi-ethnic band of kids from east Reading – loved it and competed in local and national competitions with the academy teams of national league futsal clubs. Their footballing abilities soared as they played both sports from the age of ten until sixteen, by which time a few of them were snapped up by professional football academies. To those already converted to the need to help players develop individual skills and fall in love with the game, it's a godsend. The kids generally enjoy playing it more (more touches of the ball and engagement), the parents can't shout as much (the impact of a novel environment on them is both benign and powerful), and the coach can devolve responsibility to the players because things happen so fast on court. Of course, as kids get older – and certainly in adult futsal – the importance of the coach's role and responsibility soars markedly.

Rocking up at the Warehouse for a game of micro-futsal is one thing. Playing matches is another. In Reading, after the players were bitten by the futsal bug, finding competitive games proved a nightmare. The Berks and Bucks FA, which put on the county finals leading to the regionals in Surrey, had climbed on board the futsal bus driven by the national FA. But any attempts to get out of first gear with local grassroots futsal soon stalled. It's a perennial problem for the game – as the later chapter on England shows. The lead officer for futsal in the county, Simon Wears, put up a valiant effort. The problem was that no one out among the 1,500 or so Charter Standard football clubs in the region was actively pushing futsal. Along with fellow FA coach mentors with a passion for futsal – particularly Kevin England, Andy Ritchie and Steve Punshon in the Berks and Bucks area – I took on the responsibility of encouraging coaches to give it a try. 'But is there a league?' was the stock response. 'And where can we play?' was often the next. It's a chicken and egg situation. The teams or the league? Which needs to come first for a sustainable futsal culture to be established at youth level?

The most memorable moments of frustration over several years include: arriving as a mentor for the coach of Dominic's team, Laurel Park FC under-14s, for a Berks and Bucks FA league fixture at a school to find it closed because the caretaker hadn't been notified; arriving at another venue to find no access to the goals; the referee simply not showing up; and a whole season of league fixtures being scrapped a couple of days before matchday one because too few teams had registered. Simon Wears tells me that finding and keeping facilities for leagues is always a challenge, but points out that in 2019 things have developed since futsal was incorporated in the national FA's strategy. All too often over the years, though, Fernando Silva found himself plugging the gaps. Silva is the head coach of Reading Royals Futsal Club, which he set up in 2013.

A connoisseur of both football and futsal from Porto, Portugal, he was instrumental in organising the small-sided game for kids and adults in Berkshire from 2010 onwards. His mission began after coaching his son Hugo's grassroots football team from under-7s, an experience that only fuelled his unease about the 'abusive' environment inflicted on children by aggressive parents and coaches. 'I could not just stand and watch as young kids came off the field crying because they had done something wrong,' he tells me. He knew a different way – 'I always had the futsal bug inside me' – and set up the Royals after departing from his first venture,

Reading Futsal Club, which he founded and led into the National Futsal League. While Reading Futsal Club merged with Escolla Futsal, founded by the Brazilians Gilberto Damiano and Rodrigo Sousa, and winning the national title in 2018 – Silva turned his gaze to the grassroots, putting on leagues and competitions with one eye on getting an adult team together for the big league. A one-man futsal association, Silva is one of the futsal gurus responsible for driving the game in the years when many county FAs in England seemed unable or simply unwilling to meet the demand at grassroots level. Polished league and cup youth competitions – complete with players entering the court to the Champions League theme tune – provided the next level of inspiration for young players. Silva is clear on the need to provide 'a fantastic experience' for children. 'Because futsal is not very known in this country it's very important that we look different and make them (kids and parents) want to come back again, otherwise it will be just another indoor football session.'

The 'Fernando futsal way' proved educational for coaches and parents, too. As he witnessed himself in England, a shouty coach dictating play can have a corrosive effect on some youngsters. Many parents, equally noisy and 'knowledgeable', pile in with their nuggets of destructive instruction and knee-jerk clichéd urges to 'get rid'. With one or two unsolicited tips to the referee thrown in for good measure, it's teamwork. Just not as the kids like it. One of the most remarkable sights is when this sort of football coach enters a youth futsal environment. They soon discover their figurative PlayStation joystick doesn't work. 'Get rid' doesn't work either. It's about letting the players learn on the job, not abusing every mistake. Give the ball away needlessly and it becomes hard work. On one occasion in Silva's league, my teenage Whiteknights FC team played one we were familiar with from eleven-a-side games. The opponents were physically strong. But in futsal, it's different: physicality is not clattering an opponent early doors or going long to the quick lad, as it can be in football. It's more of a physical intensity, with no place to hide on court, and a requirement for tactical nous: knowing when, where and how to trigger a high, concussive press, a swift and direct counter-attack or maybe a subtle two-player 'screen' to engineer a shooting chance in a semi-rehearsed corner routine.

The selective high press worked on this particular day, springing my boys into a quickfire 4–0 lead. After fifteen minutes of frantic, pointless pointing and haranguing, the opposition coach realised that, first, his players weren't listening; and second, that was a good thing, because he was directing them towards 1970s-style, retrograde panic-inducing safety-first football with a hint of Charles Hughes POMO. This was futsal. They had to find their own way out of sticky situations, with bravery on the ball and clever combinations. In the second half, the kids on the other team started to figure it out for themselves. These nights whetted my appetite to coach more youth futsal while exploring the sport and spreading the word of the game in my FA coach mentoring role. But it wasn't enough. I knew there was no better way to gain true insight and game understanding than immersing myself at the centre of the action on court.

* * *

My chest ached – but not as much as my forty-five-year-old legs. The clock and scoreboard didn't help. There were fourteen long minutes left. And Basingstoke had just scored, leaving us 3-2 up. It was very much game on. The next few minutes were among the toughest I've ever experienced on a pitch playing a game involving balls and goals. Our largely Polish opponents, Basingstoke, had their tails up, pursuing an equaliser with the sort of calculated rhythm and energy that could have blown us away. Coached by Polish futsal expert Andrew Micek, they were strong physically, tactically and technically. We had to match them and excel in the other key aspect of futsal: psychology.

We simply had to stay strong, keep our discipline, rotate our players to keep focus – and victory would be ours. We just needed to survive and regain composure. And the ball. It was a must-win game for Basingstoke. It was must-not-lose-by-two-clear-goals for us. The outcome of the inaugural Reading Sunday Futsal Conference 2016–17 season depended on it. My team, Real Naciones, were in top spot, three points clear of Basingstoke with a better goal difference of two. We've played many times and it's always a close and feisty encounter, the sort of game that shatters the myth that futsal is a non-contact, non-physical sport for dilettantes and trickster show ponies. My team is made up of a foreign legion of futsal players who've been together for a couple of years, and most of whom formed an early iteration of Fernando Silva's Reading Royals team with one eye on the national league structure.

Sergio Cortés is our Spanish star. The former Real Madrid academy player, now in his mid-thirties, issued a pre-match rallying cry to remind us of a former coach's ode to success. The WhatsApp message invoked the motivational wisdom of one of his youth coaches while adding a vital warning against getting overly intimate with loved ones the night before the match. We needed our energy for the match, he declared. That's Sergio; he covered every angle – on and off the court.

Ricardo Medeiros is typical of our team. Born in Lisbon, he played both futsal and football until he left Portugal for England aged twenty-four. He has lived the game. In Portugal futsal is a sporting song of the streets and courts, a melody as familiar, evocative and intense as the country's haunting fado music is sober, mournful and darkly mesmeric. When he first came to England, like Fernando Silva, he was stupefied at the lack of futsal. But it was also the stark cultural limitations imposed on eleven-a-side football in England that left him confused. He first visited Palmer Park in Reading shortly after arriving in a rain-sodden October to live in nearby

Burnham. When he returned to Reading a few months later, he was puzzled to find that the 'lovely park with the football pitches and everything' had disappeared. 'It was just after the FA Cup final,' he recalls. He had inadvertently discovered the annual ritual in England that ensures metal goals in municipal parks are swiftly taken down and locked away as soon as the dawn of spring marks the end of the football season. 'I thought it was crazy,' he says. 'We'd had rain, so much rain, storms and floods. Then snow. Ice, snow and more floods. Then the sun came out, the rain stopped a little. It's time to play football on the grass. And they take the goals away. Crazy.' This is England, I tell him. And that's why we're playing futsal today, in late January, with all grassroots youth football matches in Reading postponed due to water-sodden pitches for the third week in a row. He vows to take me to Portugal one day to show me how it should be. He's not the only Portuguese player in our team. Antonio 'Carlos' Tavares is our *fixo*, the main man at the back. A bit older than Medeiros, he grew up in 'the ghetto' in Lisbon – the Santa Filomena shanty town – playing street football with his school classmate Luís Carlos Almeida da Cunha, aka Nani, the former Manchester United and Portugal star. Carlos is up there with the strongest one-on-one warriors, both defending and attacking, I've ever played with. The others are Darran Connor, the De La Salle midfielder who later gained a big reputation on the Liverpool Sunday league scene, and his schoolboy central midfield rival, Billy Kenny, whose professional career fell foul to drug and mental health problems after a dazzling debut season in the Everton first team. Just like Carlos, both lads played on the edge of reason, boasting an artful swagger defined by graceful power, vision and fearsome street-smarts.

On court, Basingstoke are pushing hard for an equaliser, bringing out their goalkeeper at every opportunity to dominate possession in fly-keeper mode. It's working. We're getting dizzy with tiredness, frantically trying to shuffle in a half-chaotic zonal diamond defence.

I take myself off and urge on Dave Horkan, an Irish powerhouse who scored the first goal – and as a late twenty-something he has relative youth on his side. The goal we need to turn the tide comes with a rapid counter-attack, finished off by Chris Ryman with a delicately clipped left-footed shot as the goalkeeper rushes out. Dave is the first to greet Chris, both Liverpool fans, as the importance of our fourth goal sinks in. Chris savours moments like these. Our captain and my co-coach grew up near Cardiff, mastering a ball on the streets and wherever he could before signing for Swansea City as a trainee, hoping to fulfil his childhood craving to become a professional footballer. He recalls the moment the dream died. Playing for the reserves aged seventeen, he lost the ball after a mazy dribble and was condemned immediately and memorably by his coach, who yelled: 'Chrissy Ryman! We've got players to do that, *your job is to pass!*' Chris tells me he knew then that something wasn't right. Being shouted at for dribbling was killing the joy of the game. Nearly twenty-five years later, he's a futsal fanatic and dribbling whenever he can. As well as being a musician, he runs a coaching school in Reading, his Soulball sessions offering kids a creative fusion of football, futsal and street football. Dribbling is very much encouraged, whatever the age.

After the Basingstoke game we spoke about Chris's clipped finish, the use of the futsal scoop reminiscent of the English Premier League's resident futsal-formed superstar, Philippe Coutinho. It was also the skill famously used by Ronaldinho to lift the ball up and over a host of Albacete defenders and set free a scampering young buck called Lionel Messi for his first ever Barcelona goal at Camp Nou in May 2005. The futsal technique delivered the ball perfectly. It also symbolises the passing of the baton on to the next generation of superstar to hail the five-a-side format as their childhood game of choice. The image of a grinning Ronaldinho carrying an ecstatic teenager on his back in celebration encapsulates the handover perfectly. Exactly fourteen years on, Messi's two goals against Liverpool in the Champions League took him to an astonishing 600 goals for the club. The futsal influence on Barcelona and football remains undimmed.

A few days before our meeting with Basingstoke in 2017, Coutinho committed his future to Liverpool by signing a lucrative new five-year contract at Anfield, amid rampant speculation that Barcelona were keen to add the Brazilian's precocious futsal-formed talents to their roster. (They got their man a year later when he linked up with Messi in a £142m deal.) The steep learning curve of futsal tactics and techniques in our own Reading league was played out against a backdrop of almost weekly exploits from Coutinho. Even as an Everton fan, I loved watching him in action, particularly alongside the other Brazilian futsal soft-shoe shuffler, Roberto Firmino – who was bringing the microscopic details in futsal to life in the Premier League. Coutinho's winning goal against Manchester United in a Europa League clash was perhaps his finest moment in a Liverpool shirt. Hailed as a 'genius moment' by the Liverpool head coach Jürgen Klopp, it was a textbook futsal scoop over David de Gea, a finish rightly lauded for its ingenuity in the ultimate adversarial moment: the one-v-one with the keeper. 'It was unexpected,' enthused Klopp afterwards. 'It was a perfect goal.' It was futsal.

From the moment Chris delivered his own 'genius moment' against Basingstoke, we could defend deep with more confidence, while our opponents grew more frantic. The victory was secured with a late goal. We finished top of the league, with Basingstoke six points behind in second. In third place were the only team to beat us: an impressive all-Spanish side called Hakuna Juan Mata. Just like our very own Sergio, they seemed to play without breaking sweat, an automatic game nous bred on the dusty outdoor courts in the 300-plus days of annual Iberian sunshine. That league season, just like others before and since, served only to enhance my appreciation of the game of futsal. On top of this, in purely experiential learning terms, playing and coaching in an environment so rich in instant feedback, so steeped in overseas cultural capital, is worth a hundred coaching courses. As the champagne flowed for our multinational, multilingual team, I knew I was on to something. We all spoke the same language fluently now. It was the language of futsal.

CHAPTER 7
BEYOND THE TOE-POKE: FUTSAL TACTICS

THE 4-0

'Remember guys,' urges Brayden Lissington. 'Keep the width. Keep the passing options open. The movement is good.' It's a timely reminder, issued 45 minutes into a training session with Reading Royals, Fernando Silva's club. Lissington, a New Zealand international and player-coach of the Royals adult national league teams, is calmly coaxing players into understanding the fundamentals of the richly versatile 4-0 attacking formation. Some players get the basics. For others it's all new. Successful execution of its synchronised movements represents something of a holy grail in futsal.

The 4-0 formation – or the 1-4-0, including the goalkeeper – is the strategy Lissington and fellow first-team coach, Richard Oxley, want to hone. It differs from the most traditional 2-2 or 3-1 set-ups in futsal by having no pivot consistently occupying space in the attacking half. Each player rotates fluidly to confuse and draw out opponents, seeking opportunities to create and exploit space around or behind the opposition players – hugely important in a game with no offside rule. The effect on opponents in fixed positions is akin to deploying the 'false nine' in football. Lissington's reminder recaps the principles he's hammering home: maintain the width at the back;

and look for triggers for when and how to move after releasing the ball. The movements, a touch choreographed for now, ensure the player in possession has three passing options at all times.

Oxley, a veteran futsal coach originally from Barnsley in South Yorkshire but now living near Reading, grew obsessed with the small-sided game after introducing his son's football team to it as teenagers. I'm on the pitch today, one of my occasional forays in training with the Royals since they entered the national league. The precise focus is the 'butterfly rotation', named after the arc of movements by players in possession. While stationed in a nominal 2-2 formation, one of two rear players punches the ball sideways to the other on the opposite side of the court. The passer then cuts forward diagonally towards the centre. If a return pass doesn't come, the moving player shifts out, quickly stepping backwards, eyes on the ball at all times, to the side where they started but about ten metres more advanced. Meanwhile the forward player originally in that spot has rotated back along the sideline to the first player's starting position, filling the space vacated, ready to receive the ball from the recipient of the initial pass on the opposite side. The duo on the opposite side complete the same rotation, and it continues until the chance to penetrate is seized. On a tactics board, a line of squiggles tracking the movement of the initial passer, for example in the left defensive position, all the way back to his starting berth resembles one wing of a butterfly. The mirror image on the right side of the court completes the picture.[16]

My eldest son, Conor, and his teammate Harjot are also playing today. They're keen to emerge from their own futsal chrysalis, the youth game and local adult league action with Real Naciones, and sign for a proper national league team. They know the fundamentals from the 4-0 sessions I've coached with them. For me, being immersed in

---

16. See diagram on p.288

playing – and being coached by a seasoned international – intensifies my appreciation of the attention to detail (and the fitness) required to thrive in futsal. The movements we're learning help enormously with build-up play in football too, particularly in midfield and near the opposition's congested penalty area up against a deep defensive block. At this stage of today's session, it's clear that mere largely unopposed runs, all too robotic and predictable, offer only limited learning. The perceptual triggers, often an opponent's slightest misstep or failure to scan, inform a player's actions and are essential to the successful transfer of the strategy to the real game. It's the concepts behind this formation that truly matter: why we need width but little depth; the importance of an open body shape when moving without the ball; the incessant search for a penetrative forward pass or a clever, disguised two-player combination to engineer an overload; and the fleeting moments of opportunity created by attackers forming 'three in a line' diagonally across the court. It's a constant pursuit of space. A quest that requires cohesion, mental agility and cute, improvised decision-making, each sliver of time creating various unpredictable attacking possibilities – all in an attempt to hone the 4-0 as an effective weapon in a team's armoury.

The 'butterfly effect' is a metaphor with its roots in the most complex depths of physics. The American mathematician and meteorologist Edward Lorenz is credited with developing the hypothesis that longer-term weather patterns are essentially impossible to predict due to the unavoidable – and unforeseeable – large consequences of minor alterations in the here and now. Just like the name given to futsal's most perplexing offensive pattern, this lepidoptera-inspired neologism, coined in the late 1960s, also applies to the game itself. 'Chaos theory' underpins the butterfly effect, whether applied to the weather, as was initially intended by Lorenz, or to more psychological matters such as the real-world attempt to pin hugely unpredictable social, cultural and political developments on the chain of consequences triggered by minor events.

Futsal at the elite level is chaos theory in action: the butterfly rotations and the butterfly effect in unison. Each minor step, feint and darting movement can trigger a chain of cohesive sibling-moves, developing an unstoppable penetrative momentum that gives rise to a typically futsal moment: a thundering finish at the second-post (futsal-speak for the far post) or a toe-poked strike by a canny pivot after inveigling a sliver of space. It looks like chaos to the untrained eye. In reality, although the outcome cannot be predicted too early in the movement pattern, the likelihood of success is linked to regular actions on the part of players steeped in the grammar of the game. The coaching legend credited with this potent offensive strategy is the former Brazilian international futsal player Antonio José Azevedo. He's known simply as Zego. And his most famous creation – the 4-0 formation – is widely regarded as the biggest revolution in the sport's history.

Just as the minor flap of a butterfly's wings is thought to have the potential to cause a tornado on the other side of the world, small detailed actions on court can unleash momentous changes in the structure and dynamics of both teams on court. But why did Zego feel compelled to invent a completely different way of playing? In short, the game needed his inspiration. When Zego was a young, thrusting coach passing on the knowledge gleaned from a long playing career in his home city, São Paulo, the game had reached a tactical dead end. Zego had moved to Argentina for his final season as a player at Newell's Old Boys in 1981, leaving behind SC Palmeiras in his homeland. The rotation from Brazil to Argentina and back fuelled his inspiration. After experimenting while coaching in Mato Grosso and São Paulo, he moved to Spain in 1985. By then Zego's visionary ideas were a decade in the making. The Brazilian told the

LNFS programme *Pista Azul* in 2019 how the 4-0 was actually born from a moment of adversity back in 1976. Facing Uruguay in the final of the South American championships, injury-hit Brazil were forced to play with all wingers on court. Zego and co. adapted by constantly rotating positions to bamboozle the Uruguayan defensive structure, securing the title with a 6-0 victory; Zego netted twice. Once in Spain, the Brazilian's transgressive tactical acumen found an appreciative audience. 'I started with smaller teams and had to get more ball possession when playing better teams,' he told *Pista Azul*. 'Having more possession, we had a better chance of surprising.' This novel approach – 'giving players freedom to believe' – transformed a sport about to undergo a huge transition off the court, as Havelange and FIFA loomed large. Zego's movement to Europe thrust him to the forefront, practising what he was preaching: the new gospel of 4-0.

'The arrival of Zego has been, or is going to be, a revolution,' noted the Spanish international player Javier Lozano in an interview with the Toledo newspaper *La Voz de Tajo* in 1987. 'As soon as his methods are familiar, it will bring many systems, and I am one of those privileged to be able to be part of them. The futsal of Zego is nothing like has been practised up until now. Once we are able to apply all of it, we are going to give many problems to other teams.' Lozano's prophecy came true. As coach of the Spain national team – a role he took on at the age of just thirty-one – Lozano finally hauled them above the inspirational Zego's native Brazil. The Spanish were crowned world champions in 2000 and 2004, and won three UEFA European championships from 1996 onwards (more on this in a later chapter). Lozano's status as the most successful national team coach in Spanish futsal history owed no small debt to Zego's 4-0 formation.

The Croatian Mićo Martić was in the middle of a nine-year stint in Milan when the 4-0 story began. 'Zego is one of the most important people in the history of the sport,' he tells me. 'If we look back to when I first started playing futsal, back then people immediately took up 2-2 positions. It was natural. The thinking was without tactics, it was the simplest way. But step by step, it became more modern, and more 3-1 was played. The next development was this move to four in line.' Martić says he loved the new system because it offered 'a beautiful amount of possibilities, the most flexibility' to players on court. 'When I started to play it in the 1980s, I enjoyed futsal more than ever. 4-0 is good for long spells of possession, very rhythmic plays.' The success of 4-0 in Spain, where many teams employed the strategy after the hugely successful LNFS kicked off in 1989, heralded a tactical shift that propelled the sport to another level. Shortly after Zego's arrival in Spain, Johan Cruyff returned to Barcelona to radically alter the approach to eleven-a-side tactics. Running alongside these shifts was an equally stark philosophical change in coaching culture at the heart of the Spanish FA, the RFEF.

José Venancio López Hierro's hair glistens like silvery tinsel. It's been a long day but he's happy to spare a few minutes to chat while at St George's Park for the FA's futsal conference. 'In football [and futsal] everything is together so you have to work on everything simultaneously,' López Hierro explains. 'You have to design exercises to work on each objective that you have planned for. It's not just playing. The variables [of the exercise] that are used to modify the exercise objectives is what coaches must know how to manage.'

Throughout the 1990s, the games-based approach to coaching took hold as the dominant methodology at the top of the federation, complementing neatly the dominance of Cruyff's vision of how the eleven-a-side game should be coached and played. As Javier Lozano's successor as Spain's national futsal team coach, López Hierro proved instrumental in the shift that elevated games-based learning above isolated technical drills. The 4-0 formation, with the essential triggers of movement of teammates and opponents, goes hand in hand with this approach to training. At the height of his Spanish team's dominance in 2006, Lozano neatly articulated the principles behind their success: 'The main aspect to develop [in futsal] is tactics. Teach the young players to think – speed and decision making are crucial.' The game-based approach to learning was key – and futsal was at the forefront. The results of this philosophical movement, replicated on football pitches as much as on futsal courts, put Spain in pole position to dominate in both FIFA sports as the new millennium dawned. The smart thinking that brought a fresh epoch in coaching culture was reflected on the court in the 4-0 formation and the accompanying development of the players' powers to thrive in more limited area of the court. One solution to this heightened intensity was the adaptation of a technique that itself developed in the 1980s due to the changing nature of the game: the universal sole control.

The man translating López Hierro's words of wisdom at St George's Park is Doug Reed. The most travelled futsal professional in the English game, Reed is only the second player, after the pivot Luke Ballinger, to reach one hundred caps for his country in a globe-trotting career that spanned stints in Spain, Croatia, Serbia, Brazil and Cyprus. An accountancy graduate who started playing while at Manchester University aged twenty, Reed was also one of the few home-grown players in England's first professional club, Baku United. As a commentator, analyst and chronicler of the game online, he added to his extensive CV in 2020 by gaining the highly prized UEFA Executive Master for International Players qualification, designed to educate the next generation of sports administrators. The adaptation of the ubiquitous sole control technique, allowing a player to escape from a pursuer in a tight mid-court 4-0 rotation, is a perfect example of another tricky subject the thirty-two year-old veteran has mastered. 'I was taught it in Croatia,' Reed explains. 'They called it "change play". It's about keeping the ball moving when you receive it on the wing when you are getting pressed. The worst thing you can do is stop the ball. If you do that you're dead.' The control allows an attacker receiving a pass on the wing to either roll the ball inside with one sole-control movement and attack the centre, or to step on it, feint to go centrally but instead step down with the controlling foot and shunt quickly forward down the line, leaving the defender trailing. The key is to react to the pressing defender's body shape and angle of approach as the ball arrives. 'It gives you two options,' explains Reed. 'But just like I was told by Mićo [Martić]: there are no right or wrong answers. There are always different variations and you have to adapt to what is going on the pitch.'

Mastery of the 'change play' sole control was the manoeuvre Brayden Lissington was working on in the Reading Royals session immediately prior to the butterfly rotation. It's an essential building block of the game. Reed compares the skill to a more controversial futsal manoeuvre – one with clear basketball links: the intentional block, or screen, to take out an opponent momentarily and 'gain separation' in attack. Just like the 'change play', the block buys a glimmer of time and space. 'And if you can't do that in futsal, you can't be a futsal player,' Reed states. 'It's all about one-v-ones but not one-v-one dribbles. It's a one-v-one where you're challenged. The task is: can you get rid of the pressure?'

For Martić, Reed's former coach and mentor who assisted the England national team for a few years, the use of the sole for a 'change play' is simple. 'It's about survival,' he tells me a few weeks after I spoke to Reed and López Hierro. It wasn't always like this. When he first started playing in the early 1980s, pressing was rare and players could control the ball however they wanted. The sole control grew in importance as the game evolved with greater speed and intensity. It's different now. 'The game is a jungle and you have to think ahead of the opponent,' says Martić. 'The sole is vital. Sometimes it's a directive control, a change play to the other side, sometimes it's a feint to dribble to the other side. The tactical awareness in futsal is much greater today. And it's also greater than in football.'

López Hierro's prowess as a thinker and a four-times European champion coach was rewarded with an invitation to draw up the official UEFA coaching manual after the introduction of the UEFA B licence in 2012. It reads like a summary of the famed Spanish 'cognitive model', a feather in the cap of the RFEF after a decade or so of dominance in football and futsal. Nearly forty years after he started playing on the streets and courts of Bilbao, López Hierro – who was named best national team coach in the world a record five times between 2007 and 2017 – says he fully appreciates the links between Pep Guardiola's modern possession-based dominance and futsal's relentless 4-0 movements. 'There is a link. This is the key . . . the basic element of training is the exercises. Many of the futsal exercises you can apply to football.' He's speaking after putting on a showcase session using *rondos* (ball possession games) with restrictions and added players to simulate the realism of playing out from the back third in futsal. The football links leap out.

It's impossible to argue with the assertion that Zego's curiosity heralded a golden age of the 4-0. As well as inspiring adornments to the basic sole control, the rise of the 'total futsal' approach that entails all players rotating all over the court also landed coaches with a headache, according to Martić. 'The problem was big for Spanish coaches,' he explains. Zego's formation, devised as a solution for teams faced with the need to overcome increasingly athletic and energetic opposition pressing higher up the court, itself spawned a bout of tactical invention as the high-energy chess being played out on court was replicated by forensic strategising off it. 'Coaches in Spain had to think of ways to beat this attacking 4-0 system. So they started to come with solutions, such as pressing even higher, using the whole court, or sitting deeper and playing zonal defence,' says Martić. Tactical agility was becoming the new holy grail for futsal coaches. The riposte to the rise of the 4-0 was not long in coming.

THE RUSSIAN CHANGE

Semen Andreev is a Russian revolutionary. In the early 1990s, he shocked the increasingly global futsal community with a tactic that had never been seen: the Russian on-court four were regularly hauled off and replaced by a whole new set of players. The precise date of the debut of this controversial mass substitution, nicknamed the 'Russian change', is unclear. Andreev reportedly flirted with it at FIFA's second world championships in 1992 in Hong Kong. The fog of confusion surrounding its birth merely adds to the sense of mystique. On the court, it soon became clear that Andreev was not simply mainlining energy and verve into his teams in an attempt to prolong their ability to conduct a high-intensity strategy. It was more than simply fresh legs. Each group of four were armed with a different tactical plan. Andreev was switching it up, keeping the opposition guessing and therefore dominating the events on the court.

The towering Russian pivot Konstantin Eremenko, an early star of the FIFA game, proved instrumental in the Russian 3-1 set-up, grabbing fifteen goals in Hong Kong to finish second-highest scorer behind Iran's Rajabi Shirazi. Andreev craved a different way, some variety, looking for the 1 per cent marginal gains that have become customary in professional sports in the decades since technology took a bigger role in globalised competitive games. In the years after 1992, this novel approach gained Russia success and registered another key moment in the historical narrative of the sport. Coming on the back of Zego's 4-0 new dawn, the 'Russian change' completed futsal's transition to a sport which at the elite level required an adaptable and rigidly flexible approach. The 4-0 was potent – but it could be countered. Elite teams had to have more than one way to go. By the time of the 1996 world championship in Spain, the 'Russian change' was not solely the preserve of Andreev's men. The FIFA technical report that highlighted the emergence of the toe-poke shots and scoop passes with the smaller ball also noted 'complete block changes for Ukraine, Russia, Holland and Belgium' as one of the standout tactical landmarks. 'One block being mainly offensive and the other rather defensively oriented,' it noted. In the aftermath of the crumbling Soviet empire, the Russian change ensured Moscow's influence on futsal grew throughout Europe and the rest of the world.

Russia has led the way in more ways than one. Top-flight matches in the professional Super League comprise two twenty-five minute halves, a conscious decision to make up for the long travelling times in a country that spans eleven time zones across nearly 6,000 miles from St Petersburg to Vladivostok, and about 2,500 miles from north to south. An extra ten minutes' game time makes the mammoth away days that little bit more worthwhile. Throw in a few 'Russian changes', and everyone gets valuable game experience. Steve Harris, the expert futsal analyst, recalls the 1999 European championships in Spain as the moment Russian futsal truly arrived on the international scene. It was the competition that turned Andreev's experimentation into a winning legacy, he says, after the pioneering coach had handed over the reins to Mikhail Bondarev in the run-up to the tournament. Russia defeated the hosts on penalties in the final after a pulsating 3–3 draw. 'It was quite an innovation,' Harris remembers. 'That tournament victory was seen as the direct result of the Russian "revolution". Normally, players would be changed just one or two at a time.' Harris believes the tactic was borrowed from a sport big both in his native US and Andreev's Russia, ice hockey, where it is called 'changing your lines'. Mićo Martić agrees on the ice hockey inspiration. 'Many coaches are using this now,' he says. 'It's a big part of the game. I have it with Finland. One group playing 4-0, one playing 3-1, the other is playing maybe a false pivot or something like that. So we have more possibilities to change things.'

This flexibility appears to be paying off for Martić, who took over as head coach of Finland's futsal team in 2013 and took them to five consecutive Nordic Cup titles. A few months after the team's first ever victory against Spain, he also led the national team to the brink of qualification for the 2020 World Cup, reaching the play-off against Serbia after surviving unbeaten in the elite-round group of death against Italy, Portugal and Belarus. Under Martić's watch the Finnish FA has also developed a women's national league and national team while powering up the grassroots: an estimated 40,000 people play futsal in 2019, leaving the sport exceeded in popularity by only football, ice hockey and floorball (indoor hockey). Coming on top of the football team's historic achievement of making the finals of the European championships due the same year but postponed because of the coronavirus outbreak, it's perhaps a clear sign that the intuitive and clear-sighted Martić is at the centre of yet another dramatic epochal shift in the sport.

Meanwhile, I've found that the Russian change can be potent at youth level too. The ideal number for a futsal squad is nine: a goalkeeper plus two distinct fours. In keeping with the idea of giving the children more ownership over tactics and formations, I task them with organising themselves: starting positions, formation, the emphasis in and out of possession and, importantly, how often to make changes. The favourite among the boys who made it to the under-16s national finals in 2018 was to have two discreet fours, alternating halfway through each half. As they got deeper into competitions, they preferred to react to the scoreline and tailor the approach accordingly. It's one of the biggest advantages of futsal over football in terms of fast-tracking the game intelligence and understanding of young players.

FIRE AND ICE

Argentinian coach Diego Giustozzi's passion is notorious. He is also one for meticulous preparation, as can be expected of someone working at the elite level of his sport. When the Argentina men's futsal team made history in 2016 by breaking the stranglehold of Brazil and Spain on the sport's biggest prize, Giustozzi's destructively offensive defensive tactics were hailed as decisive. A full-court press, nigh on impossible to sustain for long periods, had yielded that stunning result. But it was the nuanced Y-formation that seemed to gouge the energy out of the opposition, the living embodiment of a strategy forged in the true Argentinian fighting spirit. He wasn't the first to use it. The doyen of games-based coaching in Spain, José Venancio López Hierro, had employed it with his national team in the previous World Cups, and other coaches had notable successes with it in Italy while Giustozzi was playing there.

It's a formation reliant on a front two shutting down forward passing options as a third cover player tucks in behind, centrally, offering cover and support while closing off the pass into the opposition's pivot. This defensive triangle forms a three-player V, while the back man, the *fixo* – located behind the three and forming the base point of the Y – hunts down the pivot when they enter the defensive zone, and tries to intercept passes.[17] Crucially, the front three must try to maintain two 'lines of defence' and not be duped into congregating in one single line, three players strewn across the court horizontally, by the clever movement of opponents (often executing incessant 4-0 rotations) hunting for space in behind. With the *fixo* and the goal-keeper, the team thereby maintains four horizontal lines of defence. The more advanced triangular trio are responsible for choosing how high and when to engage the opposition, trying to suddenly snuff out all passing lanes for the player in possession. The system relies on clear principles and triggers on when to track a rotating opponent and when to 'exchange' for another. The objective is to press with furious, calculated precision, to win possession in a dangerous area.[18]

For Giustozzi and Argentina, it worked wonders. Argentina went one better than López Hierro's Spain did in 2008 and 2012 by defeating another unlikely finalist, Russia, to seal victory for the sort

---

17. See diagram on p.286
18. See diagram on p.287

of persistently aggressive ball-hunting approach rarely seen in the sport's history. It marked another stage of evolution – yet another shift in the ability of supposedly lesser teams to bridge the gap with stronger nations through tactical excellence. For Giustozzi – who cites López Hierro, Inter Movistar's Jesús Velasco and the globetrotting Spaniard Miguel Rodrigo as his key coaching influences – it's very simple. 'It's about trying to get the opponent to play the way you want,' he told the World of Futsal podcast. 'It makes defending easier.' The style of play was dictated by the qualities of his players, he says, not a coach-imposed ideology.

Such pragmatism is heartening. In my own small world of coaching amateur futsal, the 'fire' of a high press, whether in a Y-formation mixed defence or an all-out player-for-player approach, can reduce an opposition to ashes. The alternative to 'fire', the one to call in the troops and chill out, is 'ice', a rallying cry issued by coach or players triggering a retreat to a patient, half-court defence. In my experience, such tactical flexibility – and ownership of the strategy by calling out – can supercharge a young player's appreciation of game nous, tactical awareness and individual and group defending techniques. Ian Bateman, the long-time lead liaison for the English FA between the association and the Premier League academies, needs no persuasion on this count. He insists defensive skills are often seen as the 'unexpected return' from futsal by professional football coaches exposed to the game for the first time.

Diego Giustozzi's high-flying journey to the top of the elite game is typical of many South American countries, especially those who formed the select group of seven nations affiliated to FIFUSA at its inception in 1971. Up until his teenage years in the early 1990s, the young Diego played futsal and football. His playing career, from twin-tracking youth to seasoned veteran professional futsal player, is bookended by stints at one of the two giants of Buenos Aires, River Plate. Giustozzi's links to football remained strong (he's friends with

Tottenham Hotspur's Erik Lamela). It pays to avoid crude hyperbole and stereotyping when analysing national sporting traits. But Argentina has long had a capacity to produce a certain style and type of player. The area near the Rio de la Plata, the estuary that marks the convergence of the Uruguay and Paraná rivers, is crucial in forming what is known in the local *rioplatense* version of Spanish as *la nuestra* (our style of play). Defined by *viveza criolla* (native cunning), it is a curious distillation of the spirit attributed to the region's history. It bears more than a passing resemblance to the notorious Uruguayan *garra charrúa*, a figurative term steeped in the tradition of the indigenous warrior tribe of Charrúa Indians whose homeland surrounded the estuary, only to be largely wiped out in the nineteenth century.

The *garra* (claw, or fighting spirit) is usually attributed to the Uruguayan pitch warrior, the intense competitive edge personified by Barcelona and Uruguay's often intemperate aggressor, Luis Suárez. Just like the estimated 250,000 Charrúa descendants living in Uruguay, Brazil and Argentina in the twenty-first century, the spirit was not restricted to Uruguay. The Italian journalist Gianni Brera's book *Storia critica del calcio Italiano* noted the nuanced differences between the near neighbours' philosophical approaches to football at the time of the birth of *futebol de salâo*. Brera's vivid metaphorical dissection of the differences between the 1930 World Cup winners, Uruguay, and the vanquished Argentina – Uruguayans are 'ants' while Argentinians are 'cicadas' – is quoted in Jonathan Wilson's encyclopaedic history of football tactics, *Inverting the Pyramid*. The implication is that Uruguay achieved a better balance between 'ant-like' defensive solidity and more ephemeral flighty flair. 'This is fundamental,' writes Wilson. 'It could be said that the whole history of tactics describes the struggle to achieve the best possible balance of defensive solidity with attacking fluidity.' If Uruguay trumped their *rioplatense* rivals on this measure in the 1930s, it's fair to say the Argentinians achieved a marked ascendancy from the 1970s onwards when they copied the trick of winning a first football World Cup on home soil. In futsal, the same power shift between the two nations has taken place over the shorter lifespan of the sport.[19]

Giustozzi's stirring incarnation of the appropriated Uruguayan *garra* spirit, and military ant-like precision, in the 2016 futsal World Cup in Colombia has spawned a host of imitators. In the 2019 World Intercontinental Cup, the de facto futsal club world cup, the other sporting pugilist in the Buenos Aires *superclásico*, Boca Juniors, fought their way to the final with a strategy cut from the same cloth as Giustozzi's bespoke high-pressing tactical cloak. To the untrained eye, the cohesive high press Giustozzi fashioned in Colombia can appear confusingly random. But the effect is preordained in hours of game-based practice in the art of reacting to triggers, angles and distances of the first pressure and the support players. It's also perhaps the natural reaction, after the dominance of the 4-0, to the rise of the Russian change, which allows for a whole forty minutes to pass with a team at maximum pressing intensity if required.

Futsal is defined by rapid transitions, requiring every player to think and act constantly as though a turnover of possession is imminent. When viewed through this prism the game appears akin more to basketball than eleven-a-side football (despite the age of high pressing overseen by Jürgen Klopp at Borussia Dortmund and Liverpool). Every player has to be ready to fulfil whatever role the moment dictates, defensively or in attack. The non-specific role in a futsal squad, the *universal*, is one that Giustozzi performed as a player. And this moniker could apply equally to the game itself, which equips players with the ultimate tool kit of universal skills readily transferable to other sports.

---

19. Both nations also share a passion for baby *fútbol*: highly competitive small-sided league contests on tiny outdoor pitches, which expose youngsters to the game's raw passion. It offers a formalised version of the traditional *potrero* culture (makeshift dusty playground pitches) – long dominant, but fading in the twenty-first century due to rampant urbanisation.

CHAPTER 8
WAYNE ROONEY'S STREET SPOT

WHEN SIXTEEN-YEAR-OLD Wayne Rooney crashed the ball beyond a flailing David Seaman at Goodison's Park End to bring Arsenal's astounding thirty-game unbeaten run to a halt, Anthony Smith celebrated wildly, just like every Evertonian. 'Remember the name, Wayne Rooney,' cried Clive Tyldesley, the ITV commentator. Euphoria, yes. But for Anthony Smith it was different. He'd seen it all before.

'That was Wayne. Amazing goal. But he did that day in, day out here on the streets,' says Smith, speaking in the precise spot in L11 where a young Rooney honed the shooting power, swerve and accuracy that left Seaman and the Premier League champions all at sea that October afternoon in 2002. Smith, a senior football development officer at Liverpool County Football Association, and a childhood friend of Rooney's, is giving me a tour of Carr Lane East in the heart of Croxteth, about four miles north-east of Liverpool city centre. We've just walked from the small car park, overlooked by Smith's nan's house, that formed what he calls 'the St George's Park of street football'. We're strolling down the road towards Stonebridge Lane in a rare burst of February sunshine when he asks, 'Do you remember the Dog and Gun pub?'

How could I forget? De La Salle High School, the Catholic all-boys school Smith and Rooney attended a decade or so after I did, is just to our right. I got to know the streets around here intimately, often hanging around at the end of the day to kick a ball about before catching the bus the three miles or so back to Everton. The Dog and Gun was the classic local 'hard' boozer, the one kids aspired to get into for a sneaky underage drink. 'We used to knock about on this corner, opposite the pub,' he recalls as we near the end of Carr Lane East. We're standing with our backs to the bright red shutters on one half of a huge Bennetts off-licence. Smith points to the floor. 'It was about here,' he says, looking up and over the road, sizing up the angle, as though ready to take a shot. 'We'd spend hours and hours, just hitting balls from here.' The lamp post a couple of feet from the kerb was the obstacle, he says. 'We'd hit balls from here and try to hit the pub door over the road, bending it round the lamp post. We probably shouldn't have done it. There were people going in, people coming out. A bit dangerous, like.'

The doorway target was about twenty-five metres away. It's a similar distance to the one Rooney scored from on that famous day against Arsenal. The lamp-post figure that afternoon was the hulking presence of Sol Campbell. The Cameroonian defender Lauren played the role of the passive and motionless bin rooted a few metres from the lamp post; on the pitch but doing nothing to affect the play. The forward run made by Everton and former Arsenal striker Kevin Campbell beyond his Arsenal namesake's central defensive partner, Pascal Cygan, imitated the distracting presence of a car zooming into Rooney's field of vision as he lined up the Dog and Gun strike.

'We'd do it for hours,' explains Smith. 'I'd hit it about one in twenty. Wayne would do it one in three. Amazing. Up and bending around the lamp post, over the road and into the doorway . . . There were people walking past, cars speeding past on the road. It was dead-ball practice with loads of interference. Great practice. Wayne was deadly. Incredible.' Smith escorts me around the corner on to Stonebridge Lane. 'Another of our favourites,' he says. 'You'll see why.' He points towards the entrance porch to Treetops Day Nursery. 'See? There's a natural goal from the shelter, underneath.' The target is bordered by yellow metal bars, forming the frame of a goal somewhere between the size of an eleven-a-side and a futsal goal. Shutters guard the windows, presumably so the brutal accuracy of a young Wayne Rooney didn't break the glass.

'We played a shooting game where if you missed your shot, you went in goal,' he explains. Rooney's penchant for a stint between the sticks was famously revealed in one of the Nike Joga Bonito adverts fronted by Eric Cantona in 2005 and 2006. His desire for all-action street football was laid bare in the ad, in which Cantona delivers a eulogy to Rooney's street style – 'Without heart, you cannot play'. To the despair of the watching Alex Ferguson, the fresh-faced Rooney, wearing a cheeky grin born on the streets of Croxteth, evicts the goalkeeper to display his acrobatics between the sticks, then deserts his station to play rush goalie, or 'goalie in and out' as it was known on the streets of Liverpool.

Turning his attention back to the nursery, Smith continues: 'So yeah, we had to get the ball up and over the wall and down into the goal. The high fence wasn't there back then. It was just the wall. So I'd go from about here.' He steps back from the wall towards the pavement kerb. 'But for Wayne, he'd go from there. About the third paving flag away from the wall. And he'd do it. Up and over the wall from so close and into the goal, with bend and swerve. Again, he'd always hit the target.'

Smith is standing on the pavement, hands in the pockets of his padded Liverpool FA three-quarter length jacket, telling me all about Rooney, school days, football and the culture that made the player famously described by his Everton manager David Moyes, in a speech to the Cambridge Union in 2013, as 'the last of the true street footballers'. We agree that the Dog and Gun shooting gallery and the nursery training ground cannot have failed to influence the prodigious striking accuracy of England's record international goalscorer. While the pub-door strike is eerily similar to that goal against Arsenal, the nursery shot reminds Smith of another goal on a famous day in Rooney's career. 'It's the third goal on his debut for United,' Smith says, referring to Rooney's hat-trick strike in his first game, a Champions League group match in September 2004. 'The free kick against Fenerbahçe. It's up and over the wall then down and swerving in. Brilliant strike. It's exactly the same.'

As well as performing tireless work out in the community on behalf of the county FA, Smith is player-manager of one of Liverpool's oldest Sunday league sides, Croxteth-based Dengo United. While chatting about football, De La Salle and the city in general, it emerges that he's the nephew of David Smith, a lad who went on to play in the Premier League for Norwich City a few years after my teenage five-a-side team, Bill Green, defeated his Arch Royal side in the semi-final of the Merseyside Police competition in 1984.

Smith embodies Liverpool's footballing addiction. The history of the city's two clubs needs no introduction. Though neither Everton nor Liverpool managed to win a Premier League title in nearly three decades after the competition's inception in 1992, Jürgen Klopp's runaway championship procession either side of the coronavirus shutdown in 2019–20 took the city's joint haul of top-flight league titles to twenty-eight – still the highest of any city in England, two ahead of Manchester's twenty-six and seven more than all the London clubs combined. A *Times* investigation in 2015 found that Merseyside led the way in producing players as well as winning teams. Although just eclipsed by County Durham when figures since the formation of the Football League in 1888 are totalled, since the millennium the city of Liverpool and its outskirts have churned out more professional footballers than any region. The research found that between 2000 and 2015, this hotbed of English football produced 314 players for Football League or Premier League clubs. Jack Walton, a colleague of Anthony Smith's at Liverpool FA, tells *The Times* the success of Liverpool as a breeding ground for talent is due to a 'perfect storm' of factors, including the greater opportunity to play and practise in the city's parks and numerous youth leagues, the 'sweet spot' size of the region – at about 500,000 people it's neither too big nor too small – and the quasi-religious fanaticism for football that comes from the presence of two hugely successful clubs.

It's not just the professional game where Liverpool leads the way. In his excellent book *On the Brink: A Journey through English Football's North West*, the author and journalist Simon Hughes points out the prolonged success Liverpool's amateur Sunday league teams have enjoyed at national level: 'Aside from London, no other city has a history like Liverpool in the FA Sunday Cup.' In its first period of dominance, between 1978 and 1984, Liverpool teams reached the final for six successive seasons. Most of the teams were named after pubs, which were still the most important focal points in working-class communities in the 1980s, offering a base and a clear identity for a Sunday football team. The first season, The Lobster from Croxteth grabbed the title. Their win was followed by two consecutive victories for an equally famous Kirkby pub, The Fantail, where a young John Coleman and Jimmy Bell played before moving on to lead Accrington Stanley after successful non-league playing careers. Dingle Rail from the south end of the city won it in 1982. Then it was the turn of arguably the city's most notorious pub, The Eagle and Child in Huyton. It was here that I enjoyed a season playing for their under-14 team with new secondary school friends before we all joined a new team run by my dad and his friends from a pub in Everton called The Bourne.

The Eagle edged Lee Chapel North from Basildon, Essex, on penalties but failed to retain the crown the following year in a repeat final against the Essex team.

A decade later, similar success was achieved by three strong Liverpool Sunday league sides: Almithak, Seymour and Nicosia (with the father and uncles of West Ham United and Newcastle striker Kevin Nolan playing). The Croxteth-based Oyster Martyrs (twice winners, twice runners-up, with a prolific ex-pro striker called Leighton McGivern and relatives of Wayne Rooney in the team), the Campfield (a pub in Everton) and Canada (a team formed by city dock workers in the 1960s) have all graced the national final since 2010, adding to the city's envious haul of victories. 'Across half a century of Sunday league football, indeed, thirteen FA Sunday Cup winners have emerged from the fields on the banks of the river Mersey,' concludes Simon Hughes. Smith is front and centre of this Sunday league addiction in the city, which is being sorely tested as rocketing pitch-hire prices combine with pressures on time-pressed lifelong volunteers to curtail the number of thriving leagues in the city – a cocktail of misfortune and harsh reality that threatens the viability of the adult eleven-a-side game nationwide.

Smith's footballing pedigree led naturally to futsal. He sees its clear links with the street football culture for which the city is famous. He first played futsal in 2007 when invited to Salford by his then colleague at the Liverpool county FA, Simon Wright, who went on to form Manchester Futsal Club. 'I loved it straight away,' says Smith. 'Although my first taste of the game was actually on a 3G pitch, it was clear that it was right up my street. I'm a winger – and futsal's a technical game, very fast. I love it.' Since that day he's never again played the traditional British version of five-a-side. 'All that getting whacked into boards and everything, it's crazy. In futsal, you're protected. It's about ability. It's so much better.'

He eventually played in the national league for Liverpool Futsal Club in 2010. Before this he had introduced his gang of street footballers at Dengo United to the game. Despite a humbling first experience in Manchester against Simon Wright's new club – 'we got battered 12–1' – they entered a league set up by Wright in Liverpool, and won it to enter the futsal FA Cup in 2009. 'We went to the regionals in the cup,' he recalls. They gained revenge on Manchester in a 2–1 victory. 'It was great. We were a gang of lads who had never really played much futsal, but we were all fit street players at our peak – a good, strong group.' They also edged renowned futsal clubs Grimsby and Sheffield to reach the finals, a sixteen-team tournament at the English Institute of Sport in Sheffield. 'We were up against Kickers from London, all Brazilians, Hartpury College, who were strong, and White Bear. We drew 1–1 with Kickers, lost 7–6 to Hartpury then we played White Bear.' The White Bear team – formerly Team USSR – was made up of players from the former Soviet Union, many of whom would go on to join London-based Baku United.[20] 'I swear, against White Bear,' admits Smith, 'we touched the ball about five times in the whole game… We only lost 3–1. And we scored with one of our five touches. But honest to God, they had us running everywhere. We realised it was different at that level. A different sport.'

These days he puts in the hard yards at grassroots level, taking on the responsibility for getting kids to play futsal. He arranged for futsal goals to be used in De La Salle's new sports hall and the nearby Croxteth Sports Centre, where I used to play volleyball as a pupil. 'This is vital,' he tells me, if we're to get more kids playing the game. After our conversation he sends me a message on Twitter remarking

---

20. Backed by Azeri finances which allowed them to recruit stars including Spain's Javi Rodríguez, and former Inter Movistar and Dinamo Moscow coach Chema Jiménez, Baku dominated the English game in the late 2000s and early 2010s. In 2014 they became the first English side to reach the UEFA Futsal Cup.

how throughout the hour or so we chatted, as the sunshine lit up 'the St George's Park of street football', we didn't see one kid out with a ball. Sadly, it's symbolic of a massive cultural shift over the last couple of decades, a dramatic change that signals the death of street football. Futsal's potential as its replacement is huge, he believes.

It's not just video games that keep the kids indoors in places like Croxteth. The streets of L11 became a no-go area in the aftermath of the fatal shooting of eleven-year-old Rhys Jones in August 2007. The young Everton fan was caught up in a gang warfare attack as he was strolling home from football training on Croxteth Park estate. The teenage assassin, Sean Mercer, was a former pupil at De La Salle who lived opposite the school gates in Good Shepherd Close. The violence that led to Rhys's tragic killing and continued to simmer afterwards, between rival gangs from Croxteth and Norris Green, traumatised the community. It hit the school hard. Up to that point, it had been renowned as an in-demand competitive footballing school churning out professional players. Its most famous night, just four years earlier, when Wayne Rooney and Francis Jeffers played up front together for England against Australia at Upton Park, is one no other state comprehensive school is likely to match. When I see my former PE teacher, John Hennigan, at Everton matches we often talk about the school and its sporting legacy. Hennigan, a former rugby union player, gives pride of place in his West Derby home to a framed photograph of Rooney and Jeffers from that historic night given to him by Wayne's mum, Jeanette, who was a dinner supervisor in the school. As for Rooney's early prowess, Hennigan says he saw immense potential, but not just in football. 'He could kick with both feet, was strong as an ox, great vision, could ride a tackle – Wayne would have made a fantastic scrum-half!'

Unfortunately for De La Salle, the gang violence that led to the murder of young Rhys Jones altered the school's image fundamentally. 'No one wanted to send their kids to the school,' says Smith. 'It was all so stupid. It was pointless violence.' The school started to recover its numbers a decade later, albeit at just half the size it was fifteen years earlier. 'There's a new headteacher there now, things are on the up again,' says Smith. 'He's even a grassroots coach himself. It's good.'

Smith's own dedication to the grassroots game keeps him occupied every Friday night. In an indoor arena in Wavertree – the area of Liverpool where Ross Barkley grew up – he hosts a county FA futsal league for kids' teams aged between eight and fourteen. It's a huge hit, and gives hundreds of kids a weekly fix of futsal on top of their weekend football matches. Although Smith recognises futsal's value as a balm to soothe the societal ills in an age of limited outdoor street play, he warns that it's not a panacea. 'It's too formal,' he says firmly, adding that the 'purist' approach to the game should be watered down to allow more of a street approach with ad hoc pitches enabling more people to play. 'That's the problem with futsal for me. It's too formal, it's almost, it's too . . .' He pauses for a second. 'It's kinda too nice. Everyone's trying to get the perfect hall or 3G pitch. 'We've got all these concrete outdoor pitches, MUGA [multi-use games area] pitches, all of them are free. And available. Why can't we go and use them? That's how to get kids playing more, whether that's football or futsal. We can't hold out for the perfect indoor surface. Sports halls can be way too expensive. So you've got to be flexible and adapt around it. One of the biggest problems is caused by the egos in the game, some people who got involved early, they think they own futsal. Every time someone tries something new, they look down their noses at them.'

The Friday night futsal is a great example. It's improvised, the games played on concrete tennis courts with futsal goals drafted in and futsal pitch markings overlaying the tennis lines. More of this is needed, he says. Futsal 'purism' is also stopping the growth of the game at adult level too, he adds. 'We get teams of footballers playing against futsal clubs in our competitions. We see that here and the football teams might beat the futsal club. And they'll say "That's not futsal. There are no patterns of play, no rotations, etc." Well, if they're playing by the rules then it's fine. There's more than one way to skin a cat. It's up to the futsal teams to adapt and try to stop them.' The other issue preventing hotbeds of footballing talent such as Liverpool from taking over futsal is the day of the week. Liverpool's passion for Sunday league football prevents the best players from joining national league futsal teams, which play on the same day.[21]

When I first met Smith half an hour or so ago, I greeted him at the entrance to De La Salle and he took me immediately to the small car park, set back from Carr Lane East down a small street running between a row of four terraced houses on the right, and a hairdresser's on the left. It's the place where Rooney famously rocked up an hour or so after that Arsenal match for a kickabout with Smith and their mates. It's here Smith compares the area to the English game's expensively appointed expanse of football – and futsal – coaching and playing facilities.

Situated a Wayne Rooney free kick's distance from the De La Salle school field, the car park is about thirty metres long. 'In this space, we'd have lads a good few years older than me. I was probably in the middle of the age range,' he explains. Rooney, eighteen months younger than Smith, was happy mixing it with the older kids. 'My brother and cousins were about five years younger than me. We ranged from eight or nine to seventeen. You learn how to play against other kids. It was brutal at times. But great for learning how to handle yourself.' Rooney's body strength, balance and mental ability to cope stood out, he says. 'This is what street football gives you. Wayne was a man before his time. Not just the aggression, the

---

21. The pool of potential futsal players is also reduced hugely by the draw towards non-league football in the north-west of England and elsewhere, with teams as low as tier 10 (six steps beneath the pro game) prepared to pay players who otherwise might consider futsal as a playing pathway.

strength, but knowing how to use his body. He was frightening. We'd play here for hours, especially as Coleen lived around here and he was always playing, showing off, trying to catch her eye. Her brothers used to play with us too. I remember in the school yard there would be about fifty kids playing and Wayne could just run through them all while keeping the ball and you'd just be like "how's that even possible?" He could do it all on his own, Wayne, no matter what. I watched him going from playing for Everton under-15s at fourteen to playing for Everton's first team at sixteen.'

Rooney himself admits that this learning combination – Everton's renowned academy talent factory and the vibrant streets of Croxteth – proved potently instrumental in his growth. As a multi-millionaire on the brink of his one hundredth cap for his country in 2014, he revealed how he still returned to Croxteth for a kickabout occasionally. 'I've always believed myself to be from the streets in terms of football,' he said. 'I've always played on the streets with friends, and still do now and again when I get time. I go and do that. That is where I learnt to play football. There was a lot of help from the academy at Everton, but the majority of my football was learnt on the streets.'[22] Smith sums up his belief in what I call the 'street spot' of environment, talent and practice based on a subtle blend of formal and informal play that he says 'set Rooney apart from the rest' of his peers. 'I spoke to someone at Everton who said we haven't had a street footballer since Rooney,' he confides. 'He was a product of the environment. People now are more concerned about kids being on the street. For me, yeah, he showed signs from an early age, but the street football was what set him apart. The working-class culture, the opportunity to play, always with a ball, always against good players, older players, stronger players. I think the fact he came from nothing

---

22. *The Telegraph*, 'England striker Wayne Rooney reveals that he likes to play street football when he returns home to Liverpool' by Jason Burt, 11 October 2014.

spurred him on even more. In working-class areas, it's a release, isn't it . . . from the day-to-day perils of life.'

Alan Irvine saw it first hand at Everton back in 2002. The Scottish former winger left his academy director role at Newcastle United to become number two to David Moyes, and he recalls Rooney's remarkable presence. 'Wayne was a special talent,' he says. Rooney was unique because 'nobody could have gone into that first-team environment like he did and not just survived, but survived comfortably'. Aged just sixteen, Rooney was 'totally fearless' up against first-team players he idolised, such as Duncan Ferguson, David Weir and Alan Stubbs. 'He simply loved playing. In training, he didn't see it as "I'm practising". He was just kicking a ball, just playing football. The very fact he was playing Premier League football and then going to play with his mates in the street says it all.'

Smith needs no convincing about Rooney's status. As we're about to depart, he fixes me with a steely gaze. 'You know what,' he declares. 'In my generation, I don't think you'll ever get a better teenager than Rooney. And I'm including Ronaldo and Messi in that… When he was sixteen, seventeen, eighteen, nineteen there was no one to touch him. I don't think we ever will see it again.'

CHAPTER 9
ROBERTO MARTÍNEZ AND THE 'FALSE NINE'

THE BRAZILIAN COACH Tite was magnanimous. 'If you like football, you have to watch this game . . . you will have pleasure if you are not emotionally involved: triangulations, transitions, saves, what a beautiful game.' He was not wrong. Speaking through the painful grimace of defeat, Tite heaped praise on the team that had vanquished his *Verde-Amarela* (Green and Yellows) one breathless Friday night in eastern Russia. It was commonly hailed as the night Vladimir Putin's bold promise to make the 2018 football World Cup one of the most memorable jamborees in its storied eighty-eight year history came to fruition in dramatic, pulsating fashion. The architect of the impeccably planned victory for Belgium's lauded 'golden generation' was Roberto Martínez. The engineer who brought the bespoke designs to life was Kevin de Bruyne.

'We gave the players a very difficult tactical plan,' admitted Spaniard Martínez, the former Wigan and Everton manager. 'When you play you have to get a tactical advantage. We had to be brave tactically, and to do that in a World Cup, the players have to believe.' What the Catalan coach didn't say that night in the fuzzy aftermath of the historic victory was that his tactical ideas, strategy and innovative gameplan were built largely on the same principles that define the game of futsal.

The victory had its 'roots' in futsal, Martínez revealed, speaking to me exactly one year on from that giddy night in Kazan, when an own goal by Manchester City's Fernandinho and a glorious strike by his club teammate, De Bruyne, sealed victory for a Belgian side that eventually marched into the World Cup semi-finals. 'Everything is about having enough bodies around the ball and finding the opportunity to free players and understanding the space, which happens in futsal a lot,' Martínez explains. The Belgium head coach is speaking by phone on a Monday morning in late July after inveigling a precious moment of space for himself. His Scottish wife, Beth, gave birth to his second daughter, Safianna, just two days ago, and the ever-kindly Martínez had asked if we could postpone the chat for a few days. Such beguiling politeness shines through during a long chat covering futsal in Belgium, England and Spain, the links to football and the 'cultural challenges' presented by the need to 'educate' parents and coaches about the long-term development of young players. Speaking as a new father for the second time, he's eager to tell me how his tactical masterstroke was born on the small-sided courts where he played routinely as a young boy in his hometown of Balaguer, Catalonia. Midway between Barcelona and the city of Zaragoza in Aragon, the town once fell under Muslim rule as an eleventh-century entry point to the caliphate of Cordoba to its south. The historic victory over Brazil we're talking about acted as a gateway for the sport of futsal to invade the world of football. Antonio José Azevedo, the Brazilian futsal coach known as Zego, turned conventional wisdom on its head by developing a formation that brought the pivot back in line with other players, in order to create mid-court overloads as a weapon against stronger teams. He made his name in Spain at a time when Martínez, Pep Guardiola and other future footballing philosophers were still playing. The influence of the false pivot in futsal culture has direct links to the concept of the deep-lying striker in football known as the 'false nine'.

When Guardiola famously invited Lionel Messi to his room on the evening of the title-deciding *El Clásico* in 2009 to inform him of his new role, the latest incarnation of the false nine was born. Messi saw himself as an *enganche* (hook) in the finest Argentinian tradition, thriving in the deeper-hanging position wide to the right. Guardiola instructed him to move central and hang yet deeper, joining forces with Xavi Hernández and Andrés Iniesta to overrun Real Madrid's midfield duo of Fernando Gago and Lassana Diarra. 'That's exactly what happened,' writes Michael Cox in *Zonal Marking*, his excellent deconstruction of tactics in modern European football. 'In a 6–2 victory that effectively clinched the league title, Messi scored two, created another for Henry from a position between the lines, and helped to give Barcelona total dominance in the centre. Real's centre-backs had no idea how to stop him.' Although each iteration of the 'false nine' is subtly different, the general notion of a deeper-lying central striker is far from a novel idea in football. Jonathan Wilson traces the history back to the nineteenth century in his book *The Barcelona Legacy: Guardiola, Mourinho and the Fight for Football's Soul*:

> From as early as the 1890s, strikers experimented with dropping deep away from their markers. G.O. Smith of the Corinthians was the first to gain a reputation for doing so, standing at the head of a proud line that included various conductors in Argentinian football in the 1920s, Matthias Sindelar of Austria's 1930s Wunderteam, Nándor Hidegkuti in the great Hungary side of the early fifties and even, arguably, Real Madrid's Alfredo di Stéfano who described his role as *delantero retrasado* – a delayed centre-forward.

In the 1970s, Johan Cruyff embodied the spirit that eventually led to Messi, the most famous number ten to masquerade as a false nine. Before Messi, Michael Laudrup performed the role more than occasionally for Cruyff's Barcelona. Elsewhere in Europe, two other high-end goalscoring machines, Francesco Totti and Cristiano Ronaldo, have been used to great effect in the position. Just like Messi, the Italian and the Portuguese have both spoken of their love of futsal. Retired Italian international and AS Roma one-club legend Totti still plays futsal for pleasure in Rome and was the subject of a public offer from the president of the Italian futsal federation, Andrea Montemurro, to represent the Azzurri in the small-sided game. Il Capitano didn't take up the offer, but he continued to excel on the futsal court in 2019. In futsal, of course, shifting in between the lines can be a constant, with the four on-court players buzzing about in complementary rotations, all of them at one with the principles of movement and space creation that define the 'false nine' gameplan.

You can clearly see that Martínez shares with Guardiola a sub-conscious connection to this futsal way that smoothes the path towards strategies focusing on the achievement of numerical superiority through positioning on the pitch. 'Futsal is part of our development,' he admits. 'From the age of eight to sixteen futsal is a very powerful tool to develop you as a young player. At sixteen it becomes a Y crossroads. Some players feel they want to play futsal professionally, some forget about it and go to play football professionally, others will stay as an amateur and maybe continue playing both. We see it as noble. It's just part of our development. We both played it from age eight and see it as natural, as enjoyable. It's an element that has developed us.' Just as Guardiola's Messi disman-tled Real Madrid's defensive rigidity, so Martínez's masterstroke tore up Brazil's gameplan, forcing Tite to bring on Roberto Firmino at half-time. It was clear that the extra man in midfield created by the false nine was helping Belgium expose the space behind the Brazil full-backs. 'I think it was 2016 the last time they conceded two goals, it was against Paraguay,' recalls Martínez. 'We were trying to take

Brazil into an uneasy feeling. With Brazil if you put eleven players around your box it's very difficult to break you down, but it's what they're used to.'

It's one thing having the plan – carrying it out is a different story. 'I never lost a game on the tactics board, it's the execution that matters,' Martínez admitted immediately after the game. Which is where Kevin de Bruyne comes in. 'He has such an intelligence of the game and knows how to use space and make penetrative runs in those difficult positions,' Martínez tells me. 'It gave us a lot of opportunities for one-v-ones and Romelu Lukaku and Eden Hazard plenty of opportunities to run wide and have a chance at taking people on. Brazil couldn't defend both wide and centrally at the same time. The plan was to make Brazil feel uncomfortable.' Martínez was fully aware of De Bruyne's futsal background. Manchester City's arch creator has spoken about the futsal he played as a boy in Drongen, on the outskirts of Ghent, as vital to his peculiarly enhanced skill set. 'The technique you learn as a little kid,' De Bruyne told the Sky Sports show *Soccer AM*. 'I played on the streets and played some futsal when I was younger, so I've got a little bit of that. I think it helps when you're in tight spaces to create something out of nothing.' Martínez is unequivocal. The futsal background has helped De Bruyne's 'element of decision-making needed to really hurt the opposition', he continues. 'Sometimes when you watch Manchester City play, it's phenomenal to see how structured and how well worked the teams are, and you have this incredible piece of uncertainty which dislodges the opposition in Kevin de Bruyne. This comes from that quick-thinking brain which was developed by the technical qualities in futsal, and the evolution he has had in his career.'

De Bruyne's midfield teammate on that night in Kazan, Axel Witsel, has a similar story to tell. Witsel grew up immersed in both futsal and football. His father, Thierry, combined lower-league football with twelve years playing futsal in the Belgian top flight, one of the first national leagues in Europe when founded in 1968. Just over fifty years on, it boasts a few fully professional clubs among its largely semi-professional roll call and is dominated by FP Halle-Gooik, a club founded in 2004, a year before the serial title winners for a decade Action 21 Charleroi became the first and only Belgian club to lift the UEFA Futsal Cup. Witsel followed in his father's futsal footsteps around this time. In 2019, speaking as the fulcrum of the Borussia Dortmund midfield, he told bundesliga.com: 'I was always watching my dad and then playing on the futsal pitch indoors. And also the street, because I was always playing outside with friends. I think futsal and the street help you a lot technically.' The former Everton and Belgium winger Kevin Mirallas also played both sports as a boy, reaching a crossroads age fifteen when presented with two offers to represent his country at youth level: one from the football team and one from futsal. He chose football, but insists the futsal influence remains in his game.

When Martínez is not plotting Belgium's path to a historic first international prize in the run-up to the now-postponed 2020 European Championship, he is 'very busy creating projects' to bring through a new generation of Belgian stars. Futsal is a huge part of the Royal Belgian Football Association's strategy. Bob Browaeys is the technical co-ordinator who helped overhaul the association's approach in 2000, fuelling the growth of the so-called 'golden generation' by instilling a coaching culture that prizes small-sided, games-based practice (the one-v-ones and two-v-twos that Martínez spoke about), player-centred learning and creating a street football feel for kids to enjoy. Martínez works with Browaeys to oversee the talent development programme, a rigorous approach that's vital in a smaller nation that cannot afford to let potential go untapped. Its focus on tackling relative-age bias is a prime example, seeking to ensure younger kids in the school year or relatively late maturers are not left behind.

From 2008, the national youth teams have run squads made up of players born in the traditionally neglected second half of the year to ensure any hidden gems are given every opportunity to shine. The international winger Yannick Carrasco's progress was accelerated as a participant in the first year of this system. De Bruyne was also a late maturer, failing to trouble the national youth team selectors until the under-19 age group. The other major focus is futsal. Backed by Martínez, Browaeys is ramping up the amount of futsal played by the football stars of tomorrow. 'We want to encourage our national teams to play more of it because it is also a fantastic learning environment for our players and we need to integrate it much more,' Browaeys told Sky Sports in 2018. Martínez rejoices in the fact that this wider role in the Belgian FA 'allows me to be involved every day'.

While Martínez clearly boasts a strategic flexibility, buried safely and deeply in the Catalan's futsal-formed consciousness, it's not simply about the one-off shock tactics on display in Kazan. He is keen to expand on how the twin-track upbringing in both sports infused his general coaching philosophy. 'Futsal forces players to become incredibly comfortable on the ball, so you cannot rely on the errors of the opposition,' he explains. 'It's only four-v-four so if you're not great on the ball you're going to struggle and find it very difficult to break the opposition down. This makes you think and find a way to use the ability of each player to become better than the opposition four. That's fundamental to futsal.

'I think that's something that I brought into my coaching,' he continues. 'I always want to find a way to win through accumulating the outstanding qualities of each player, rather than developing a system or a way of playing where the players simply have to fit in and become average with what they were doing, their jobs. If you've got an outstanding defender or tackler, it would be very difficult to ask them to play fantastic diagonal balls. Or the other way round, asking a fantastic passer to battle all the time to recover the ball and tackle. When I started out in coaching, this was the influence. How could I get the outstanding qualities into a team, get the sum of all individuals to be better than the other team. The mentality of being a team comes first, of course, being a unit, working for each other and knowing the strategy. But I simply ask each individual to master what they are outstanding at. Not the other way around.' So it's clear that futsal is great for coaches, great for players, great to watch – and it's even wonderful for parents, says Martínez, helping to alter their understanding of what a coach is doing to the extent that it could slowly change a win-at-all-costs culture. 'Everything in futsal is about controlling the ball and using the space,' he says. 'This is the basics of how you see football, right? So a parent will watch futsal and then they will appreciate more how a player can utilise space, receive and turn with the ball, and how you can manoeuvre with the inside, outside, top or the sole of the boot, as the ball doesn't bounce and is always on the ground. It's educational.'

Just like listening to Martínez himself. But futsal is not an optional extra, he points out. It's essential not only because it can dilute the win-at-all-costs culture at the younger ages, but also because of the socio-cultural changes the world over.

The combination of casual and organised futsal and football he was weaned on can no longer be taken for granted, even in Spain. 'This was fantastic to develop street football and one-v-one techniques and I think we're losing that,' he says. 'The players are not allowed to have that practice on the street any more. I think this has an effect that means they play in a more structured way. They try to learn how to play a certain way in a system, not to develop as a player and how skilful you become on the ball.' Whether on the streets or in the halls, futsal has clearly been fundamental to the past development of the present Belgium and Spain football teams. But it's also a game that has to be part of the future in such a changing world, according to Martínez. We can't say we haven't been warned.

CHAPTER 10
ENGLAND: REWRITING THE DNA

GRAEME DELL IS chilling out in the hotel shortly after breakfast. His room is small but comfortable, allowing for some last-minute preparation for the big game to come. His mind wanders back to the handful of matches he's overseen as the England men's futsal head coach, the harsh lessons and heavy defeats testing the former football coach's stomach for the fight ahead. Outside his window, the balmy autumn sunshine illuminates the southern Portuguese resort of Tavira, nestled in the eastern reaches of the golfing paradise that is the Algarve. There is a polite knock at the door. Dell shuffles over to open it and sees Orlando Duarte. They hardly know each other. Duarte is the coach of Portugal, England's illustrious forthcoming opponents, whose tactics Dell has been busily poring over in a vain attempt to find a hole in their strategic armoury. 'He's got his futsal shoes in his hands and is carrying a clipboard,' recalls Dell.

'Hi, Orlando . . . how are you?'

'Hello, Graeme. C'mon, we're going training.'

'No, no . . . we're not training now. We're playing against you. Tonight.'

'I know, I know . . . you're coming training with us. You're going to watch us train.'

Dell smiles, expecting Duarte to say he's taking the piss. There's only silence. Dell accepts the invitation, shuts the door, gets changed quickly and races to the lobby ready to go. 'When I got down,' Dell remembers, 'all of his team were there. Every single one of them came over and shook my hand. Every one. And when we got on the bus to head to the training session, Orlando looked at me and said: "Unless we share the knowledge, you're never going to learn as a nation." He pointed around the bus and went on: "Look at these players… you don't have the same players as I do. And even if you had the same knowledge, you can't do the same things. But you have to have the knowledge. You have to develop it." And he was bang on,' says Dell. 'This was a massive learning experience of having to share.'

Despite the advantage of Dell's fresh insight, England's paucity of game nous was cruelly exposed that evening in a 24–1 demolition. 'People say it was embarrassing losing by that score. We got battered, yeah. But we'd scored one goal against Portugal. They were fifth in the world. That was an achievement for us.' Dell's passion for futsal – and football – is still alive nearly fifteen years on from that humbling in the Algarve Four Nations tournament in October 2004 – still England's biggest ever defeat. It's far from an outlier though. England won only one of their first fifty competitive matches – an 8–7 victory in Birmingham against Greece in late 2007. It was the official England team's forty-fifth encounter, the previous matches all ending in defeat apart from a ding-dong 5–5 draw with Cyprus in 2006.

Portugal's growing reputation in world futsal was confirmed a few weeks after the 2004 Algarve rout in the FIFA world championship when the *selecão* missed out on a second consecutive semi-final by a point, edged out by eventual finalists Spain and Italy in a classic second-round group of death. Speaking after the England demolition job, Duarte summed up the gulf between the two nations. 'England aren't the sort of team we can realistically measure ourselves against,' he warned. 'They're new to the world of futsal.'

The future of English futsal was laid down that day. And the timing could not have been more urgent. Just three weeks earlier 'the last of the true street footballers' had served notice that his era-defining talent was starting to burn, with that debut hat-trick for Manchester United. Dell could not have known at the time, but the informal street play so explosively demonstrated by Rooney's emergence coincided with a vital first stepping stone for the game that could yet become its more formal replacement. A decade and a half later, with numerous bumps in the road navigated, futsal in England has its own experts to call on, with their own backstories and life lessons to offer solace to other nations with a similar conundrum to tackle.

'I sometimes forget about the journey we've been on,' admits Dell, sipping a coffee in a café at Bisham Abbey National Sports Centre, the sumptuous Berkshire complex that was English football's base camp back when Dell became the youngest coach in England ever to achieve the 'full' coaching badge in the mid-1980s aged just twenty-one. 'I laugh at myself when I think about it. My first truly competitive futsal match was like being smacked around the face with a wet fish.' A regular five-a-side player as a boy, Dell glimpsed futsal while travelling in Spain, Portugal and Italy in the 1980s. But his interest grew after he 'stumbled across' the world university futsal championships in Málaga in the early nineties. 'It was only about eight teams, two men and a dog watching, but it was proper futsal. It was fascinating.'

He knew there were 'pockets of interest' in the UK. 'But everything I'd heard, read or seen about it was simply five-a-side on a futsal pitch... when you looked at it the players were rubbish. They didn't understand what they were trying to do.' One of the hotbeds of innovation was Pendle in east Lancashire, a sleepy district nestled at the end of the M65 after it weaves north-east from the historic football hotbeds of Preston, Blackburn and Burnley. Geoff Payton, a former apprentice footballer at Burnley who combined refereeing with duties as manager of Pendle Leisure Centre in Colne, set the ball rolling on futsal in the area after entertaining the visiting Australia national team in Europe for the 1985 FIFUSA futsal world championships. The FA knew of his interest and directed the visiting Australians his way. After setting up local leagues, Payton established the English Futsal Association and recruited local semi-professional footballers to compete in the FIFUSA world championships in 1988, taking the place of late drop-outs Mexico in the tournament in Melbourne, Australia. Although not backed by the FA, it was the first appearance of an England team at an international futsal competition.

A few years later, Pendle's futsal pioneer set up a British women's team to play a FIFUSA-run international tournament, also in Australia, in January 1997. The players were drawn from colleges in the north-west. Payton scouted potential players while refereeing and was 'astounded by their talent' on court, he told the *Lancashire Evening Telegraph* at the time. 'They liked it and the rest is history.'

In fact, this is prehistory in the eyes of the FA, where only FIFA-backed futsal merits recognition. Coincidentally, Dell is speaking on the day he held an emergency conference call with the head of judicial services at the FA over the recent noise about an organisation suddenly offering non-FIFA youth futsal in England, under the banner of the Paraguay-based AMF. It's something Dell expected to happen one day, and he accepts the FA must 'take a hit' for 'not sorting itself out' by fully embracing futsal. The growth in interest in the game at the FA is marked though, he insists, and England is light years ahead of where it was when he first got involved in futsal. It's a period he recalls with candour. 'In the early 2000s when the FA started to look at futsal,' he remembers, 'Geoff Thompson, who was the FA chairman, also sat on the UEFA panel and was under moral pressure to get involved, to join the futsal party, so to speak.' It was a turbulent time at the FA. Thompson's reign as chairman was bookended by the dismissal of Glenn Hoddle in 1999 after comments about disabled people in an interview with *The Times*, and the appointment in December 2007 of the Italian coach Fabio Capello on a lavish contract reportedly worth £6m a year.

Dell recalls answering a fateful phone call from the FA in 2003. 'I thought they were taking the piss,' he admits – a little like he presumed Orlando Duarte was winding him up the following year. 'They said: "We want you to coach the England five-a-side team." I said: "What England five-a-side team?" And they said "futsal". So that was it really.' His experience coaching the British Universities Sports Association's men's football teams at the World University Games since 1995, and in the professional game – as first-team coach at Wycombe Wanderers and head of the centre of excellence at Queen's Park Rangers under Don Howe –made him a wise choice. Within weeks he was in Kuala Lumpur with a ramshackle group of youngsters, making up a squad that wasn't so much an official England team as an FA select squad. 'A baptism of fire,' laughs Dell. England finished eleventh in a twelve-team tournament, with Argentina coming out on top. Diego Giustozzi – who would go on to coach the Argentina national team to World Cup glory in 2016 – scored in the 3–2 final victory over arch-rivals Brazil. Uzbekistan trounced the FA squad 10–2 in the first game and Iran put fourteen past them in the second. A sole victory came in the final match, where Indonesia succumbed 3–2 to the nascent bulldog five-a-side spirit and endeavour.

The first official England game took place a few months later during the UEFA futsal championship qualifiers in Albania in January 2004. It was another eye-opener. 'We landed in an airfield in the middle of a valley,' recalls Dell. 'It looked like we'd landed in a farm.' After a 'three-hour drive on a fifty-two seater coach, travelling on unmade roads', they reached the training in venue. 'It was a coastal resort in the middle of nowhere. The power got turned off in the middle of the afternoon and back on again at seven p.m. Freezing cold. We were sleeping in the hotel and we were literally wearing our tracksuits in bed it was that cold.'

The welcome didn't get any warmer. The hosts were in no mood to indulge the English visitors, who wore their nation's footballing reputation like a target on their backs. The Albania episode served up a cruel first lesson in international futsal, at the same time exposing UEFA's amateurish planning in the arena of competitive futsal qualifiers. The UEFA futsal club competition was in its third year, while the 2004 futsal championship for national teams was just four editions old after starting in 1996. The kick-off in England's first game was delayed because the power didn't come on until early evening. 'That was fair enough,' recalls Dell. 'But then we look around the venue . . . on all the seats there's an A4 sheet of paper with the black Albanian eagle on a red backdrop. When we pick up the paper, you could see printed on the back of it the words "Fuck off England". Seriously. All the crowd were waving these things during the match.' Welcome to the world of futsal, merry old England. They lost 8–6. The second game, against Cyprus, brought another defeat, this time 8–4. None of the teams in the group qualifier made it to the tournament finals in Ostrava, Czech Republic, in 2005. England's dismal showing was hardly a surprise. 'The reality was we had no infrastructure, we had no players,' admits Dell. 'The quality of play was rubbish. But the FA made clear we were in it to keep it going.' Dell began 'scouring non-league football for good technicians who, while they didn't understand the game, had the fitness and game awareness and understanding so we could put something together. And to an extent that worked.'

But it only took the team so far. The heavy defeats continued, and the learning curve showed no signs of flattening out. There were limited signs of progress domestically, however. The first FA Futsal Cup was held in 2003. Sheffield Hallam defeated another Yorkshire team, Thomas Rotherham College, to take the mantle held unofficially by Tranmere Victoria as best team in the country. Founded by the club's chairman, Geoff Hughes, who transformed a lowly Sunday league football team in Birkenhead, Merseyside, into the foremost futsal club in the country, Tranmere were ahead of the English FA in promoting the game. In 2002, they hosted and won the country's first international tournament – up against Scotland, Ireland, Northern Ireland and Gibraltar. A month later they also hosted the might of the Iran national team for an exhibition match. And after winning a tournament organised by the Sheffield and Hallamshire FA, Tranmere became England's first representatives in the UEFA Futsal Cup, inspiring the FA to finally get involved in the game. When they did, in 2003, eleven teams were invited to the Aldershot army barracks for the first FA Futsal Cup. 'No one came to watch,' says Dell. The Yorkshire teams were joined by Tranmere, Pendle Santos (from Geoff Payton's Lancashire hotbed) and two teams from Grimsby, another early adopter of futsal, fuelled by the passion of an inspirational coach called Kevin Bryant. Dell helped the FA build up the event over the next five years. But it only went so far. 'I recognised the FA futsal was behind where I was at as a coach: no coach education in place, no national league, so I went off and did my own thing . . . I felt I'd done my bit,' he says. 'And Pete Sturgess came in with his full-time role at the FA, [and he] was able to make changes in the programme that were needed.' Within months, Dell was invited back into the fold to work on futsal coach education.

Although Dell's stint in a key FA role was less tumultuous than that of the man who hired him, Geoff Thompson, there's a certain symbiosis about their experiences. A couple of months before Dell stepped aside as futsal coach in 2008, the embattled FA chairman resigned, saying he was 'handing the torch over burning more brightly than when I received it'. For Dell, looking back, the sentiments were strikingly similar. 'I'd done my bit,' he reiterates. 'And we'd progressed. It was time for someone else to take over.'

* * *

'Which hat are you wearing today?' enquires Pete Sturgess as he thrusts his hand towards me.

'Oh, I dunno, Pete. Guess it depends on what you say . . .'

We're in a function room at Reading FC's Madejski Stadium as Sturgess, the star turn at the Berks and Bucks FA coach conference, chats briefly before delivering a talk on grassroots football to eighty or so coaches. Sturgess is the FA's lead technical coach for the foundation phase (children aged between five and eleven), and this is his latest staging post on a nationwide roadshow trying to bust the myths about what the England DNA means for the mums' and dads' army of grassroots football coaches from Cornwall to Carlisle trying to make sense of the game to benefit their children. In 2014, the FA launched a best-practice programme described as England's unique genetic code, its DNA, to create a 'golden thread' between the national teams, from the under-15s up to the England men's and women's senior teams. With a nod to other nations' successful coaching models, particularly those of Germany and Belgium, it highlighted the grassroots youth game as a crucial starting point. Sturgess is here today to fill in the blanks between five 'core elements' key to creating a new breed of English player and coach: 'who we are', 'how we play', 'how we coach', 'how we support' and 'the future England player'. I'm armed with a notepad and recording every utterance. So my answer was no lie: I'm here as coach, mentor and, if the need arises, journalist too.

'If you are not prepared to show children kindness and understanding at ages five to eleven, the golden years of learning, if you're a coach who is intolerant of mistakes – then do you know what? Coaching is not for you.' It's firm but fair. Stephen Moody (my co-coach at Woodley United FC) shares a wry smile and a raised eyebrow with me. Sturgess is firing the latest salvo in the battle against the win-at-all-costs brigade that has long held grassroots football in England captive, stunting long-term player development for a generation as the era of the uncoached street player gave way to the age of Charter Standard clubs. All too often, an army of well-meaning but ultimately regressive volunteer coaches imposes on children an adult-centric view of the game, stomping all over the enjoyment youngsters crave. Sturgess's crusade to 'educate' coaches is nothing short of a quiet, thoughtful revolution. The FA's online learning platform – which I use to aide mentees in their coaching – is a revelation, with close to 20,000 subscribers regularly interacting on its pages filled with age-appropriate coaching sessions, insightful articles and evidence-based analysis on why kids want to have fun. The message linking 'freedom to play' and 'master the ball' with the creation of better players in the long term is finally getting through, slowly but surely. The start of this assault on the old-fashioned approach to coaching can be traced back to 2008 and the birth of the pioneering youth award, filling at a stroke the embarrassing void of child-centred, age-appropriate content available in the FA's expansive – and to some, expensive – coaching courses. Suddenly, running alongside the rigidly formulaic, didactic coach education programme, from the introductory level one to level five (UEFA Pro), was an extensive, evidence-based embrace of games-based learning. It was a method of attaining the FA's recently introduced four-corner model of holistic player development, adding much-neglected social and psychological elements to the physical and technical focus that had always been present. The courses were a breath of fresh air. A few years later, the nationwide youth football review spelled the end of publication of league tables up to under-11 level. A 'retreat line' was introduced at the younger ages to encourage playing out from the goalkeeper by forcing opponents to wait in their own half until a keeper takes a goal-kick. The other huge change placed greater focus on smaller-sided games, stemming the mad rush to put pre-adolescent children on an enormous eleven-a-side pitch with goalkeepers half the height of the crossbar.

On top of these successful practical measures, the DNA was built on the valiant but ultimately vague Future Game template, revealed in 2010. Future full England team manager Gareth Southgate was at the heart of the operation as England under-21s coach. He had a special remit to work on youth development with the technical director, Dan Ashworth. At the DNA launch, Ashworth – who was hired by the FA from West Bromwich Albion and went on to depart for a similar role at Brighton in 2019 – was up front about the intent: 'We get hung up on "is it 4-3-3 or 4-4-2?" No, it is a philosophy and principles of play.' The extent to which the changes directly influenced the performances of the junior England teams is impossible to discern. But success swiftly followed. The remarkable run of success for England's youth teams in 2017 put the youth development programme on the map. Dominic Calvert-Lewin's victorious thirty-fifth minute strike against Venezuela in the final of the under-20 World Cup announced the arrival of a much-coveted new breed of young player. A month or so later the under-19s, led by the impressive Chelsea starlet Mason Mount, edged out Portugal to become European champions. Earlier that year the under-17s reached the European championship finals, with a young Jadon Sancho named player of the tournament. There was a fresh vibrancy to England's youth teams. In between the under-19 and under-20 final victories, however, Aidy Boothroyd's under-21s proved that the old world order might take a little longer to overturn: England lost in a European Championships semi-final. On penalties. To Germany. This blip aside, the purple patch of success was difficult to ignore.

Pete Sturgess is here today preaching the same messages for the grassroots game. And it's working. 'We want kids to love the game and learn how to play,' he says. 'Where's the sense in telling kids to just boot the ball away when under pressure? Where's the sense in telling a kid "you're a defender" age six? Where's the learning?' The quest to get children 'staying on the ball' is one that invites scorn and intrigue in equal measure in youth football. All too many coaches feel it's better to treat primary school children as though they are mini-adult professional players, bombarding them with visceral urges to 'pass, pass, pass it', to 'dig deep' and 'want it more than the opposition', all the time being sure never to 'try anything fancy' while on the ball. Sturgess pulls no punches. For a man obsessed with letting young children explore and experiment in an enjoyable environment, he's not playing about. 'It's not staying on the ball until you run up a blind alley and lose it,' he states firmly. 'It's actually saying: every individual in my team needs to be capable of keeping the ball for us. And we can do it in small groups, in a collective. This is the bit we're missing out. It really isn't "stay on it until you lose it". But in the early stages at age five, six and seven, that's what it's going to look like.' The explicit nature of his instruction is heartening. It's a boldness that has developed as the DNA project has gained a more sympathetic hearing. He talks like a man who's given up trying to whisper and coax change out of grassroots coaches. But he's also more than just words.

Later that day he puts on a showcase session out on the 3G artificial pitch with a bunch of under-9s, focusing on staying on the ball in physically demanding one-v-one situations in a tight box five metres square. This is Sturgess with his oversize, wide-brimmed football hat on. The smaller, close-fitting item of headwear he fetches from his wardrobe – one he wore with pride and distinction for the best part of a decade as national team head coach – might as well be emblazoned with the letters F, U, T, S, A and L. All his urgings about more time on the ball, more touches, more dribbling opportunities, more enjoyment and '10,000 experiences' link neatly to the small-sided game. He warns the assembled coaches that futsal must be an 'essential part of the diet' young footballers in England are weaned on if they are to blossom into players possessing the 'robust technical base' required. It's a message I first heard when I interviewed him in 2012 after he watched my under-10s team compete in the national finals.

Sturgess's efforts are assisted by another luminary of the professional youth coaching world, Paul McGuinness, who joined the FA from Manchester United's academy after a decade coaching the under-18s. The son of former United manager Wilf, he is equally strident about the role futsal can play in developing youngsters. 'It's absolutely vital,' he tells me at St George's Park while watching a futsal session by Sturgess strikingly similar to the 'stay on the ball' game he demonstrated in Reading. 'Because it's all the basic building blocks of the game. The technical skills, the one-v-ones . . . it's vital.' McGuinness talks about creating 'predator players' through repetition of opportunities in futsal, which offers 'instant feedback' for players – and coaches – to assess where they are strong and weak. 'It's clear when it breaks down what the problem was,' he explains. 'If you start eleven-a-side before you've learned these skills, you won't be able to see the wood for the trees.'

McGuinness is not new to the small-sided format. In 2002, he was involved in the pioneering pilot study with Manchester United under-9 players that found four- and five-a-side games yielded much greater opportunity to practise the 'predator' skills he craves than eight-a-side matches. On average 500 per cent more goals were scored, scoring attempts were up 260 per cent, and other actions were much more frequent too. The number of passes was up an average 135 per cent, dribbling attempts 280 per cent and individual one-on-one encounters – the bedrock of the game – soared by 225 per cent. A few years later McGuinness introduced games uncannily similar to the game of futsal to the older age groups. 'We used to play on a basketball court when I was at United with Marcus Rashford, Jesse Lingard,

Paul Pogba and so on. But we would play seven-a-side or six-a-side . . . we called it Joga Bonito. It was a version of futsal, if you like. But you're getting the different skills in there, with the hard floor, the combinations and so on. Futsal is a more tactical game. At United, it was more like street football, a scramble. With a football, not a futsal ball. So here, in futsal, it's more about tactics. We've seen today two-v-one tactics, three-v-twos, little overlaps, running someone out of space allowing someone else to come into the space . . . all of these small bits you will see on *Match of the Day* tonight.'

* * *

Mike Skubala's eyes darken. 'It's the simplicity that kills,' declares the England coach. Four rows of heads nod in unison as murmurs of agreement and snorts of acceptance fill the air. The challenge is clear. England's futsal players are summing up after a bout of video analysis of their opponents in the 2020 futsal World Cup main round qualifiers. It's the final training camp before their chance to make history. England have never got beyond this stage.

I've been with the team at St George's Park for the day. Exactly four years earlier, I spent a whole weekend with them at the equivalent stage in the qualification process for the 2016 tournament in Colombia. England's forthcoming nemesis in 2015 was Ukraine, the overriding focus of the weekend being how to escape the suffocating high press of the powerful eastern Europeans. England may have crept up a few places in the world ranking since then, but their status against the stronger teams is unchanged: they are still the underdogs. Most teams in the top fifty will press them high, fully expecting their suspect technique and tactical rigour to break down often enough to make the potentially perilous full-court press well worth the risk.

In the lecture room of the All England Suite, the players are issued with the challenge of watching edited clips of two of their three forthcoming opponents, Italy and Belarus. They sort themselves into two groups. Russell Goldstein, a schoolteacher by day, makes for the door, heading for a different room to study Belarus while joking that he's not staying here with 'someone from the *Guardian* in the room'. I resist the urge to man-mark him and instead stay put. The Italy clips appeal more anyway. Skubala's only intervention is to ask for 'one or two seniors to go in each group'. Doug Reed stays, along with the veteran captain, Raoni Medina, one of the handful of naturalised foreign citizens to have represented England at futsal. Born in Brazil, Medina turned professional in football at Sporting in Portugal – where he played in the same youth cohort as Cristiano Ronaldo – before falling out of eleven-a-side and back into the game he played most as a boy. The skilful pivot has been at the forefront of the game, for England and the dominant London-based club side Helvécia, for over a decade. Skubala sits calmly, acting as a facilitator, a guide encouraging the players to take ownership of the process, nudging them towards answers only when he feels they're missing a trick or getting sidetracked. Calvin Dickson, a left-footed winger/pivot with a maths and physics degree, and Richard Ward, a City of London bank worker with a sideline in depositing the ball in the back of the net for his country, offer swift and vocal insight. It's a masterclass in coaching off the court.

This scenario is a walk in the park for Skubala. Like all futsal coaches at the top of the game, he embraces the challenge of acting fast in what he calls the 'pressure cooker', where he has thrived since his playing debut for England – his first taste of futsal. As a non-league footballer training to be a teacher, he took up Graeme Dell's invitation to play for England, confident in the knowledge that he 'could handle a game of five-a-side'. Despite losing 6–1 in Thailand – 'futsal was different . . . it was much harder,' he told the Coaches Voice website – he loved it instantly. Aged twenty, he accepted he couldn't make a living playing football or futsal and went to university to study sports science and psychology, eventually swapping life as a teacher for a post as Director of Football and Head Football Coach at Loughborough University, where he also led the Great Britain Universities football team. Throughout these years he racked up sixty caps for the England futsal team while also displaying the versatility learned in futsal by playing non-league football 'as a winger, a centre mid or even a number ten at times.'

Once Skubala stopped playing, Pete Sturgess recruited him as assistant coach of the national team. Futsal challenged him more as a coach than football, he says. The need to focus constantly in a scenario requiring coaches to make up to eighty substitutions a game is a burden he relishes. After the summary of Italy's potential strengths and weaknesses are completed, Skubala stands up from his desk-bound position with a laptop and points the group towards a grid on the clipboard. It's extremely lopsided. The column marked 'strengths' is a riot of warnings, whereas the 'weaknesses' section contains four lonely entries. 'That's why they are seventh in the world,' Skubala declares. 'It's difficult to pick holes in Italy's game.' Once Goldstein and the second group return to share their findings on Belarus, Skubala restates the big message of the morning's training session, when he implored the goalkeepers, particularly the first-choice Mark Croft, to 'own the game in the build-up'. He wants the goalkeepers to break out of the high press that all three teams, particularly Italy, will no doubt inflict on them. Just like their patient passing game, Italy's suffocating high press is predictable yet extremely effective, the physical manifestation of the brutal tactical punishment meted out in high-grade futsal. The lethal simplicity that Skubala talks about.

The session they are about to begin at 5 p.m. – the second of the day – is about preparing tactical tweaks to face their third group opponent, Hungary. Skubala's tone changes as he demands the players park all thoughts of Italy and Belarus. 'Now. Please. Now. Hungary.' The ensuing chat – and session – concerns how to shackle Zoltán Dróth, the hulking pivot who poses Hungary's biggest threat. If I were Skubala's coach mentor, I'd be full of praise for a robust display of flexible, adaptable coaching in preparation for facing fearsome challengers. As it was, I simply thanked him for the insight, wished the team luck and departed with a promise to talk again after the mission near the Amalfi coast.

In the end, England's attempt to shatter the glass ceiling was undone by their opponents' brutal cohesion, and the tactical intelligence of their star players. Zoltán Dróth was largely nullified in the opening game, his markers sticking to the gameplan of forcing the Hungary number eleven on to his unfavoured left. But an early second-post finish by Dróth's teammate, Imre Nagy, set the tone of the three-match tournament. As though a metaphor for England's pursuit of the big European futsal nations, the second-minute tap-in left them playing catch-up. Two second-half goals (one from Dróth) completed a 3–0 loss. England needed a result in the following game to retain hope of claiming one of the two qualifying berths in the four-team tournament.

The Italian job came next. Again, it was an opposition player cited as a threat a week earlier, 1,500 miles away in St George's Park, who struck – effectively ending England's chances of qualification. Alex Rodrigo da Silva Merlim, a Brazil-born winger known simply as Merlim, was singled out by the England players as the Italians' weapon of choice. Frustratingly, England held Italy at 0–0 until half-time, the pledge to manage the game and make it 'scrappy' played out for real. Then Merlim pounced. Not just once, but twice. Both world-class strikes, one with the right foot, one with the left. The game was over. Italy got a couple more before England pulled one back with a penalty. A 5–2 defeat to Belarus in the final group game completed the misery. But there was no demoralising hammering in the manner of those painful winless early years under Graeme Dell.

Skubala told me afterwards the games were always going to be a 'tough gig' and compared them to a non-league football club trying to beat the pro clubs in the FA Cup. 'It's possible, but not often.' As for Merlim? 'He was class, but we kept him quiet tactically until we got tired. I suppose that's why his club pay him 20k a month!' And why he was named third best player in the world that year. Yet again England were undone by moments of quality from teams with more highly paid game-changing individuals in their ranks. The loss of Stuart Cook to a knee ligament injury a few weeks earlier had left England facing an uphill struggle. Arguably England's equivalent of a Merlim, the Mancunian *fixo* is England's game-changer, with an extraordinary array of fleet-footed magic on court. He was lauded in 2014 with a headline in the *Daily Mirror* asking: 'Is this England's best footballer?' Shining for Manchester Futsal Club at the time, Cook's talent contrasted with the underperforming England football team.

Cook tells me he was always drawn to small-sided games. As a late developer, he was small and technical and 'fell out of love with football aged fourteen' to pursue five-a-side cage football 'four or five times a week' against adults in tough parts of Manchester. 'I had to learn to look after myself pretty quickly,' he says. He turned to futsal just over a decade ago, aged twenty-two, after a big growth spurt and found it suited his game. 'It's so much more enjoyable than eleven-a-side. You don't have to run fifty yards first. It's like getting straight into the battle.' Turning out for various clubs in England, at times he was paid expenses to play futsal on a Sunday for the likes of Helvécia (where he played for three years) and semi-professional football on a Saturday. With a secure day job, a mortgage and four children, the thirty-three year-old admits he has spurned many offers to turn professional (from futsal clubs in Italy, Slovakia, Iran, Malta and

Cyprus) and from Crewe Alexandra in English football. 'Financially, it was never viable,' he says. Cook's equally cogent decision-making on the court has long been key to England's chances of reaching the next level. Without him, the Italian job was always likely to be a mission too far.

* * *

The defeats on court in Italy exposed the size of the task still confronting the national team a decade and a half after their humbling in the Algarve. One of England's biggest persistent challenges in truly adopting futsal lies away from the court: the cultural dominance of traditional five-a-side. The era of the big furry tennis ball may have long passed, but in 2020 the form of five-a-side it symbolises was still going strong, played with a regulation football, restrictions on players entering or leaving the penalty areas and on the height the ball can travel. Then there are the side boards inviting the ice-hockey-style crushing of opponents. It's the cage football Cook loved so much. The small-sided pinball-style encounters described in *When Saturday Comes* magazine by the writer Lionel Birnie as 'football for the masses' with a long history of reducing 'professional footballers to the level of amateurs'. From the long-running Evening Standard Fives, started in 1954 and later won by West Ham's Moore and Hurst, to the *Daily Express* national five-a-side tournament, and eventually the hugely competitive 1980s Soccer Six games, small-sided football holds an alluring cultural significance for generations in England. The rare, televised activities of the eleven-a-side pros is replicated a thousand times over by friends, work colleagues and organised teams at the casual, grassroots level. The slow death of the Sunday league eleven-a-side culture in England, hastened by the soaring cost and dwindling availability of decent grass pitches, has boosted small-sided football. In 2015 Sport England revealed

1.5 million adults played it in the UK, two-thirds of them in England. The hugely popular FA People's Cup, which runs male and female competitions from under-10s up to adults, attracts 50,000 players a year. In 2018 Mike Skubala notched a small victory in his quest to plant the futsal flag firmly in the ground occupied by traditional five-a-side football, lobbying successfully for a futsal tournament to be included for the first time.

Later that year, Skubala also presented the Fast Forward with Futsal strategy, a six-year plan to grow the game launched with full backing from the FA. Its five targets for 2024 were set out: 150,000 people playing futsal regularly; an increase from the current 900 to 15,000 futsal coaches qualified at FA Level 2 or UEFA B (Level 3); an England men's futsal team in the top twenty of FIFA world rankings, up from fifty-fourth, and the creation of an England women's team in time for the 2021 UEFA women's futsal championships; finally a woolly commitment to a 'defined network of facilities, covering every county FA.'

Women's futsal has been sorely neglected in England. Unsurprisingly, perhaps, in a country where women's football was banned by the FA for fifty years until 1971. Sue Campbell, the FA's director of women's football in 2018, is quoted on page seven of the brochure, opposite the page listing the five priorities sitting above the famous eulogy from Lionel Messi stating how playing futsal 'on the streets and for my club' formed his unique skill set. 'Futsal can play a key part in our strategy to grow the women's and girls' game – developing the players of tomorrow,' declares Campbell. The aspiration to get more people playing, male and female, is bold. In 2018, there were 574 adult teams registered in England, 77 female, 394 male and 103 mixed gender. Among children, although no overall figures were recorded by the FA – an indictment of the hands-off approach to the sport thus far – in 2016 more than 10,000 youth players, boys and girls, were thought to be involved in futsal via Charter Standard football leagues, taking a winter break in January and February to play futsal indoors instead of kicking their heels when football matches fell victim to the wintry ice and rain. The document strikes a more ambitious note than the target of 150,000 players with talk of 'participation potential in England', citing FIFA's finding in 2016 that sixty million of the 300 million people enjoying any form of football worldwide were playing futsal. This 20 per cent figure is replicated in Spain, the brochure says, and if it were to be achieved in England, 885,000 adults would be playing futsal. Among the total football-playing population from age five upwards – 11.4 million – that equates to 2.3 million futsal regulars.

The major drawback for the adult game has been the quality of the national league. The first official FA-backed national league was formed in 2008. It was men-only and came two years after a short-lived unofficial attempt, the Futsal Premier League. In 2019, the FA overhauled the national league structure by backing a new National Futsal Series. Some teams from the previous FA-backed league – described to me as a 'poor product' by Graeme Dell – set up a rival National Futsal League. Skubala hopes the new structure will enhance the futsal product but accepts that there was a 'lack of understanding within English culture about futsal'. The association focused on the coaching rather than the facilities, infrastructure and strategy, he says. The game was almost 'decommissioned' at the FA after the inaugural futsal coach conference in 2014, he says, and the game was seen as a much lower priority than women's football. This period of stasis explains my intense frustration for two or three years trying to get regular futsal competitions up and running in Reading.[23]

---

23. The Covid-19 pandemic plunged the Fast Forward with Futsal strategy into jeopardy in 2020, as the FA embarked on a radical cost-cutting agenda in the run-up to the senior national team's Euro 2022 play-off qualifier, away at North Macedonia. The cuts raised fears that the FA was about to 'decommission' futsal again.

'We've struggled to give futsal an identity,' Skubala admits. 'Schools might be doing it, but using five-a-side goals, or bouncing it off walls, which is no different from conventional five-a-side.' Underpinning the strategy for the game is his list of 'five key principles' that define the game: the smaller futsal ball with less bounce, the hockey-size goals, the laws of the game, the hard surface, preferably indoors, and the use of lines not walls to form an 'island' pitch. 'And then we add the futsal-specific coaching on top of that.'

He says part of the aim is to clarify 'what futsal gives you'. Skubala makes a clear pitch for what futsal means in a British context. His quest is aided by Wales – where veteran professional and national team star Rico Zulkarnain set up his own Newport club in 2019 – joining Scotland and Northern Ireland in establishing futsal leagues and national teams ready to compete in 'home nations' tournaments. 'As a sport it can give you the returns to develop footballers, but if you play around with it . . . futsal will be a game that gets lost,' warns Skubala. 'It needs to be done as a sport in its own right to give it the football development value.' The biggest football clubs in England appear to agree.

* * *

A decade after 'the last of the true street footballers', Wayne Rooney, kicked down the door to the first team, Everton were one of the first clubs in England to embrace futsal. Alan Irvine led the way as the club's academy director. 'There was a lot of talk about futsal at the time,' Irvine tells me during a coach mentors' gathering at St George's Park. With the full encouragement of the futsal-savvy new Everton manager, Roberto Martínez, Irvine headed to Barcelona to see for himself. He was blown away. 'At the younger end it was technique, technique, technique. At the older end, it was a really great counter-attacking game. It was rapid.'

The attributes visible on court, from the elite Barcelona futsal first team to the youth players, mirrored the demeanour of the best foreign players at Everton. Irvine says the midfielders Mikel Arteta and Steven Pienaar shone due to their sublime abilities to shield and protect the ball. 'They could keep the ball much better than players tonnes bigger and stronger,' he says. 'That was one of the things we wanted to get out of futsal.' Everton's youngsters loved it as something fast, fun and different. It can also fill a societal void. 'I'm a Glasgow lad,' Irvine explains. 'It dismays me the lack of players coming out of Scotland now. Particularly Glasgow.' Like many observers at the heart of the game, Irvine is clear about the cause. 'It's the death of street football,' he insists. 'It has changed the way players develop, unfortunately.'

All inner cities, including Glasgow and Liverpool, 'would benefit from a strong futsal programme', he says. 'Scotland used to produce dribblers. I'm convinced they developed because of street football. We didn't have the facilities. We played fifteen-a-side on a postage stamp. That's where we learnt to protect the ball, to stay on the ball . . . and here we were all these years later at Everton trying to create an environment for that to happen.' With the FA's Ian Bateman pushing the game in the professional academies, many more clubs then joined the party. The common misconception of futsal as simply 'five-a-side with a funny ball' has been discarded, Bateman told me. Outside the prized 'category 1' academy status, Nottingham Forest FC – twice winners of the European Cup but perennial contenders in England's second tier since 2000 – have led the way by introducing futsal one day a week for academy players from under-9 to under-16. James Barlow, lead futsal coach at the club's academy, says the aim was to complement football training by using futsal to 'allow players to explore a moment of the game, under stress in a smaller area, in a more condensed, decision based, transitional game with high repetition'. The futsal programme has been embraced, with the club's under-18s even playing a game against England under-19s futsal team (futsal beat football 9–4). 'Futsal is an incredible part of their diet while learning the game,' Barlow insists.

It can also be simply more fun, a factor not to be underplayed in the age of callous academy football business models – expertly uncovered by the author Michael Calvin in his searing book *No Hunger in Paradise*. Skubala's ambition is to roll out the 'dual pathway' nationwide, following the approach of other big futsal-playing countries. 'All kids should do both then choose which one to go into,' he says. 'In Spain no one really plays football in schools ... it's futsal. In Brazil, it's 100 per cent futsal in schools then outside, more similar to here, football and futsal throughout the week, then at age thirteen/fourteen you pick futsal or football.' He cites Max Kilman as a perfect example. Within two years, the defender jumped from playing futsal for England – along with non-league football – to the Wolverhampton Wanderers first team. 'People think he's just come from non-league but he has actually twin-tracked [in futsal and football], like the Brazilian model. Everyone talks about him playing for England in futsal but it wasn't just that. He was playing week in, week out in national league for five years. He wasn't just training in futsal for football. He was playing futsal for futsal. There's a big difference. He was serious about it.'

Should Kilman's progress continue, he could become the third former futsal international in the twenty-first century to also wear the national shirt in football. Celtic's Australian number ten Tom Rogic, lauded for his creative intent by his manager Brendan Rodgers, made the leap to the Socceroos after starring for the 'futsalroos', scoring a hat-trick against Kuwait in the 2010 Asian Football Confederation championships in Uzbekistan. Rogic told the *Sydney Morning Herald* that futsal could be 'the missing link' for young Aussies looking to make it in football. Meanwhile in

France, Wissam Ben Yedder, the predatory striker handed his debut for the eleven-a-side national team in 2018, played several times for the French futsal team as a teenager and embodies a bold new emphasis there. More on this later.

Kilman's story also busts the myths about futsal being all about small, technical players. 'Max breaks the mould,' says Skubala. 'He's nearly six foot five, he's a centre-half . . . his case shatters the illusions of what futsal is about.' Just like Stuart Cook, Kilman learned the art of survival as a smaller teenager playing against bigger kids. When I interviewed Kilman for the *Guardian*, he told me he saw 'clear links' between the freedom and creativity of street football he played near his home in north London and the futsal he picked up at the age of fifteen. 'I was just five foot six. I was quite a technical player – I had to be. I learned how to play.' But in the elite adult game it's a different story, insists Kilman. 'A lot of people interpret futsal as all about skill, about dribbling, who can have the best individual player, the most flair. I feel that's completely wrong. At the top of futsal, you don't have time to make dribbles. You get the ball, you turn, you shoot, you react, you defend. You don't have time to start doing step overs, rainbow flicks and all these street skills in the highest level of the game. Unless you're Ricardinho, that is!' The game supercharged his defensive instincts, bravery to receive the ball under pressure and speed of decision-making, he says. It also fuelled his tactical awareness. 'This can be much more important than the technical side of things,' he states firmly.

Kilman's 'twin-tracking' route to the Premier League is becoming a trend. Zak Brunt, one of the teenagers whose bruising experience features heavily in *No Hunger in Paradise*, eventually found solace in futsal while playing academy and non-league football. After starring in the national futsal league and for England under-19s, Brunt signed for Sheffield United and made the first-team squad in 2020 aged eighteen. At Arsenal, the midfield prospect Charlie Patino hailed four years of futsal at Escolla Futsal Club alongside academy training at the Gunners as instrumental in his progress after signing his first professional contract and making the *Guardian*'s list of twenty Premier League talents to watch in 2020.

It's no surprise Kilman wants Skubala and the FA to intensify its commitment to futsal, especially in schools: 'If England ever want to compete with the likes of Brazil, youth futsal is vital. From what I've heard, in Brazil they play futsal until age thirteen or fourteen and they easily transition into football if they want.' Kilman practises what he preaches. When he's not training with the legion of Portuguese stars at Wolves, he's doing his bit for the future of the English game by encouraging his younger brother, Michael, to follow his lead. 'He's only seven but he's good, and enjoying it. He's twin-tracking as well like I did, playing both futsal and football. He's started a bit earlier than me. So he might be even better!'

CHAPTER 11
BRAZIL: THE GOLD MINE

THE FIRST ONE hit at four minutes past eight on a chilly Wednesday evening. By 8.07 p.m., lightning had struck twice, in a chaotic 180-second burst of natural, destructive force. Despite the devastating explosions rocking the Estadio Santiago Bernabéu, no one was hurt. Instead, the powerful strikes illuminating the famous arena triggered unconfined delirium, as a young Brazilian nicknamed '*O Raio*' (the Lightning) shunted Real Madrid two goals to the good before their Turkish opponents, Galatasaray, could take cover. Storm Rodrygo had hit town. About eighty-five minutes later, the outstanding eighteen-year-old notched a third goal to complete a 6–0 rout and became the second-youngest footballer in history to score a hat-trick in the UEFA Champions League. In doing so, he edged out Croxteth's very own Wayne Rooney by thirty-eight days, and nestled proudly behind his legendary fellow Madridista, Raúl, whose quick-fire haul in 1995 (just 114 days after his eighteenth birthday) remains unchallenged. This perfect hat-trick, scored in early November 2019 – left foot, right foot and a header – was widely heralded as the arrival of the latest Brazilian prodigy in world football. It's a list stretching back well over half a century to Pelé and Rivellino, the standout stars of the 1950s generation when the first *futebol de salão* leagues were bringing competitive action to the streets and courts of Brazil. In the twenty-first century, it seems any new Brazilian talent is hailed as 'the new Neymar' – the most prodigious of the modern breed. Before Neymar, the tag was 'the new Pelé/Zico/Ronaldo/Ronaldinho'. And as sure as night follows day, the latest nascent samba starlet's talents on the eleven-a-side stage can be traced right back to the futsal courts of his homeland.

Rodrygo is the newest top-of-the-range model wheeled off the famous Santos production line. Joining the club where some of the greatest football players in the world began, the eleven-year-old prospect immediately impressed, not in the football academy, but on the smaller court in the club's futsal department. By the time he was thirteen he had switched to football, captaining the academy teams up to age of seventeen, playing two years above his age group due to his rare abilities. Real Madrid's €45m bid in 2017 proved too much for Santos to resist.

The 'new Neymar' tag was predictably trotted out again after Rodrygo's historic performance in Madrid. A more nuanced response was to compare his rise with the struggles of the misfiring Eden Hazard – the man whose portrait the youngster once proudly kept as the lock-screen image on his phone while still at Santos. The flickering prodigy was suddenly shining brighter than the *galáctico*, offering a consistent vision of what Los Blancos *thought* they were getting with the prized signature of the Belgian magician. The story goes that Rodrygo was alerted to Hazard's imminent arrival while he was still at Santos on loan after agreeing a deal to join Madrid the following summer. Guillem Balagué, the Spanish football journalist, reported to the BBC that the youngster was told the wide left position would be Hazard's, and that he would need to make do with alternative starting positions. 'So Rodrygo started developing his skills as a false nine, a number ten and on the right, adapting his game so quickly,' Balagué said. The results showed on that November night in 2019. Excelling from a wide right position, Rodrygo flitted across the middle too, before playing the last half hour in the left-side berth vacated by the substituted Hazard. Zinedine Zidane's post-match eulogy hinted further at the youngster's adaptability. 'He plays well in every sense,' said the French World Cup winner and Real Madrid manager. 'We know his qualities in attack well, but he also works hard in defence and helps out with a lot.' Such flexibility and all-round game nous was nothing new to the Madrid regime. The thick scouting dossier on Rodrygo's attributes carried the headline 'mental agility and intelligence'. In and out of possession, the youngster betrays the benefits of a childhood immersed in the relentless breeding ground of the 40 metre by 20 metre court.

The beneficiaries of Madrid's largesse, Santos, are well aware of the need to put futsal front and centre of its youth academy. In the same year Rodrygo's departure was sanctioned, the São Paulo-based club went public on its plans to revolutionise its youth structure by merging the futsal and football pathways. The club's academy manager, Marco Antônio Maturana, believes the merger will put the next 'Menino da Vila oriundo do futsal' ('village boy from futsal') on the path to the big time at Santos FC. 'When we remember Robinho [the former Manchester City forward] and Neymar's childhood, the first thing we remember are these kids scribbling on futsal.'[24] The trio of current first-team footballers who started in the futsal academy – Yuri Alberto, Gabriel Barbosa (Gabigol) and Rodrygo – were cited as evidence of the need to promote futsal. Of course, the first and arguably the biggest star to emerge from the club was *O Rei* himself, Edson Arantes do Nascimento, the skinny fifteen-year-old who became Pelé. Since the 1950s, the production line has rarely failed

24. Santos FC.com.br, 'Departamento de Futebol de Base e de Futsal são oficialmente integrados' by André Mendes, 9 March 2018.

to yield quality. The reputation for a remarkable academy structure churning out players schooled in the art of fast, fluent attacking prowess – a feature of futsal at its finest – was cemented in the early 1960s when a Pelé-inspired team earned plaudits for winning consecutive Copas Libertadores. For the whole of that decade and beyond *Os Santásticos* (Fantastic Santos), as they were christened, embarked on a lucrative globetrotting tour to fund Pelé's growing salary demands.

Since that era, the production of homegrown players has continued, but so too has the constant battle with financial constraints. One of the toughest decisions came in 2012, when club president, Luis Álvaro de Oliveira Ribeiro, closed the women's football team and the one-year-old men's futsal section to bankroll a new contract to keep the club's latest rising star. It was a significant moment. The futsal team had just won its first ever Liga Nacional de Futsal title. The nineteen-year-old prodigy they were so eager to please? It was Neymar Jr, who professed his loyalty to the club before upping sticks for Barcelona twelve months later. In 2015, the women's team returned but the futsal section was stripped back to the youth academy. But it's the emphasis on young stars playing futsal that marks Santos out as a specialist in unearthing gems. The scouting network is key. Roberto Antônio dos Santos, known simply as Betinho, epitomises the vigilance and desire required to find the talent.

Betinho discovered Neymar after first setting eyes on him at a match on Itarare beach in São Vicente. The youngster was not playing. It was his father, Neymar Sr, who was on the beach strutting his stuff. But Betinho was impressed with the gliding athleticism of the skinny six-year-old dancing up and down the stairs beachside. And when he first saw him with a ball at his feet, Betinho was blown away. 'My heart started beating like mad,' he is quoted as saying in Luca Caioli's book, *Neymar: The Unstoppable Rise of Barcelona's*

Brazilian Superstar. 'I saw the footballing genius that he could become. First Robinho, and now another pearl, both in São Vicente. You find footballing talent where kids are most in need. Here there is a gold mine of talent.' Although Betinho has since swapped his role at Santos for a job working for Neymar Jr's own company, the club's commitment to hoovering up the best futsal-formed kids from the São Vicente 'gold mine' and further afield is even greater now the academies are merged.

Neymar's experience, meanwhile, is typically Brazilian. Three things fuelled his love of the game: the small futsal ball, his beneficial location (courts and the freedom to play) and grinding poverty. Back in 2017, shortly before his departure from Barcelona to PSG, Neymar spoke of futsal's formative influence in an interview with *FourFourTwo*. 'It has developed my technique, quick thinking and short moves,' he said. 'Futsal is fundamental to a footballer's life. It had a big importance in mine. When you're out there playing, you're forced to think fast and move even faster – if you lose a second, then the ball will be gone. It's a more dynamic game, and there isn't as much space as in the games that I play for Barça. You need to react quicker on the field.' Real Madrid realise it's not all about Santos when picking up futsal-formed stars. Reinier Jesus, an eighteen-year-old signing from Flamengo in 2020, boasts a famous parent as well as his own short history of the small-sided game. Mauro Brasília, Jesus's father, scored a goal in the FIFUSA world championship final in 1985 as Brazil defeated Spain.

The list of high-end footballers with a futsal upbringing in the South American nation where more people play the game than eleven-a-side seems limitless. Among the talents to have shone in the English Premier League, Philippe Coutinho is most often cited. Footage of the young Carioca gallivanting on court aged twelve is there for all to see on YouTube. In 2020, he told UEFA how he 'based all his football learning' on his futsal schooling at Clube Sargento do Rocha and Mangueira before joining Vasco Da Gama. Lucas Moura is another. The Tottenham Hotspur FC striker attributed his fleet-footed deception to a futsal upbringing after a sublime hat-trick in the dramatic Champions League semi-final defeat of Ajax in 2019. The Brazilian duo propelling Everton FC in 2021 under Carlo Ancelotti both bear the hallmarks of the close-quarters nous mainlined into a futsal-formed youngster's bloodstream. Richarlison thrived on the small courts in Nova Venécia, Espírito Santo. Midfielder Allan learned his breathless, all-action style in futsal too before linking up with Coutinho in Vasco Da Gama's youth section.

When Rodrygo struck for the first time that heady night at the Bernabéu, the source of the assist was hugely significant. The long, raking ball from the left came from the boot of the veteran Brazilian Marcelo. The nominal left-back (it feels risible to define his role as a single position) switched play after a micro-pause in possession involving a futsal calling card – a split-second sole stop and roll – to buy a precious moment before releasing the ball with immaculate timing. The symbolism is stark; it was the passing, not just of a foot-ball from one side of the Bernabéu pitch to the other, but of the long-cherished torch of Brazilian futsal flair from one famed generation to another.

Marcelo's long-stated ambition is to return to his first love, futsal. In an evocative ode to his formative years, he told The Players Tribune website how futsal brought him unbridled joy. 'I have a pro-found memory of the smell, and the feeling of the ball at my feet,' he writes. 'Little Marcelito was out there every day.' For what seemed like an eternity at the peak of Real and Barça's joint domination after 2008 – when Marcelo's compatriot Dani Alves joined him in Spain, signing for the Catalan enemy – the Spanish *El Clásico* carried an intriguing sub-plot. Which wing-back would come out on top: the left-footed Madridista's savvy sole-control, or the right-sided Alves's attacking nous? Both were official futsal-manufactured products, packaged up to shine on the eleven-a-side game's biggest stage.

'*Respeita o véinho*' was the pre-match plea, according to the Brazilian sports site *Globo Esporte*. But Alessandro Rosa Vieira, aka Falcão, or 'the Pelé of futsal', didn't really need to urge the young Rodrygo to treat him with the respect afforded to a vintage wine at an annual exhibition futsal match labelled Dribble Kings. The uniquely stylish left-footed predator known as the Falcon is widely regarded as the best futsal player ever. Rodrygo didn't need telling. In Brazil, futsal stars are huge names in their own right. They don't always switch to football. The only man to ever come close to Falcão's dizzying level, Portugal's Ricardinho, betrays his own view on the matter by carrying a tattoo on his left calf declaring 'The Number One: Falcão 12'.

The statistics bear out the hype too. The Falcon's two strikes against Paraguay in 2018 took his international goals tally to a world-record 401 in 258 appearances for Brazil over a stellar twenty-year period, leaving him nine clear of the prolific Iranian pivot Vahid Shamsaei. The record goalscorer in World Cup history, with forty-eight goals in thirty-three matches over five tournaments, he picked up the mantle of his predecessor Manoel Tobias by winning double awards of Golden Ball (best player) and Golden Boot (highest scorer) in consecutive tournaments, the second coming in his first of two World Cup wins in Brazil 2008. While Tobias's elegant dominance and goalscoring were revered, the Falcon offered more, in both defence and attack. And the man with the golden touch came into his prime just as the rise of Google gave birth to the age of social media, with Facebook, Twitter and Instagram transforming the visibility of a sport so well suited to iconic moments of jaw-dropping ball wizardry. Shortly after retirement in 2018, Falcão's mark on the game and national psyche was acclaimed by none other than Neymar, who took the opportunity in an interview with the media in Brazil before a match against Uruguay to hail the great Falcão's influence on both sports. 'I'd like to say thanks for the beautiful show he put in the courts throughout these years and for being a huge reference to all of us,' said the PSG forward.

Falcão's list of achievements in futsal is endless. As the sport's first truly global figure, his exploits forced futsal-blind sports fans to sit up and marvel at the audacious skill set of the Brazilian number twelve. Domestically, he won an astonishing nine league titles with five different clubs. From 2005, only the two titles won by Sorocaba – where Falcão assumed an ambassadorial role after retirement – stopped him picking up every Liga Nacional de Futsal title over ten seasons; the Falcon's every move seemingly followed inevitably by the accolade. Most notably, he chalked up four titles in six seasons with Santa Catarina-based Jaraguá. The following season, 2011, saw the thirty-three year-old steer his beloved Santos to victory in the brief but glorious futsal flirtation with an LNF franchise terminated by Neymar's wage demands. In 2006, as the standout star in the game, aged twenty-six, Falcão even fulfilled his youth ambition of playing professional eleven-a-side football. After answering the siren call to sign a six-month contract for São Paulo, where he played alongside Brazilian greats such as the goalscoring goalkeeper Rogério Ceni, he managed thirteen appearances without truly settling. The pitch, if not the stage, proved a little too big for his liking. The team went on to win the São Paulo state Campeonato Paulista and the international Copa Libertadores, although Falcão had returned to the comforting confines of futsal by the time the season climaxed.

The São Paulo dalliance was not Falcão's only brush with a giant of world football. In 2015, the two-times champions of Europe under Brian Clough, Nottingham Forest FC, announced the signature of the Brazilian to much intrigue in England. But the thirty-eight year-old Falcon was not about to don his boots in the second tier of English football. The Kuwaiti owner of the club, Fawaz Al

Hasawi, had persuaded him to represent Forest at the annual Al Roudan futsal tournament. Unfortunately, an injury restricted the Brazilian to cheering his new teammates from the sideline in Kuwait, as Chelsea FC's Diego Costa smashed five goals past Forest, in a thrilling reprise of his own youth futsal antics as a boy on the streets of Lagarto.

Perhaps Falcão's most famous performance in yellow and green came in 2012 as his powers were waning – a passing of time illustrated in his role slightly left of centre stage, in Brazil's attempt to win the FIFA World Cup for a fifth time. Nonetheless, despite his game time being limited due to injury he proved he was still the difference between Brazil and the array of fast-improving nations inspired by Spain's tactically astute disruption. The quarter-final opponents, the old enemy Argentina, boasted young stars in their ranks such as Cristian Borruto, who fired Argentina into a 2–0 half-time lead at the Huamark Stadium arena in Bangkok. Brazil's crown was in danger of being yanked off and spirited away by their increasingly noisy neighbour. That was until Falcão stepped off the bench to see if he could turn the tide for Marcos Sorato's men with ten minutes remaining. Turn it he did.

His mere presence on court seemed to unsettle the Argentinian players, a sense of unease flashing across their faces whenever the ball was at the Falcon's feet. The comeback started with an opportunistic strike by Neto, the man who went on succeed Falcão as Golden Boot winner, ensuring that Brazil topped the scoring charts for the sixth consecutive tournament. The equaliser came swiftly, the scorer almost as predictable as the manner in which it was stolen. Falcão's thirty-third minute strike lifted the roof off the arena and sealed an unstoppable shift in momentum. It was also a goal that screamed futsal more than any other, one where an extra pocket of space and time were available only to one man in the world in that split second. After a one-two with Fernandinho, he received the ball about eight metres out, his marker Maximiliano Rescia touch tight and blocking his route to goal while two team-mates hovered. With Falcão's delicate sole cushioning the ball to his left, he didn't quite turn as much as half-shuffle, a poacher cocking his gun rather than fixing the prey in the crosshairs of his sight. As Fernandinho bolted inwards for a return pass, Falcão's body faced the sideline squarely. With nowhere to go but sideways, or back to Vinícius to continue the relentless passing-and-movement routine, seeking out a precious yard of space to shoot. Falcão's extraordinary vision kicked in. He spotted something different – a demi-semi-half chance surely invisible to anyone else in the arena. As his right foot swivelled on the floor with the elegance of a pirouetting ballet dancer, a swift poke of the left-footed toe end – an image so familiar to futsal fans – lifted the ball audaciously back towards goal, arching through a futsal ball-sized gap between the bewildered Rescia's legs, and into the net before keeper Santiago Elías could even move.

The mortals on court had fully expected the next move of Falcão's left foot to be stepping over the ball to gain his balance. For a brief, euphoric moment, he seemed to alter the architecture of human movement skills. It was 2–2. This interruption to the natural order of things ceased as Falcão pounced again to send Brazil through to the semi-finals. A more earthly sole-control and toe-poke in the final rescued Brazil's hopes at 2–1 down to Spain with three minutes left on the clock. In extra time, the Brazilians sealed a fifth World Cup with a Neto goal nineteen seconds from the end. Fittingly, Falcão was on the court at the time – and his role in the celebrations reminded the watching world of his unrivalled talents.

For Marcos 'Marquinhos' Xavier Andrade, the celebrated coach of the Brazil national futsal team, Falcão stands tall as the figure who embodies the trademark Brazilian approach of *inteligência* (intelligence) and *sendo livre* (freedom) that defines futsal. 'Falcão had all the qualities that the futsal game requires,' he tells me in

2019. 'Technique, intelligence, physicality, mentality. We have very good athletes in Brazil now, but some don't have all the requirements like Falcão. It's going to take a while to find a player like him.' Marquinhos's description evokes the renowned Brazilian spirit of *ginga*, a word commonly associated with futsal and football skills and used to describe the balletic, self-preservatory gyrations employed in capoeira, the Brazilian martial art with an African heritage. The spirit of this artistic ritual of expressive intent is one I saw for myself in 2015 on a trip to Rio de Janeiro, where I watched kids and adults play beach football incessantly and, on Copacabana beach, joined in the games of *altihna* (team keepy-uppies) and *futevôlei* (head tennis) myself. I couldn't resist.

Speaking to me after a guest coaching session in London with the strongest team in England, Helvécia, Marquinhos tells me futsal is about using *inteligência* to seek out and exploit two-v-one opportunities all over the court. Futsal is a speed game, he tells me. It's also hugely psychological. It's about *pensamento, tempo, acção*. He's talking about 'thinking, timing and the action'. This transfers directly to football, where the space and time afforded is much greater. In Brazil, futsal is everywhere, he says. 'All over the country. In schools, community clubs, local associations . . . until nine or ten they play only futsal. At this age they are introduced to football and then have a mix for a few years. Then they reach a crossroads, where they choose football or futsal. It's about fifty-fifty. Half choose futsal, half football.' This is why Brazilian futsal is the renowned *treinador* (coach) for the eleven-a-side game, he says. We talk about Falcão, and about the long list of exports to football, from Pelé and Rivellino to Rodrygo. The sport deserves more respect, he insists. 'What all these players, along with sessions like this one today, show is that our relationship with football is that we are providing a service free of charge.' Futsal is far more than simply football's *treinador*. It's seen as very much a separate sport, with football sections conspicuously absent from the big LNF futsal clubs. Marquinhos acknowledges that the traditional culture of playing *futebol de salão* 'everywhere and anywhere' with the *bola pesada* – 'and since the 1990s the bigger futsal ball' – is changing markedly. 'In Brazil we still have several remote, small towns where there is no violence and the kids can still play outside . . . but in the big cities it is more difficult to find space because of the gang violence. About 80 to 90 per cent of pro football players you see now came from the suburbs, the *periferia*, where there is less violence.' So who is emerging to replace the retired Falcão in futsal? 'Leandro Lino is perfect – for his age. He has loads of potential. Today in Brazil he is the best player.'

Since we spoke another young *ala* for the Brazilian champions Magnus Sorocaba, Leozinho, burst on to the scene to win best young player in the world in 2019. 'We have a good squad but not good as a team yet,' warns Marquinhos, who also heaps praise on the Magnus and Brazil captain, Rodrigo, and the Barcelona pivot Ferrão. Rodrigo is a formidable *fixo* with ferocious shooting power who led Magnus to a third consecutive Intercontinental Cup in 2019, adding to his first with fellow Brazilian giants Carlos Barbosa in 2012. Nicknamed *La Pantera* (the Panther), Ferrão hails from Chapeco, in the heart of the state in Brazil known as 'La Tierra Santa del Futsal' (The Holy Land of Futsal): Santa Catarina, where the people are defined by the long history of immigration from Italy and Germany once coal was discovered there in the nineteenth century. Along with his fellow Chapecoense pivot, Pito, who plies his trade at Barcelona's big rivals in Spain, Inter Movistar, he hails from an 'inexhaustible quarry' of futsal stars. In 2019, Marquinhos told Gustavo Muñana, a Spanish journalist and futsal analyst for the SEUR website, how people from the region had an 'inherited innate quality to fight adversities' that shows itself on the futsal court due to the relative dearth of high-profile football clubs in the region.

It's not the only place in Brazil to create superstars of the game. Paulo Roberto, the main attraction in the early years in the Spanish LNFS, is arguably Brazil's greatest ever exported futsal star. Nicknamed '*Maravilla*' (Wonder) while starring for his adopted nation, Spain and ElPozo Murcia, the Rio de Janeiro-born Roberto's left-footed wizardry helped elevate *fútbol sala* to another level in Spain. Yet his arrival there was a fluke, coming after he interrupted a kickabout on a court in Rio to speak to a scout from Marsanz, a club based in Torrejón, near Madrid, who had telephoned to proposition Roberto's good friend, Robson. He seized the chance to sign after a reluctant Robson recommended him instead. *Maravilla* thrived in Spain, where the courts were slightly bigger than in Brazil. 'I had more space to dribble,' he later told *Diario AS*. He reportedly turned down the advances of Atlético Madrid president, Jesús Gil, to switch to the eleven-a-side game, instead leading his adopted national team to a first world championship victory in 2000. It marked the climax of a decade in which he had rivalled another Brazilian – Manoel Tobias, 'the Ronaldo of futsal', who hailed from the north-eastern state of Pernambuco – as best player in the world. The most prolific Brazilian pivot in this era was arguably Lenísio Teixeira Júnior, known simply as Lenísio, who starred in Spain alongside Paulo Roberto at ElPozo Murcia, then at Cartagena. He also won three league titles with Falcão back in Brazil, with the Santa Catarina giants Jaraguá, between 2007 and 2010. Lenísio's younger brother, Vinícius, amassed over one hundred caps for Brazil, and was still playing into his forties. Chapeco's Ferrão hails Lenísio as his inspiration, telling the Pasion Futsal website in 2020 how he watched his idol 'change the game' by becoming 'one of the most complete pivots ever', with all the versatility required by the modern game. Ferrão's bespoke version of this subtle combination of elegance and power was no more evident than in an Intercontinental Futsal Cup clash against China's Shenzhen Nanling Tielang in 2019, when the Barcelona man dispossessed an opponent before scooping the ball over the advancing goalkeeper's head and into the net. Five sublime touches in as many seconds left a quintet of opponents dumbfounded. A clip of the goal on Instagram attracted three million views. At the next World Cup, it could be Santa Catarina state's pivot power that fires Brazil to glory.

THE *ORIUNDI*

The night Mauro Camoranesi first pulled on the famous royal blue number seven shirt, a page turned to reveal a new chapter in the storied history of Italian football: for the first time in forty years, a player born overseas had represented the national team. The twenty-six year-old midfielder's debut against Portugal in February 2003 reopened the contentious debate about whether *oriundi* (the Italian word for an immigrant of native ancestry) should be allowed to represent the country of their forebears. Argentina-born Camoranesi, a skilful winger at Juventus who went on to start for the Azzurri in the victorious 2006 World Cup final, became the first such recruit since the 1960s, when AC Milan's Angelo Sormani was called up due to his Italian ancestry, despite being raised in Brazil. The former Inter Milan, Juventus and Bayern Munich manager Giovanni Trapattoni's bold selection instantly scraped open a long-festering wound.

A little over a week later, the *oriundi* issue also loomed large in the much smaller world of *calcio a 5*, the name for futsal in Italy. While a paroxysm of outrage greeted the Camoranesi moment – why should the mighty three-times World Cup winners 'need' foreign imports? – in futsal the policy of looking outwards for talent had thrust the national team to prominence as the main European challenger to the world champions, Spain. It was a growing obsession, particularly with Brazilians of dual nationality, that would eventually give rise to a pejorative new nickname for the Italians: the 'Brazzurri'. Before the month was out, a São Paulo-born winger for Lazio in the *calcio a 5*

Serie A had fired Italy to a first European title, capping a remarkable transformation since their dismal failure to reach the 2000 world championship. Vinícius Bácaro's goal against Ukraine sealed the victory as the *oriundi*-inspired Italians romped to glory, winning every game in the tournament and conceding only three times. Just as it did with Trapattoni, the team selection threw the spotlight on the coach, Alessandro Nuccorini, as the tentacles of the intensely emotional *oriundi* debate gripped the small-sided game. Yet with the Roman goalkeeper Gianfranco Angelini and captain, Salvatore Zaffiro, keeping the flame alight for homegrown players, the domi-Nation of imports was only partial, a mere shy flirtation with testing the ethical boundaries in pursuit of glory.

A more full-blown embrace of this bold selection policy was to come. The initially muted response to Nuccorini's recruits can perhaps be explained by futsal's much lower profile in the psyche of the Italian press than the national obsession of *calcio*. Moreover, Italy was a land of *calcetto*, or *calcio a cinque*, a traditional five-a-side football similar in identity to the British version. This, rather than futsal, was the dominant small-sided activity among the masses, played on artificial turf with a bouncy football, particularly in and around Rome.

It is in the capital city that the roots of futsal's Italian rise took hold. The sport of tennis also played a prominent role in futsal's growth, quite literally providing fertile ground for *calcio a 5*'s tentative green shoots to flourish and eventually blossom in the environs of Rome. The story goes that Nicola 'Nicky' Pietrangeli, the double French Open champion revered as one of Italy's best tennis players ever, led the way as an early adopter of futsal in the early 1980s by adapting outdoor courts to play it when the tennis was rained off. The Tunisia-born Roman's stroke of sporting improvisation is thought to have helped spread the game throughout the city, with many more tennis courts converted to meet demand for futsal as an alternative to *calcetto*. While the extent of Pietrangeli's role in futsal's rise is difficult to quantify, his legacy lives on. Rome's famous multi-sport Stadio Pietrangeli, named in his honour, hosted the Italian women's futsal team's debut match against Hungary in 2015.

The tennis influence doesn't end there. 'Fulvio Colini is the most famous and successful Italian coach in our history,' says Valerio Scalabrelli, an expert Italian futsal analyst. Colini only took up futsal after turning his back on life as a tennis coach in the mid-1980s. Yet the Italian competes with Spanish futsal visionary José Venancio Lopez Hierro for the title of true pioneer of the mixed-defence tactic honed to perfection over a decade later by the former Serie A star Diego Giustozzi, who led Argentina to the historic World Cup win in 2016.

The Divisione Calcio a 5 – backed by the Italian football federation (the Federazione Italiana Giuoco Calcio) – operates a Serie A for both the men's and women's game, with regional divisions in Serie B and a network of local feeder leagues. Although the men's top division is fully professional, its status is demeaned by the fact that the DC5, as it's known, is a branch of the federation's LND, the national amateur league, which devotes itself to the management of non-professional football in the country. Colini's tactical wizardry formed the backdrop to a 'real revolution in the panorama of Italian futsal' in the early years of the new millennium, explains Scalabrelli. With the Brazzurri upsetting the odds on the international scene, the Brazilians transformed the domestic league, the imported *ginga* spirit and positivity energising futsal at the grassroots. 'We started replacing the term *calcetto* with "futsal",' recalls Scalabrelli. 'We then played it exclusively indoors and the discipline started to be practised more throughout the Italian peninsula.' The first decade of the millennium treated Italian futsal fans to 'three huge novelties', he says: 'The continuous arrival of South American players; the presence of foreign coaches; and the increased competitiveness of non-Roman teams. Torino, led by the Spanish coach Jesús Velasco, was the first side from outside the Lazio region to win the title. He repeated the success in 2002 and 2003 with Prato.' The Brazilian Zego coached at Verona for a spell. Mićo Martić was busy cutting his teeth as a club coach in Italy too after a decade playing at Verona, AC Milan and Bergamo futsal clubs.

The former tennis man Colini's finest moment came at Montesilvano, on the Adriatic coast, where they made history in 2011 by becoming the first and only Italian club to win the annual UEFA Futsal Cup. Captained by Marcio Forte, a stalwart of the Italian national team born next door to the Santa Catarina 'Holy Land of futsal' in Paraná state, the multinational team shocked Lisbon's Sporting in the final after defeating Benfica in the semis. Colini's astute tactical nous later fired Luparense, Pescara and the Pesaro-based Italservice to Serie A titles in the space of six seasons, sealing his status as the most revered and successful club coach in the country. Both Colini and Giustozzi have more than a favoured defensive strategy in common. Their mutual appreciation of the need for tactical flexibility was honed in the place seen as an unrivalled breeding ground for esteemed tacticians since the 1950s, the Italian coaching headquarters of Coverciano. It proved an alluring combination: players schooled by Brazilian futsal culture coupled with revered Italian coaching nous, a *treinador* double-act to rival any in the global game.

* * *

Meanwhile, back on the international stage in the mid-2000s, Nuccorini's progress with the Brazilian-tinged Italian national team continued apace, a runners-up spot in the 2004 world championship in Chinese Taipei confirming their seemingly unstoppable rise. The overseas recruitment intensified. By 2008, FIFA officials had registered outrage, as Nuccorini's strategy of embracing the *oriundi* who dominated Italy's Serie A reached the point where not one member of his squad for the World Cup in Brazil was born in Italy. If they had reached the final, the Brazzurri would have been up against the home nation, Brazil, meaning every player involved – in the Maracãnzinho Gymnasium in Rio de Janeiro – would have been born in the land of *Verde-Amarela*. It would have brought to life Marquinhos's figurative description of Brazilian futsal as the *treinador* of the world game. As it happened the Brazzurri had to settle for third place, clinching victory in the play-off against a Russia team led by Pula, a São-Paulo-born pivot who had switched nationality, proving that the Brazilian export industry was also alive and well further east in 2008.

The *oriundi* debate has a long history in Italy, dating back to the days of monarchy under the ruling Casa Savoia (House of Savoy), whose royal blue colours the national football team adopted rather than the red, white and green of the national flag. The subsequent Azzurri (the Blues) nickname was coined in the middle of the first major Italian diaspora, a four-decade long exodus starting in the 1880s, when about fifteen million Italians departed. Many settled in South America, adding to the numbers of football players in places such as Montevideo, Uruguay – and ultimately inspiring Professor Ceriani to go indoors and create the first version of futsal. The second big wave of emigration, after the Second World War – involving another estimated fifteen million emigrants – can be seen as forming the quasi-European feel of regions in South America such as Santa Catarina. In 2010, Italy boasted an estimated seventy million *oriundi* worldwide. The first recognisable Italian football *oriundo* arrived in 1920 – a decade before Ceriani gave futsal to the world – when the Swiss-Italian midfielder Ermanno Aebi took to the field in a friendly against France, scoring a hat-trick in a 9–4 victory. On the back of the fascist dictator Benito Mussolini's passionate desire to promote the Azzurri's footballing success as a powerful symbol of potent nationalism and identity, returning foreigners

– known as the *rimpatriati* (repatriated people) when coming from the United States – were fully embraced in Italy's national team. When the Azzurri lifted the Jules Rimet trophy for the first time on home soil in 1934, this ruthless approach to 'recruitment' was vindicated. Five of the squad inspired by Il Duce's open-door policy were *oriundi*. The selection process for the national team was mirrored by the Serie A football clubs. The most striking post-Second World War example is José João Altafini, who represented Italy in the 1962 World Cup after moving to AC Milan from Palmeiras, having helped Brazil to victory in Sweden 1958 as the second youngest squad member after Pelé. Overseas recruitment continued until the mid-1960s, when Serie A banned foreign signings in an attempt to arrest the national team's decline. The ban was relaxed in 1980, allowing Serie A teams one foreigner each. This was increased to two before European Union rules took precedence to allow overseas players, *oriundi* included, to flood into football's Serie A during its peak years of the 1980s and 1990s. By 2020, dozens of players born overseas had pulled on the Azzurri football shirt, between them collecting more than 300 caps and seven World Cup-winning medals.

It's not just football and futsal where controversy rumbles over the *oriundi*. In rugby, about thirty players have been capped for the men's team, 50 per cent of them Argentinian. In basketball, of the sixty-plus caps given out to players with dual nationality or as a result of the naturalisation process, nearly 90 per cent of their recipients hail from the United States or Argentina. The mix in football is global, with a focus on South American recruits. But in futsal, the green-and-yellow samba flair is the overwhelming choice. In 2021, the number of *oriundi* with a cap for the Italian men's futsal team was approaching one hundred – all bar two, both Argentinians, hailing from Brazil. After the years of excess, the Brazzurri flag was still flying, not quite at full height, but fluttering midway down the pole, thanks to the breezy presence of the inspirational captain,

Gabriel Lima, and star winger (and England's tormentor in chief) Merlim, both born in the land of *ginga* spirit. Roberto Menichelli, the coach who took over from Nuccorini in 2009, steered the tiller slightly back towards home. The second European title in 2014 was secured with six home-grown Italians in the squad, the rest all naturalised Brazilians. In the final, Lima and Merlim were joined by Saad Assis and Daniel Giasson in the starting five, the sole non-Brazilian being the influential goalkeeper Stefano Mammarella.

For Brazil, the trading of its high-value goods overseas is nothing new. It's a history that runs from the blood-stained riches of its sugar industry, built on the backs of millions of enslaved Africans in colonial-era Brazil, to the vibrant coffee trade it dominated at the start of the twentieth century and on to the mass export of soybeans and iron ore one hundred years later. The lucrative twenty-first century trade in polished ball-playing gems discovered in Neymar's São Vicente and numerous other 'gold mines' adds yet another commodity to the list. In the eleven-a-side game in 2017, Brazil's status as prime exporter was confirmed by researchers at the International Centre for Sports Studies (CIES) Football Observatory. A total of 1,202 Brazilians were playing professional football overseas, the biggest proportion of the total number of expatriate players plying their trade in the 137 leagues in ninety-three countries analysed. The biggest single destination was Portugal. In futsal the figures are more difficult to pin down, but it's easy to identify Russia and Kazakhstan as conspicuous importers of Brazilian game nous to help fast-track their national teams to glory in the modern game. Their Group C clash in the 2016 Euros in Serbia, with the Rio de Janeiro-born Leo Higuita to the fore, showcased up to six of the ten players on court at any time who were originally from Brazil. Later that evening in the same venue, Italy lined up in the opening Group D game with three Brazilians – Merlim, Lima and Fortino – in their starting five. At the opposite end of the Belgrade Arena court stood four more naturalised Brazilians: Eduardo, Augusto, Amadeu and Rafael. Their opponents, Azerbaijan, were the latest team to look towards Brazil for a quick fix. It wasn't long before they were nicknamed the Brazeri, a riff on the Azeri team's selection tactics following the Brazzurri's.

In 2018, while Italy still led the way with six Brazilians in their squad, the Brazeri contained five. Along with Higuita and co. in Kazakh colours, plus six more shared by Russia and Romania, the Brazilian influence was still huge throughout Europe. Only Portugal among the big hitters stood alone as the nation never to have given a cap to a native of the land that shares their language. Just like in Italy, the Brazeri strategy, inspired by the Brazilian coach Miltinho, yielded instant success. In 2016, shortly after he took over from the Spaniard Tino Perés, who also coached the serial Azeri Premier League champions Araz Naxçıvan, Miltinho led the team to the quarter-finals at their first ever World Cup in Colombia. The fourteen-man squad was 50 per cent Brazilian. The newly naturalised Brazilian pivot Thiago Bolinha was eclipsed in the goalscoring stakes only by the majestic Ricardinho, Eder Lima (another naturalised Brazilian playing for Russia) – and the greatest Brazilian of them all, Falcão.

CHAPTER 12
GOAL-ATTACKER: THE HIGUITA WAY

THE FIRST STRIKE stings the huge palms of the Brazil-born Russian goalkeeper Gustavo as the match suddenly bursts into life, with Kazakhstan trailing 2–0 after two goals in a minute by their big rivals and former Soviet overseers. Kazakhstan's Brazilian coach, Cacau, has just used a timeout to unleash the formidable figure of Higuita, another boy from Brazil. Higuita's brutal right-footed effort, a thunderbolt from one naturalised Brazilian goalkeeper to another, precedes a fierce attack that leaves all ten players hunkered down in the Russian half in the Belgrade Arena at the 2016 UEFA Futsal Championship. Higuita is in control, commanding the court. He receives the ball again centrally, this time a couple of metres further into opposition territory. As three Russian shirts converge, two sliding in for emergency blocks, Higuita feigns to shoot, but flicks the ball wide to Douglas, yet another naturalised Brazilian wearing the Kazakh silvery-grey. As the defensive pack regroups, Higuita collects the ball again. He's in the opposition half, so the four-seconds limit on possession no longer applies. Locking the ball beneath his sole, he looks up, scans the scene and pauses. The Russians freeze. Will he shoot? Or is he faking it? He does neither. It's a third way: a classic 'shot to miss', the ball arrowing powerfully towards the left upright, safely screened from Gustavo's grasping reach, where the lurking pivot Zhamankulov shunts it home with his midriff. Three moments: the shot, the feint and pass, and the shot to miss – together making up an alluring triptych illustrating the talent of the most supreme example of the flying futsal goalkeeper the sport has ever known.

Leo Higuita was born Leonardo de Melo Vieira Leite in Rio de Janeiro in 1986, to a family of Flamengo fanatics. Before long young Leo was driving his parents to distraction by smashing his first football – a precious fifth-birthday gift – up against the wall for hours on end in the yard of their tiny family home. It was there in São Paulo, where they lived for a couple of years due to his dad's work, that he fell in love with a ball. They returned to Rio de Janeiro when he was six, and young Leo's hyperactive style and passion in goal soon earned him the moniker 'Higuita' in honour of René Higuita, the famously acrobatic and eccentric Colombian eleven-a-side goalkeeper of scorpion-kick fame.

But the futsal Higuita was not simply a carbon copy. Revered in Kazakhstan, his insistence on wearing the number two shirt is a numerical statement of a fiercely renegade spirit. Although his Colombian namesake proved influential, the Brazil-born three-times best goalkeeper in the world cites another figure as the inspiration for life between the sticks. 'Zetti is the guilty one for me becoming a goalkeeper,' Higuita tells me. Zetti, or Armelino Donizetti Quagliato to give him his full name, excelled for São Paulo FC in the early 1990s, in between stints at city rivals Palmeiras and then later at nearby Santos. Zetti's handling skills shone in volleyball, basketball and, of course, futsal before turning to football aged fifteen – eventually establishing himself as the understudy to the legendary Taffarel in the Brazilian national team at the 1994 USA World Cup. Between them, Zetti and Taffarel helped Brazilian goalkeepers finally cast aside the cloak of ridicule worn most ostentatiously by Felix, the errant jester of Pelé's otherwise extraordinary 1970 World Cup-winning team.

In the opening group game of the 2016 futsal Euros in Belgrade against Russia, Higuita was one of six naturalised Brazilians on court, with Cacau pulling the strings from the sideline. The twenty-nine year-old goalkeeping icon displayed his usual array of creative guile in possession, flicking scooped passes up and over the head of any Russian player who dared to press. As ever Higuita, the master of versatility who changed nationality after moving from Belenenses in Lisbon to his Almaty-based club side, AFC Kairat, held all the answers. The only thing missing was his customary goal. Kazakhstan's debut game in the Euros ended in a 2–1 defeat, but it didn't stop the new boys and their peculiarly dominant style leaving an indelible impression. Recovering to reach the semi-final, the Kazakhs lost to eventual winners Spain before beating the hosts, Serbia, to clinch third place. It was in this game, in front of 11,000 joyous fans, that Higuita opened his account by firing home a forty-metre volley straight into the gaping Serbia goal after saving a shot from Slobodan Rajčević. On top of a direct assist and two hockey assists (assisting the assister), he proved himself as the top number two in world futsal, having a hand in four of the five goals in a 5–2 victory. His goal was one of the eight he tells me in 2019 he has scored for his adopted country, on top of twelve more in elite UEFA Futsal Cup competitions and many more domestically in Kazakhstan.

Higuita is a giant of the modern game. The famous goal-line crouch, bent forward on all fours, gloveless hands (common in modern futsal) touching the floor, neck craning to track the ball, often precedes an act of brazen agility to repel a shot, all the time protected by the volleyball-style pads adorning his knees and elbows. But it's with the ball that he has altered the DNA of futsal at the highest level. When the goalkeeper turns *arquero líbero* (sweeper keeper) in futsal, they transform the mood on court. The opposition invariably retreat to a deep, zonal defence in fear of the sudden five-v-four overload – the goalkeeper's presence adding 20 per cent extra to the team's attacking punch.

Originally used only by teams chasing the game, the fly-keeper, or 'powerplay', carries the risk of leaving an unguarded goal, and is a source of huge controversy in the game. Traditionally, teams replaced the goalkeeper with a substitute attacker (wearing a distinctive shirt) to initiate the 'powerplay'. But when the keeper can actually play, as Higuita can, it opens up another world of opportunity. Some purists say its overuse kills the speed and free-flowing attacking feel of the game, as teams secure dominance of possession throughout the match. 'The five-v-four game bothers many clubs and teams,' Higuita acknowledges with a knowing chuckle, before turning serious. This nonconformist serial winner remains unrepentant about how he has redefined the role of the keeper: by being '50 per cent crazy'. That fifty-fifty split is important: the other half is audacious genius. 'This is really a revolution in futsal,' he insists. 'We didn't create it, but we put it into practice without fear and successfully. We know the huge risk and yet we take it. Cacau trusted me as his own "flying goalkeeper" to make a difference and put the name of Kazakhstan and Kairat among the best in the world.'

This incursion started when Kairat bustled into the elite European scene with a surprise victory in the 2013 UEFA Futsal Cup, the forerunner of the Champions League. To prove it was no fluke, they sealed the prestigious Intercontinental Cup the following year, and recaptured the UEFA crown in 2015. The Kairat coach, Cacau, took over national team duties too and employed the same pioneering fly-keeper tactics that had worked so well against teams such as the Spanish giants Barcelona and Inter Movistar. Whereas the Colombian Higuita was nicknamed 'El Loco' for his often extraneous madcap antics, his Brazilian namesake's modus operandi is ruthlessly efficient:

a rebel, yes, but not a selfish dissenter. His successes on court mark him out as the ultimate team player, intent on securing victory by whatever means necessary. Speaking through his translator, the goal-keeping coach at AFC Kairat, Luizinho Cruz, Higuita points out that other clubs are 'hiring goalkeepers who have the same style as mine and this has now been accepted'. Along with two other Brazil-born star keepers, the outstanding Lisbon-based duo of Guitta at Sporting and Roncaglio at Benfica, Higuita's way is seen as increasingly unas-sailable. So how did the Flamengo FC fanatic from Rio de Janeiro choose futsal over football, then build a new life 9,000 miles away at the intersection of two alien continents – Asia and Europe – before busily transforming the very structures of his chosen sport?

His first experience of 'butterflies in my stomach' brought on by being in goal was unforgettable. 'Social Ramos Clube was where my dad used to play futsal with his friends from work every Tuesday,' he recalls. 'And I kept running and playing around the club while he played. They used to have futsal "grassroots" categories. One day, some eleven- or twelve-year-old kids invited me – I was just six years old – to play futsal with them as a goalie. I loved to play as a goalie, jumping a lot just like Zetti! That day I did a lot of brave saves. I was half nutty, 50 per cent crazy.' Social Ramos Clube was where the great Ronaldo 'O Fenômeno' started out some four years earlier, at the age of twelve. Higuita shares a futsal background with another Brazilian superstar to light up Estadio Santiago Bernabéu. 'I played futsal with Marcelo in Fluminense FC,' he tells me. 'I was fifteen and he was fourteen. He was completely above other kids with his skills. He dribbled like Falcão used to do, with perfect technique.' The pair keep in regular contact, watching each other's progress in their respective sport's UEFA Champions League jousts. Higuita is narrating his back story just a few weeks after signing a lucrative new contract to keep him at AFC Kairat until 2024, a deal that saw him labelled futsal's first 'million dollar man' because of the release clause inserted in the

contract – tying down a giant of the game who is far more than a mere goalkeeper.[25] The Dutch futsal coaching guru and former player Vic Hermans, in his book *Futsal: Technique, Tactics, Training*, labels the role the 'goalplayer'. Just as the number ten, or *enganche*, is synonymous with Brazil, so clearly is the goalplayer, or, more pertinently perhaps, the 'goal-attacker'. The Higuita way, the style formed by his bold and flexible '50 per cent nutty' approach, marks a growing trend – in futsal and football – that shows precious few signs of stopping.

* * *

'Pepe Reina was the first,' says Andy Reading, the England futsal goalkeeper coach and proud holder of the record as the first English futsal professional.[26] 'It was like this . . .'. Reading drops to the floor and forms a K-shaped human wall, staring up earnestly through his dark-rimmed spectacles. 'It's the block shape in preparation for a shot,' he explains patiently while demonstrating the techniques now common currency in the rarefied world of Premier League football. Reina's impact at Liverpool was profound, recalls Reading. 'He was the first real exponent of it.' It's a vision of shot-blocking excellence formed on the futsal courts. The Madrid-born Reina's style, the sweeper-keeper with immaculate distribution – and a tendency to save shots with his feet – marked him out as distinct from the man seen as the first truly great *arquero libero*, Bayern Munich's Manuel Neuer.

Germany's goalkeeping supremo grew up under the influence of the nation's second biggest sport, handball, playing it as a boy and

25. Big transfer fees are rare in futsal. Only the biggest clubs can afford to offer contracts of more than a year – leaving many players free to move at the end of a season – or meet a contract release clause bigger than €100,000 to sign a player mid-contract.
26. In 2004 Reading departed Tranmere Victoria Futsal Club, along with a teammate Jay Corran, for Transylvania, signing for ACS Odorheiu Secuiesc, champions of the newly founded Romanian Liga I.

telling Munich-based tabloid paper *Tz* in 2011 how he 'tries to imitate handball goalkeepers' by using his feet in one-v-one confrontations in football. Reina was different. The Spaniard's strikingly similar techniques were almost certainly learned as a boy playing the younger sport of *fútbol sala*, which of course drew on the seven-a-side game for its goalkeeping DNA back in the formative days of Juan Carlos Ceriani in the 1930s, and again in the 1980s, as Spain and FIFA refashioned the look of the sport. The art of futsal goalkeeping is even more visible in the style of his successor as resident Spanish supremo in the Premier League, Manchester United's David de Gea. The Old Trafford shot-stopper built up a catalogue of exemplary saves over the best part of a decade, defying the best strikers in the world in a manner often deemed unorthodox.

Reading obliges when I ask for more detail on De Gea's go-to moves. 'OK, really simplistically . . . if it's a hard shot around the feet you'd use a forward kick-through . . . If it's another hard, low shot – but low and to the side of the keeper – then you'd be thinking about a lateral split save.'[27] This is classic David de Gea. 'If the ball is fired in further away again, you'd probably think about saving with the hands. But in the middle of all this, you're thinking as a keeper, if you pick up the line and power of the shot early enough you can drop into a K save or block save. That's where one knee goes down to give added protection centrally.' That's the block, split and kick-through saves all boxed off. Reading presses on. 'The block, or K save, is also very useful in one-v-one situations. Classically, eleven-a-side keepers in one-v-one will hit the deck and, dare I say it, expose a lot of goal. But in futsal, if you do that you're exposing too much, and up against a clever and nimble player they'll take advantage. So the K or the block increase your percentages of coverage of the goal.'

---

27. A split save is an action akin to doing the splits where one leg collapses to the floor, knee bent, and the other leg stretches out wide to deflect away a shot.

All of which pretty much sums up the apparently left-field brilliance of De Gea, whose teenage talent attracted the attention of the Spanish futsal World Cup-winning goalkeeper Luis Amado. Nicknamed *A Parede* (the Wall) by his Brazilian rivals at his peak for Spain and Inter Movistar, Amado used a joint appearance on the sports station Radio Marca in 2010 to give the nineteen-year-old Atlético Madrid prodigy a pep talk and reflect on how similar the youngster's style was to his own. De Gea played *fútbol sala* in Madrid from the age of seven at La Escuela De Fútbol Atlético Casarrubuelos, although he was much better known for his prowess at the other end of the court as a goalscoring pivot. With one particularly outrageous shot-stopping performance at Tottenham Hotspur in the early days of Ole Gunnar Solskjaer's tenure at Old Trafford, De Gea left many footballing pundits bemused. In an echo of the footballing mainstream's confused response to Ronaldinho's Stamford Bridge toe-poke, admiration for the Spaniard's agility was tinged with a suspicion that it was all just freakish luck and renegade opportunism. For Tony Elliott, the ex-professional football goalkeeper and lead goalkeeping coach for England futsal, there's no debate. 'De Gea isn't getting coached in futsal now, but he's remembering the type of actions that he learned in his youth,' Elliott told Sky Sports in a save-by-save analysis of the United stopper's technique. It's simply evolution, he says. 'The game changes and the decision-making process of the goalkeeper is quicker than ever now because of the speed of the modern game. Ultimately, what that has created is a different type of goalkeeper.'

De Gea is not alone in applying a futsal filter to goalkeeping in the Premier League. The distinctively more vivid and dynamic Brazilian image of the futsal goalkeeper stands out in the combined form of Leo Higuita's compatriots. Alisson Becker's supreme ability with his feet is starkly Higuita-esque (without the goals, of course). His exquisite supporting role behind Virgil van Dijk and Liverpool's Champions League-winning defence earned Alisson the honour of

FIFA's best goalkeeper in the world in 2018–19. Thirty miles along the M62 from Liverpool at the Etihad Stadium in Manchester, Alisson's rival for the Brazil goalkeeper's jersey Ederson was a couple of years into the starring role as Pep Guardiola's number one in the fresh adaptation of the Catalan's long-running show titled *juego de posición* (positional play). The Manchester City keeper's lineage throws up another striking similarity with Higuita. Born near São Paulo, Ederson started out in futsal – 'that helped me a lot,' he told the *Daily Telegraph* – and played football as an outfield player. 'I used to play as a *goleiro-linha* [fifth man], it's a goalkeeper that plays a lot with his feet. So, we used to attack with five players and defend with five. From that period, I had my shooting skills and good footwork.' As a boy, Ederson idolised Rogério Ceni, the prolific Brazilian goalscoring number one whose exploits at the opposite end of the pitch eclipse even the prolific Higuita. The record goalscoring keeper in football history, Ceni registered 131 strikes during a twenty-five year tenure at São Paulo starting at the age of seventeen. He became a regular in 1997 by ousting the incumbent, Zetti, the man who inspired Higuita's own *goleiro-linha* tendencies. Of the 131 goals, sixty-one were free kicks, one was from open play and the rest were penalties. It's not just with his feet that Ederson excels. Andy Reading informs me that the Brazilian style of goalkeeping diverges from the Spanish positional-play template in one big way: the readiness to repel invaders by bolting from goal to snuff out danger. 'In a one-v-one situation,' explains Reading, 'if the goalkeeper picks up the flight of the ball, they will race out in a double-knee slide to go one-v-one with the attacker. That's very Brazilian.' Ederson does it. Alisson too. But neither uses the knee-slide wipeout as often or as conspicuously as futsal's biggest exponents of the art: Higuita and his Lisbon-based Brazilian compatriots, Sporting's Guitta and Benfica's Roncaglio.

The wider world of football has noted the changing face of goalkeeping at elite level too. Recognising the greater contribution to the

build-up play, either by passing in and around pressing attackers or by launching lightning-quick counter-attacks, the Technical Study Group report on the 2018 World Cup in Russia also flagged up a new phenomenon: 'the X-block', an alternative name for the K or wall block directly imported from futsal. 'On countless occasions, goalkeepers came out on top of one-on-one situations inside the penalty box through good positioning, timing and use of the "X-block" technique,' the report concluded. The former Netherlands striker Marco van Basten, one of the analysts, pointed out the disadvantage for goalkeepers of deep defensive blocks making attacking situations 'so crowded that they cannot see the ball'. For goalkeepers, the deep defensive block has almost turned football into a futsal match, with the ball constantly popped about within twenty metres of the goal.

Higuita sees this. The increasing intensity in football makes it 'very similar to futsal, with a lot of dynamism, speed and short-distance reactions', he says. The rise of the block save symbolises a bigger convergence of the roles, where he finds similarities in '80 per cent of the game actions of a keeper'. As would be expected with the finest ball-playing goalkeeper in the history of futsal, Higuita is keen to point out the links in attack too. 'Goalkeepers need to play more with their feet within the goal area in football,' he says, noting the change to the goal-kick laws introduced in 2019. It's a development recognised by another English Premier League keeper. Shortly after securing a £20m move from Arsenal in 2020, the Aston Villa number one Emiliano Martínez revealed the source of his ability on the ball. 'I played futsal for many years back in Argentina,' he told Sky Sports. 'So I'm comfortable with my feet.' Whether it's an instant shot-stopping block or a fundamental presence in build-up play, the futsal goal-player's repertoire of abilities with their feet have grown increasingly relevant to the eleven-a-side game – where the traditional final defensive barrier is now seen more frequently as the first line of attack. The feet are fast becoming as important as the hands.

CHAPTER 13
PORTUGAL: THE REBEL GAME

THE TEENAGER STANDS awkwardly on one leg. Proudly wearing his England training kit, he listens eagerly, one of his bright yellow Joma futsal shoes planted firmly on the hall floor. The other, his right, hovers in the air, protruding slightly away from his left knee. Another boy stands a metre away, poised with the ball, ready to attack. 'OK . . . if the opponent is defending like this,' says Jorge Braz, coach of the Portugal national futsal team, touching the delicately balanced defender, 'which way will you go?' Braz is conducting a masterclass at the futsal coaching conference in St George's Park, home of the English game. The FA's diligence in attracting such a big name yielded an unexpected bonus: just a week earlier the 'achievements' section on the coach's CV gained a new entry reading 'UEFA European futsal champion 2018'. The mastermind of Portugal's historic first futsal title is showcasing his methodology to sprinkle some stardust on the day. He doesn't disappoint. The question posed to the imbalanced England under-19 player on court catches the assembled coaches off guard too. Braz makes a big point about the fine margins of evading a touch-tight pursuer – in this case, by observing where their body weight is tipped. It's a striking demonstration of the meticulous approach that separates the good from the great at the highest level.

The quietly spoken Braz is a bundle of contradictions. With a puppyish face, the elegantly bald forty-five year-old exudes an impassive yet energetic calmness, a studious professor with a scrupulously open mind. Confident, yet eager to learn. Born in Canada, he speaks perfect English while oozing Iberian sophistication, having worked for the Federação Portuguesa de Fútebol (FPF) since 2006. Braz is finally emerging from the shadow of his mentor, the esteemed Portugal coach Orlando Duarte, the visitor who shocked England's Graeme Dell back in 2004 with a surprise invitation to watch his *seleção* train. It was Duarte's appointment as head coach of the national team in 2000 that led to Portugal gatecrashing the party of the international jet set a few months later, just thirteen years after the national team's first game – a 4–0 defeat to Spain. Duarte inspired the team to a shock third-place finish at the 2000 FIFA world championship. It took another decade – helped perhaps by Duarte's decision to blood a young Ricardinho in the national set-up in 2003 – for Portugal to make a breakthrough in a tournament, finishing runners-up to Spain (who else) at the 2010 European championship in Hungary. Futsal – and particularly the 4-0 formation Braz prides himself on using – is a game of space and advantage, he says. 'When we see in the game, really obvious situations one-v-one, they are often not taken,' he says. This is one of his golden rules. 'I don't say you have to go against the opponent one on one. I say you gotta try. We have a saying in Portugal. You say to the opponent: "You're gonna fly!" That's Ricardo Quaresma, the footballer. Each time he receives the ball, he looks at them and says: "You're gonna fly . . ." And this guy then takes two steps back.' Braz explains how this allows his team to create space to attack. The readiness to go one-on-one is essential.

Quaresma is the maverick of Portuguese football, the man nicknamed *Puto Lelito* (Gypsy kid) by his former Sporting teammate, Cristiano Ronaldo, in honour of his compatriot's Roma heritage. He

became known more widely in Portugal as *O Cigano* (the Gypsy), cementing his status as a footballing outsider, a renegade superstar calling out the wrongs in an arena that can all too often be defined by crushing cultural oppression. Quaresma makes things happen on the pitch: a notoriously one-footed ball-hogger with a penchant for the *rabona* – the scissor action that allows the ball to be chopped, chipped or punted with the farther foot, wrapping around the standing leg – and the beautifully precise, curling, swerving outside-of-the-foot pass or shot known as the *trivela*. Quaresma, who replaced his injured friend, Ronaldo, in the twenty-fifth minute of the Euro 2016 football final, delivered a *trivela* in stunning fashion in the crucial final group B game in the 2018 World Cup against Iran. 'When I find myself in a situation with three choices,' Quaresma explains, 'I will always choose a dribble or a trick over a square ball or a twenty-metre pass back. Life is all about risk.'[28]

That same sense of high-stakes experimentation was transferred between futsal and football, to devastating effect, by Cristiano Ronaldo. A dazzling risk-taker at Sporting in Lisbon and Manchester United before evolving into Real Madrid's relentless goalscoring machine, Madeira's most famous son is unequivocal about futsal's benefits. It was his childhood game. 'The small playing area helped me improve my close control, and whenever I played futsal I felt free,' says Ronaldo. 'If it wasn't for futsal, I wouldn't be the player I am today.'[29]

As the St George's Park session gathers pace, Braz moves the players into a mass game of one-v-one (every pair with a ball, with a keeper in either goal). A riot of noise ensues, the squeaking of futsal shoes on the immaculate blue court surface filling the cavernous hall with teenage energy. 'It's just like on the streets,' shouts Braz. 'Go

---

28. UEFA.com, 'Quaresma charisma lifts Porto' by Graham Hunter, 8 December 2006.
29. FIFA.com, 'The football greats forged by futsal', 30 October 2012.

play, dribble, take the advantage, score. It's your game . . .' It's a clear attempt to summon up the maverick spirit of Ricardinho, Ronaldo and the Gypsy kid. For the England youngsters on court – all born since the start of the millennium – their formative ball-playing diet will be denuded of the vital sustenance of street football. Their eagerness is heartening. Futsal is filling the street void yet again.

After the session, Braz restates this commitment to positive play. It was 'very fashionable' for a few years in Portugal 'to pass, receive, pass, receive and pass', he says. 'But if I receive and the defender is ten metres away. Why pass? Pass for what? The main goal in possession is to create space and take advantage.' He moves seamlessly on to explain how his Portugal team seized the advantage to win the futsal Euros seven days earlier. 'This was the happiest moment of my life but not just for me, that's not my way,' he says. 'It's a really happy moment for the futsal family of Portugal . . . This was our moment.' The big story is the freaky coincidence between the final showdown and its football equivalent eighteen months earlier, when Ronaldo memorably roared his teammates to victory against France after injuring his knee in the match. The team made history while the talismanic goal machine hobbled on the sidelines. Braz's *seleção* also secured a first ever European title without their cornerstone. The masterful Ricardinho succumbed to an ankle injury and was forced off too, agony etched on his face, just as it had been for CR7 at the Stade de France in July 2016.

'I was very confident because of the way the team was prepared,' recalls Braz. 'Spain are a great team. Russia [Portugal's semi-final opponents] are a great team . . . but for our side, we always believed. All the staff. And we did it. We believed it would fall our way . . . Afterwards, people said, "It was the same as Ronaldo . . ." this is interesting, all the astrals lined up for this to happen but we worked very hard to be prepared.' Portugal's first Euro futsal title caps a

remarkable hat-trick – after the football Euros in 2016 and the FIFA beach soccer World Cup victory in 2015 – and is credit to the overhaul of youth participation in futsal and a decision taken to prioritise home-grown players rather than naturalised Brazilians. 'We were already a traditional futsal country,' says Braz. 'It is only thirty years though. That is nothing.' Braz says the current rise of the game in Portugal dates back to 2011, when the president of the Portuguese FA, Fernando Gomes, vowed to make futsal 'the most popular sport in school sports halls' and a game of huge 'social relevance'. The 2018 Euros victory 'is the clearest sign that we're doing it well', he says. At the grassroots, the federation's work paid off handsomely. With just 11,000 players affiliated nationwide in the late 1990s, the Gomes edict transformed participation. By 2013 the figure was 28,000. In 2019, 35,000 adults and children were registered as playing futsal. As with all countries, thousands more will be playing unaffiliated. A spokesman for the federation told me in 2019 that more than 700 schools now boasted a futsal programme for pupils. The pursuit of greater 'social relevance' for the game is aided by the prominence of professional futsal in Portugal, where seven of the fourteen clubs in the top-flight Primeira Liga have full-time men's teams.

This is crucial, says Braz. The Portugal model of pro football clubs running a futsal team – as well as teams in other sports – would be great to see in England, he says. 'With some football clubs – Benfica and Sporting are the main examples – their budgets are so high that football can help the other sports.' Braz implores me to visit Portugal to see for myself. I make a note of the invitation. Only time will tell whether England seizes the advantage futsal can offer a nation. But for Portugal, under Braz's careful stewardship, one thing is certain: futsal is on the attack, moving forward, telling the rest of the futsal world: 'You're gonna fly . . .'

* * *

'*Boa tarde*, mister,' the youngster chirps, smiling as he thrusts out his small right hand. Nuno Ramos beams back, stands up, shakes the boy's hand and enquires about his health and wellbeing. The boy nods happily. 'But why are you wearing this?' snaps Ramos, pointing at the boy's green shirt. 'We are Benfica, not Sporting . . . why green?!' The boy's half-frown quickly gives way to a winning smile when Ramos laughs. The youngster walks off, relieved, happy, excitable, and skips through the double doors into the futsal hall to prepare to play.

Ramos tells me he's got a few minutes until he needs to prepare for his session. The mutual respect between a nine-year-old boy and an adult coach seems symbolic. This is what a coach-child relationship should look like. And it's also one, I discover over the subsequent three hours, that is etched into the fabric of Sport e Lisboa Benfica, the sporting institution known as Benfica. As well as being the biggest football club in the country, *As Águias* (The Eagles) boast successful handball, basketball, volleyball and roller hockey sections along with its professional men's futsal team. Along with its big rival Sporting, Benfica dominate Portugal's sporting world. Futsal and football are hardwired into their DNA.

It's great to finally see what all the futsal fuss is about in Portugal, here in the heart of one of Benfica's satellite camps, a university facility in Lisbon hired out for academy training. I'm here with two futsal teammates from Reading, Ricardo Medeiros (on translation duties back in his home city) and Chris Ryman, who is here to soak it all up. Within minutes the action on court kills off any lingering suspicion I might harbour that futsal is not a specialist sport. The fun and ABCs (agility, balance and co-ordination skills) in the *jogo lùdico* (playful game) were multipurpose PE exercises. But the subsequent sight of a repetitive passing and sole control game for the on-court players while the budding keepers squat near a goal working on their dynamic flexibility to perform the lateral split save

proves beyond doubt that this is a sport in its own right. Yes, many skills can transfer to football, but it's not football they're learning. It's futsal-specific practice. And why not? It's the Benfica futsal academy after all.

I remark to André Rodrigues, the under-15s coach standing with me, how enjoyable and engaging it is for the boys. It's non-negotiable, he tells me. 'Their first experience [of the sport] is this . . . it has to be good,' he says. But why does Portugal stand out, I enquire. 'Every school has a court, every school plays futsal. It is the game of the schools. It's their start. This is how they learn . . .' So what are the golden principles, the bedrock of the game, in the eyes of a youth coach at one of Europe's most prestigious football and futsal institutions? 'It all starts with the one-v-one duel,' Rodrigues explains. 'How to beat the opponent. Only when we have learning on this, do we proceed to the two-v-two, and up towards five-v-five. But all of the time we stick to the sub-principles relevant to each dynamic. It is all about how to play.' The principles of small-group tactics are the foundation of football too, a fact that brings home the unarguable links with the eleven-a-side game at the heart of a global sporting giant that has become a byword for prodigious youth talent. In the three years after 2015, Benfica made more than €230m from sales of academy players, from André Gomes, who signed for Valencia before heading to Everton via Barcelona, to Manchester City's Brazilian futsal-style keeper Ederson. And this was before the club sold the teenager João Felix to Atlético Madrid for €126m.

Futsal clearly plays its part in opening the door for talent to be welcomed into the Benfica family. Sometimes the young futsal players are seen as more suited to football and encouraged to switch, Rodrigues tells me. Some boys come the other way, dropping into futsal after being released by the football section. The latter change becomes more difficult once they are teenagers, because the intensity and tactical nuances of the small-sided game can prove too much for

the eleven-a-side player to cope with. Out on the court, the under-10s are busy playing in one of their three sessions a week at Benfica, immersing themselves in the game and the culture of the club. Ramos tells me later that his ethos for coaching kids is about three things: ensuring they grow as respectful people; evolving their 'mastery of the ball'; and having fun. A fourth, he says, is winning the Lisbon championship. But how does he bring this philosophy to life in the sessions? '*O jogo rebelde*,' he exclaims. The rebel game. 'Just like on the streets, where we have holes, pavements, obstacles, problems to overcome. The players need difficulties here – just like on the streets,' he continues. 'It's important.'

A competitive edge is also essential, Rodrigues tells me, pointing out one of the youngsters on court battling to dispossess an opponent and start a counter-attack. 'Look . . . it works,' he whispers. The boy in question is one of several under-10s on trial tonight, all local kids looking to impress the coaches and scouts up against the regular academy players. 'When they get older, towards the age group I coach [players aged thirteen to fifteen] we start to use statistics too. The importance of competition keeps them focused. As well as winning the games in training, we measure and count for them. The intensive exercises will be there to keep it fun and keep players engaged and competing.' So what do they measure? The 'second-post finish' is crucial, he says. 'How many times do we shoot to the second post? How many times does a certain player react and make it to the second post to finish? What about the first touch? The first control? Is it clear, does it take the ball in an oriented control to the place the player wants to go? How many good, how many bad?' It's the same focus on second-post finishes and the oriented sole control Mićo Martić, Jorge Braz and other futsal luminaries have told me about. The under-10s games finish. Ramos chats briefly to the players, who are all glowing after ninety minutes of doing what they love, hundreds of touches of the ball, thousands of decisions to make, all with

enjoyment and learning at the heart of it. And with zero instruction from anyone other than the coach, with the watching parents respectfully observing in complete silence.

As a legion of new coaches appear at our side of the court, I'm introduced to several of them, including Rodrigues's (numerous) assistants and the head coach of the all-conquering Benfica women's team, Bruno Fernandes. The under-15s boys are about to play against the women tonight, a break from the usual routine because many of the strongest female players are away on international duty with Portugal, preparing for the first UEFA women's futsal Euros. As the new arrivals appear on court, a customary changeover ritual begins. With the under-15s and the women standing in a line on court, the under-10s boys file past, shaking hands with every player and coach – including me, Chris and Ricardo. The handshakes are simply a symbol of positivity, respect and sportsmanship linked to number one in his three-point philosophy, explains Ramos.

The contest between the boys and the women is extremely competitive. The star contingent absent from the women's team includes the goalkeeper Ana Catarina (named the best keeper in the world just two months previously), the elegant *fixo* Inês Fernandes, the *ala* Sara Ferreira, the fearsome pivot Janice Silva and the rising star of the game, Fifó, who at just nineteen was named third best player in the world in 2018 and 2019 and was expected to eclipse the Brazilian Amandinha as the face of female futsal in the coming years. Fernandes, the coach, says the players on court are also strong, with some of the younger players from the B team out to impress, including one or two seventeen-year-olds. With an average age of twenty-one in the first-team squad, they are closing in on a hat-trick of consecutive national league titles, Fernandes tells me proudly. Although the amateur women's game here is still way behind the men's, when Portugal catches up with Spain and Italy, where pockets of professionalism exist, Benfica will no doubt be ready

to advance. Fernandes tells me he wants the team to be the best in Europe. 'That is our aim,' he says sternly. All-conquering at home but falling short in Europe clearly sits uneasily with him. I remember this conversation five months later, when Benfica announce he has stepped down as coach of the women's team. Before we depart after the women's match, the under-10s coach Ramos fills me in on the three boys who will be asked to sign for Benfica after tonight's showing. I'm intrigued. The under-15s coach Rodrigues had tested my scouting capabilities by asking me to choose which players showed promise while we were watching. They selected two of the boys I'd picked out. The third one had passed me by. 'He was trying things all the time,' explains Ramos. 'We like that.' They're all local boys. Two from grassroots clubs and one from Belenenses. It's at this point, Ricardo's ears prick up. Os Belenenses ('the football team of us Belém citizens') are his club.

One of only two Portuguese clubs outside the lauded Trés Grandes – Benfica, Sporting and Porto – to have won the Portuguese championship (Boavista clinched the title in 2001), Belenenses are the capital's third club. The dramatic title victory in 1946, edging out Benfica by a single point, was due largely to the inspirational coach Augusta Silva, known as *O Imortal* (the Immortal), and the goals of the main forward, Artur Quaresma. As well as his goals, Quaresma also bequeathed to the nation another bundle of footballing joy: his great-nephew, Ricardo *O Cigano*, the man hailed by Ronaldo, Jorge Braz and a generation of Portuguese fans.

In 2019 though, the long and storied history of the club where José Mourinho and his father also both played counts for nothing. Turmoil gripped the club, when the limited company holding the rights to the professional football side of the club – the SAD (Sociedade Anónima Desportiva or Anonymous Sports Society) – wrestled the Primeira Liga team away from the rest. The futsal club was unaffected, along with the handball, basketball, athletics and

rugby sections, but the number one priority in all similar multi-sports clubs is football, and the Belenenses split ranks as one of the biggest scandals ever to befall a Lisbon team. Six months on from the divorce in the summer of 2018, the newly created Belenenses team, which retained ownership of the historic Estádio do Restelo in Belém, was scrabbling around in the sixth tier of football, while the team spirited away was still challenging Benfica and Sporting in the Primeira Liga under the name Belenenses SAD, playing home games in an eerily empty national stadium. It's a stark morality tale of Portuguese football, raising questions about history, culture, roots and the price of ambition and power. Nuno Ramos's selection of the nine-year-old Belenenses boy to make the step up may not make big news. But it's further evidence of the clear pecking order in the Portuguese sporting hierarchy, where the biggest and strongest readily consume the weakest. On today's evidence on court, the mighty Benfica's studiously child-centred approach to *o jogo rebelde* at least offers a partial counterweight to the idea that sport is always only about the ruthless pursuit of power and glory. With the game of the streets, at least, it's still about enjoyment of the people.

THE MAGICIAN

'Sorry.' I hold up my hands for mock effect while walking in light drizzle, engaged in introductory chit-chat about yesterday's international futsal match. The grateful recipient of my apology struts alongside, to my left, leading the way but struggling for a moment to finish his sentence in a non-native language after I'd asked how he felt the game went. 'Ppphhh . . .' He rolls his eyes skywards, towards the gaggle of stubborn grey rain clouds. His team lost 6–1. 'Phwaahhh . . .' He exhales loudly, shrugging his stout and muscular shoulders. 'It could not be . . .'

'Any worse?' I venture.

'Yes! Any worse.' He smiles. 'You knew. But you put the words . . .'

'In your mouth,' I say, nodding. 'Sorry. I will not put any more words in your mouth. Promise. What is it in Portuguese by the way?'

'*Pior que aquilo é impossível,*' he replies.

The man I'm speaking to is Ricardo Filipe da Silva Braga, otherwise known simply as Ricardinho, or *O Mágico* (the Magician), the futsal superstar crowned best player on the planet for five consecutive years from 2014–18. We're strolling past two pristine eleven-a-side football pitches towards the futsal hall, a white-walled beacon of excellence at the Federação Portuguesa de Futebol (FPF) headquarters in Rio Maior. I check my watch instinctively, without looking at the time – a tic I've recently developed. I'm happy to be here, but also hugely relieved. When we set off a full four hours ago, heading north from Lisbon, I was expecting a one-hour drive. Ricardo, my Portuguese futsal teammate, was in full tour-guide mode as he drove me and our other curious teammate, Chris, on a whistle-stop tour of Lisbon's vast array of grassroots facilities, including indoor futsal venues, roofless outdoor courts, dual-use basketball and futsal facilities, and grass and artificial football pitches. The diversion turned into a full detour when we stopped off at Santarém, a historic town on the River Tagus, to meet Ricardo's cousin, Luis Peralta, a semi-retired prison warden and former football and futsal coach. From a vantage point high up on a fortress that serves as a monument to *O Conquistador*, Afonso I, the first king of Portugal, Peralta pointed out the several white concrete futsal courts dotted around the town on the banks of the mighty Tagus. '*Fútebol de salão,*' he proclaimed. '*Bola pesada.*' It was yet more evidence of the powerful futsal culture. With time ticking on (and concerns about whether we would ever get to Rio Maior growing), Peralta whisked us to his flat for an impromptu four-course meal, with wine, port and coffee for refreshments. Once the passionate Benfica fan had decided he wanted to come with us – declaring 'I love Ricardinho' – he swept us thirty miles north-west

in his grey Toyota Avensis, with just twenty-five minutes until my interview with the best futsal player on the planet.

We arrive with three minutes to spare. Ricardinho is waiting. The five consecutive awards as the world's finest player is far from the only staggering statistic he owns. Yesterday evening he earned his 160th cap for his country in a decade and a half of excellence yielding 135 goals. Domestically, he led his club, Madrid's Inter Movistar, to five straight Primera División titles in arguably the strongest national league in the world. A few months after we meet, Ricardinho's transfer to the Paris-based French team ACCS sent shock waves around the world of futsal. But in his previous life at Benfica, where he broke through in 2003, he racked up five titles too, the total haul of national league medals reflected on his shirt number: he is the most famous number ten in futsal. R10 is also the biggest name in the sport by far since the retirement in 2018 of the Brazilian Falcão – 'my idol, the best player in futsal history' according to Ricardinho.

Once we're sitting in the futsal hall in Rio Maior, he kicks off with the previous night's defeat at the hands of 'the daddy of futsal', Brazil, a team Portugal have never beaten. 'We showed them too much respect,' he admits. The ascendancy of the former colony over the nation of empire in the battle of the lusophone nations is not confined to the small-sided game. In football, the *Quinas* have got the better of the *Canarinhas* only four times in nearly twenty meetings. Despite the heavy defeat – and the return match the next day, which Brazil also win 4–0 – it's still easy to make a case for Ricardinho being the best player on the court. Brazil's inspirational captain, the grizzled goalscoring *fixo* Rodrigo, shone in typical fashion, defending, scoring and displaying a sublime range of passing that included several disguised *caneta* (literally 'pen') nutmegged balls threaded through an opponent's legs. Guitta, the rival to Kazakhstan's Leo Higuita as best keeper in the world,

engaged in a one-on-one showdown with Ricardinho all night. And the Chapecoense Barcelona man Ferrão, who dispossessed Ricardinho as best player in the world later in the year, excelled as the head boy among Brazil's line-up of impressive young students such as Leandro Lino, the man hailed as a rising star by the coach, Marquinhos Xavier. But it was only *O Mágico* who required special scrutiny, his presence on the ball triggering a spike in attention from the 3,000 people in the Pavilhão João Rocha, Sporting's home arena. It was a full house, in keeping with the attendances common at league matches in Portugal and other futsal nations, but way short of the highest ever crowd at a match. That was in 2014 in Brasilia's Mané Garrincha stadium, where 56,000 watched as Brazil took on Argentina on a court erected in the middle of the football pitch.

In his recently published autobiography, *La magia acontece donde hay dedicación* ('Magic happens where there is dedication'), Ricardinho talks of his joy at following Cristiano Ronaldo by leading his nation to European glory despite an injury in the final. It also features much about the young Ricardo's life as a child in the village of Fânzeres and the town of Valbom (where his family moved after a house fire when he was ten). It's the life of an impoverished street footballer whose 'most faithful companion' was a ball. In his youth, his teachers would complain to his parents because his obsession with playing on the streets at every spare moment meant he rocked up at classes 'sweating like a chicken', and dripping all over his notebooks. The middle child of three boys, he would play football with them all day long. But Ricardo's devotion stood out. Just like Wayne Rooney – born no more than six weeks after *O Mágico* in autumn 1985 – and countless other football-obsessed children the world over, Ricardinho wasn't choosy about how he played. For Rooney in the football-crazy city looking out to sea from the north-west coast of England, it was kicking half-flat balls about in the shadow of De La Salle school in Croxteth. For Ricardinho, growing up near Porto

on Portugal's north-west coast, a proper ball was a rarity. He was often forced to make do with socks, tape and, more controversially, the precious apples and oranges his father brought home from work at the market in Porto. 'It did not have to be a ball,' he says in the book. 'It could be anything: it was enough that it had a round shape.' He was obsessed, playing before, during and after school – when he would meet his friends at the top of a nearby hill on 'a small improvised field' they called *a encosta* (the slope). 'We played until dinner time. We turned the garden benches into goals; the park was our stadium: a stadium in which the fences, swings, lamp posts and pots of flowers were not an obstacle to give wings to our imagination. Each one assumed the role of his idol . . . my friends and I shared the dream of many children of the world: to become football players.'

I start to ask about his childhood love for FC Porto, but he nips in before I've finished the question, leaving Ricardo the interpreter for dead. 'Of course, I pursued football. I have always said my dream was to be a football player. However, I haven't chosen futsal. Futsal chose me. I tried to play football and "they" told me I was too small to play it. And when futsal chose me, I said, if this is what I'm going to play I want to be the best at it.' And the best he is. 'If you joined Ronaldo and Messi, that's how Ricardinho is in futsal,' Jorge Braz, the Portugal coach, told me shortly after the victorious Euros in 2018. The pressure of comparison to the two giants of world football doesn't faze Ricardinho. 'No, it would be worse if you compare me with any António or Pedro. Comparing me with Ronaldo and Messi just gives me reasons to be happy!' These sentiments formed the crux of a feature on Ricardinho I wrote for the *Guardian*. But we spoke much more widely about his rise to the pinnacle of the game, the man whom Jorge Braz mentioned at St George's Park as the embodiment, along with Ricardo Quaresma, of the much-vaunted Portuguese one-v-one prowess so essential to futsal. Ricardinho thrives in high-pressure situations. He says he sees 'everything in

tenths of a second' when playing. In the previous night's match, his desire to invite pressure was obvious, picking up the ball close to his own goal, welcoming one-on-one confrontations. 'You must show your opponent exactly the opposite of what you're feeling,' he explains. This is something we try in Reading in our own amateurish way, I tell him, but he seems puzzled. A laughing Ricardo explains in Portuguese that we'll show him later precisely how our own version of this bravado once backfired with embarrassing consequences.

For now, Ricardinho needs no second invitation to expand on how and where it all began for him: about the rollercoaster ride that propelled a football-crazy kid out of the impoverished streets of Gondomar; through his challenging teenage years as 'always the smallest' (he's now 1.67 metres – 5ft 6in – half an inch shorter than Lionel Messi); the dedication that led him to Japan to earn the fortune that set him up for life; the mental and physical challenges of maintaining his impeccable standards, including what he calls his 'Achilles heel', an addiction to coffee; and the millionaire's lifestyle as the biggest futsal star on the planet. When he was lauded in *Forbes* magazine as *O Pequeno Gigante* (the Little Giant), the headline ran alongside a photograph of the boy from the Gondomar streets, now a picture of sophistication dressed in a smart tuxedo.

He takes us back to the day a light came on in his life. The day that triggered the switch from the teenage darkness and rejection imposed by his beloved Porto to an age of enlightenment after being bitten by *O Pequeno Bug* (the Little Bug). The date was 25 April, the anniversary of the Portuguese Carnation Revolution, the military coup that overthrew the decades-long far-right Estado Novo regime. It was the first year of the new millennium, a quarter of a century on from the landmark revolt. As Ricardinho recalls, it makes 25 April a significant date in Portugal's history in more ways than one. 'I played a seven-a-side football tournament on the bank holiday. By reaching the final, we beat a futsal team and their coach was a woman called

Carolina Silva, the Gramidense coach, who looked at me and said: "This kid should be playing futsal".

'With Carolina, I found what I wanted. It was futsal. When I started, my passing focus was mainly long passes like football, until Carolina started to tell me what futsal was about. You have to move much more, you have to support the middle and touch the ball just a couple of times . . . all these things. Obviously, I had plenty of flair and wanted to have the ball over and over again and dribble one player, two players, running up and down the pitch. But it was there, with Carolina, that I understood that I wanted to improve in this sport. 'I had played futsal in schools and with friends. But this was different. When I played after school, my mum would come out around midnight and call me to come home to bed because next morning I had school. My life was always playing, just like a regular kid. One time I got into big trouble, though. It was the day of my cousin's baptism and we needed to leave home around noon. It was ten a.m. and as you imagine we had loads of time. Haha. So I went down to the *campo da bola* [football pitch] right next to my house and I was there just to see the other kids playing. So I was all impeccably dressed by my mum. Just like we usually were, actually. Although we didn't have much money, my mum had bought me brand new shoes and I told her: "Mum, I'm going just down to the *ringue* to see the kids playing." She said: "Ricardo, you *benze-te* [bless yourself], don't even think about *jogar á bola!*" "'No mum, don't worry," I said. So, off I go, down to the *ringue*, and I start watching the kids playing futsal. It is all going fine, but then one of the kids' mums calls him in, and now one of the teams is a player down. They ask me if I wanted to play and I say: "OK, I'll start in goal." The game starts and only a few minutes into the game my shoes are a mess already! After the game, I went home and told my mum: "The shoes are hurting my feet, I'm going to swap for my trainers and I'll use them for the baptism." She replies: "No way! You are wearing your

new shoes for the event." When she looks down at my shiny new shoes, she roars: "I AM GOING TO KILL YOU, RICARDO!"

'One of the messages I always try to get across is: I was raised in a very poor family. I don't want pity when I say life was hard, and that I didn't have trainers, etc. I want people to see that I was very poor, yes, but that I always found ways to get what I wanted. So if someone tells you that you're too small or tiny to play football or futsal, don't let these people affect you . . . you should fight, go for it. Don't ever give up on your dreams and what you want for your life, and don't let anyone pity you, because here we find a way to get to our goals. That's the message from me.' It's one we all hear, loud and clear.

The ability to cope under pressure is vital, but it's a ceaseless quest for a creative edge which also marks Ricardinho out as the best. The man with a showreel of audacious goals on YouTube – backheels, *rabonas*, *cabritos* ('goat kid' in Portuguese, the name for the skill of flicking the ball over an opponent), fearsome toe-poke finishes and intentional glancing deflections – remains under no illusions about his creativity, insisting he was not born this way. It's been a process of dedication and experimentation, he says, fuelled by the people in his life. From his parents, Américo and Olga David Braga, to Carolina and 'Master Zego', the pioneer of the 4-0 formation who teamed up with Carolina and mentored coach and player throughout their formative years, right up to his coach at Inter Movistar, Jesús Velasco (another 4-0 disciple coached by Zego in Spain), and the national team's Jorge Braz, many key people have given Ricardinho the platform to extend his talents.

Although not in the same financial bracket as his millionaire friends at Real Madrid, he's a handsomely paid sporting icon in Spain, where futsal is a high-profile professional sport with a passionate following. The move to Nagoya Oceans in Japan safeguarded his future. Their offer of €30,000 a month in 2010 – it was the second approach for

his services, he says – was swiftly rejected and replaced by a package he admits has set him up for life. The Ricardinho brand is difficult to quantify, according to Daniel Sá, executive director of the Instituto Português de Administração de Marketing (IPAM). Although now a global phenomenon, Ricardinho's value is still well below that of Ronaldo and other leading footballers. Sá told the Portuguese daily *Diário de Notícias* that *O Mágico*'s marketability was in the same bracket as the likes of Miguel Oliveira, the Portuguese champion motorcyclist. No mean feat for playing a sport yet to achieve Olympic status, in a league – Spain's LNFS – where the average basic top-flight salary was reportedly €3,200 a month in 2018–19.

In many ways, Ricardinho's journey mirrors the sport's rise. Since the day he was plucked from obscurity by Carolina Silva at the dawn of the new millennium, futsal has been transformed from a neglected, impoverished, largely amateur pastime to one gaining greater recognition for its links with developing football skills, and as a professional sport in its own right. Whether it makes the Olympics any time soon or not, Ricardinho's legacy in the game is secure. Though the biggest personal brand in a sport embracing the digital age, Ricardinho's passion, dedication and approach-ability seem to reflect a more traditional bygone era. On court, he's a cartoonish figure of squat, pent-up power and finesse, the invet-erate street hustler as hypnotically dominant with a futsal ball as he was once mesmeric with a tiny bundle of socks and tape. It's a vision of what the eleven-a-side game used to resemble before the greed, the cynicism and the agents seized its soul. The football of the Wayne Rooney breakthrough years, a raw and refreshing energy of the street urchin gatecrashing the big league. The football of the Ronaldo *O Fenômeno* decade from the mid-90s onwards, scaring and scarring defences in equal measure with the ball at his feet. Futsal seems somehow closer to this renegade spirit, a little freer, more pure, less predictable, than the present iteration of association

football – despite Lionel Messi and Cristiano Ronaldo's valiant efforts. Futsal is the rebel game.

Off court, the ball of energy dressed in a black, green and red FPF *seleçao* tracksuit does not relent. There's a breathless verve about Ricardinho. It's clear, he can talk the talk too. Just before the end of the interview, there's time to hand him a smartphone so he can describe arguably his greatest moment. Before I've finished explaining, his furrowed brow gives way to a cheeky smile, his eyes widening as he nods knowingly. He knows where I'm going. He's just as quick to scroll the footage forward. 'It's the right foot,' he declares, pointing at the screen. 'Look at the right foot.' He's talking about the seasoned international Marko Pršić, his hapless Serbian opponent in a feisty group game at the 2016 Euros in Belgrade. The Ricardinho standing here hits pause on the action at the point where the advancing Pršić offers up his right leg. The Ricardinho on the screen also halts, poised, left sole glued to the ball, right foot planted on the jet-black court, having feigned twice to explode towards goal, where three Serbian players are perched zonally, waiting, watching, fearing the worst: 'In this moment I saw him attack the ball with his right foot. By doing this, his body moves this way.' It was the moment of truth. The time to hit the multi-button combination play he'd practised so often. One the Portuguese number ten knew could instantly destabilise his marker and trigger a brazen act of explosive dexterity, flicking the ball up and over Pršić's head to leave the dazed Serbian flailing to the ground as he chests the ball, lets it bounce and smashes it high into the Serbian net. 'I knew it would happen . . . I've imagined all that,' he beams.

The skill, he says, was inspired by the footwork of Issy 'Hitman' Hamdaoui, a freestyler and briefly Ricardinho's teammate at Inter Movistar in 2014. *O Mágico* delivered a glossier, more ruthless update on the training session Akka 3000, as it is known. His 2.0 version, complete with added potency and game realism, amounts

to an act of breathtaking sporting audacity. A glorious moment of mathematical symmetry – four touches to dupe four opponents in four seconds from start to sensational finish – that typifies his unique talent. And one that brings to mind the exhortation by Jorge Braz at St George's Park to seize on the micro-details in one-v-one encounters. 'It's not hard to do that dribble,' insists Ricardinho. 'The difficulty,' he continues, 'lies in finding the right moment in a match where you're under pressure from the 10,000 people watching. I know players way more skilful than me who know a lot more tricks – but under that pressure it's much more complicated.'

At club level, Ricardinho's finest four seconds came with three minutes remaining in the fifth and decisive play-off for Inter Movistar against Barcelona, at the climax of the 2016–17 LNFS season. The victim – his fierce rival Ferrão – is beaten by a high-risk *caneta* on the wing with the scores level. Ricardinho skips away, then fires an unstoppable toe-poke finish past the Barça keeper – securing yet another title for Inter and confirming his own place in the pantheon of futsal's greatest ever game-changers.

Ricardinho hands the phone back. The FPF press officer, Bruno, says we have a few minutes left before he must return to the squad to prepare for the second Brazil match – so, naturally, we get a ball out. After a spot of juggling and showboating from *O Mágico*, we make good on our promise to recreate our own version of his trademark one-v-one powerplay yards from his own goal line. I take the ball from Ricardinho – a sentence I feel proud writing – and tell him he's the opponent, ready to press me when I receive the ball from Chris. They're both central near the halfway line. I'm about six metres from goal, also central. Luis Peralta, Ricardo's cousin, obliges by standing out wide, taking up the passing option to my left. Ricardo is just behind me (playing himself, which adds to the realism somewhat). Chris rolls the ball back to me and cuts forward. Collecting it with

my sole, I look up beyond an advancing Ricardinho and dance backwards on the ball. I grimace a bit because I'm recovering from a popped calf muscle about six weeks ago.

Ricardinho senses my hobble-dance is not the most elegant and quickens his pace. Ruthless. Ricardo vacates the goal, edging wide right to offer a safe passing lane. I see this and feign to go left to a waiting Luis before swiftly rolling the ball backwards with my right sole, preparing in an instant to punch the ball out to Ricardo. Losing touch and sight of the ball for a millisecond, it trickles agonisingly, embarrassingly beyond my reach, backwards and over the goal line. It doesn't even hit the net. I throw up my hands in mock disgust, to emphasise the fact that we're re-creating the farrago for Ricardinho's benefit. He seems appreciative. In fact he loves it. He laughs long and loud, perhaps a little too long for my liking. I dribbled the ball into my own goal – just like I had done in that crucial match back in Reading. I decide to take *O Mágico*'s piss-taking banter as a backhanded compliment. He doesn't really think I'm stupid. He's in awe of my bravery in possession. I like this game of trickery. He's fooling me, just like he was trying to bamboozle the Brazilians last night. This is Ricardinho, the fleet-footed master of disguise who escaped teenage footballing rejection to find refuge, fame and fortune in the rebel game he has helped propel into the professional sporting limelight of the twenty-first century.

CHAPTER 14
SPAIN: FÚTBOL SALA, LA FUNDACIÓN

WHEN MARC CARMONA speaks, it pays to sit up and listen. So that's exactly what I do, nestled in the principal lecture room in the swish educational wing of La Masia, the nerve centre of FC Barcelona. In theory, the youngsters here will go on to honour the famous Barça colours and add to the legacy of one of the most storied institutions in global sport. The building is actually the second iteration of La Masia, the famous rural farmhouse where the likes of Lionel Messi, Andrés Iniesta, Xavi Hernández and the legion of Pep Guardiola's tiki-taka foundlings were reared on a nutritious diet of tactics and tapas. Carmona is the most successful coach in the Barcelona futsal team's history, the master tactician responsible for an unprecedented period of glory in *fútbol sala*, one of the club's five professional sections. 'One day Iniesta trained with us here because Nike wanted to present a special award for futsal,' recalls Carmona, reflecting on the symbiosis between the two sports played with a ball at the feet. 'We trained with a lot of respect because you can imagine, if we were to injure Iniesta!' he laughs. Iniesta's mutual respect was tangible. The midfield maestro admits that playing futsal as a boy gave him an innate game nous that later set him apart in the cut and thrust of peak Pep-ball. In the futsal hall next door to La Masia, Iniesta didn't

struggle as such – 'oh, he was very good,' remembers Carmona – but afterwards he expressed appreciation for the difficulty of playing futsal at the elite level. 'What I love is their skill with the ball, the intensity of the moves, the sidesteps, the blocks, the passing,' Iniesta told Nike. 'I take my hat off to futsal players because it's extremely difficult. Watching it on TV is different to when you train or play it for real.' In another hat-tip to the small-sided game, he pointed out that as a professional footballer the 'tactical elements and movement in the game gets lost on you'.

Carmona's period in charge of the futsal team overlapped with his friend and fellow coaching icon Guardiola's equally astounding impact in the eleven-a-side game. In a twelve-year stint as *fútbol sala* head coach, starting in 2004, the former footballer (until the age of nineteen) and futsal player (until twenty-nine) took Barcelona's futsal club from the second division to the top flight as it joined the growing ranks of professional futsal teams in the Liga Nacional Fútbol Sala. With a haul of seventeen domestic and European titles, including a four-year purple patch from 2010 when they lifted three consecutive LNFS championships and two UEFA Futsal Cups, Carmona's record mirrors Guardiola's own four-season spree, securing three straight La Liga titles and two Champions Leagues. It's no surprise that this era of dominance yielded Spain's historic first World Cup football victory in 2010, snatched courtesy of a dramatic late winner in the final in the 'battle of Johannesburg' against a pugnacious Netherlands team – a goal scored by Andrés Iniesta himself, of course.

In the Spanish equivalent of a collection of *fútbol*-themed Russian dolls, the 2010 history-making eleven-a-side national team stands tallest. A peep within reveals Guardiola's all-conquering tiki-taka tyros, a shade smaller in scale of success, but arguably more beautiful to observe – their beating heart imprinted with the red and yellow stripes of Catalonia. And inside this, the next miniature

version, stand the *fútbol sala* micro-giants of Carmona's making, the Barça team that arguably defines the Catalan culture of the club more intensely than Messi and co. Three teams, all nigh-on identical in their socio-cultural formation and ball-hogging elegance, yet distinctly identifiable from their signature patterns with a ball at their feet. They're the Spanish/Catalan 'dolls', alive with the imagery of futsal that identifies Barcelona as perhaps the ultimate symbol of the fusion between *fútbol sala* and *fútbol*. The eleven-a-side team's prowess – male and female – has long been built on *la fundación* (the foundation) offered by the small-sided game, whether that's with youngsters schooled on the dusty courts of Catalonia or imported talents from South America such as Argentina's Lionel Messi, Uruguay's Luis Suárez or Brazil's Ronaldo, Ronaldinho and the flying full-back Dani Alves. In 2010, when Barcelona players – most of whom were La Masia graduates – made up nine of the starting team that won the World Cup, another remarkable feat was achieved: Messi, Xavi and Iniesta filled the shortlist of three for the Ballon D'Or – the first time one club had achieved this since AC Milan in the late 1980s. La Masia may well have been the finishing school, but futsal acted as the nursery where their ball mastery was first nurtured. Carmona is speaking to me, aged fifty-two, as head of coach education – or 'the organiser', as he puts it modestly – at the self-styled *Mes que un club* (more than a club), working across all its professional sports: football (male and female), futsal, basketball, handball and roller hockey.

My eldest son, Conor, is here with me to see some futsal and soak up the delights of the Catalan capital – a week before his under-16s team, which I coach, are due to play in the national finals of the English FA's youth futsal tournament. It's a significant staging post on our quest to learn how to speak the language of futsal more fluently and examine how deeply the game is ingrained in Barcelona's identity. Carmona readily accepts the links but is determined to point

out that *fútbol sala* differs from football at the elite level in more than name alone. 'We are both played with the foot, our goal is the same,' he explains. 'But, well, it is another sport ... In football one player can rest for two minutes. It is fine. Nothing happens. In futsal, if you rest for three seconds, you die.' So what is the biggest difference between the sports? He takes a moment. A verbal representation of *La Pausa* ('The Pause' in Spanish), the deceptive micro-delay on the ball employed by elite players to disarm opponents before enacting a killer move in futsal and football. 'Maybe, maybe the most important thing is the play *without* the ball,' he replies calmly. 'Think about it. In football during the play there are a lot of players who do not move. In futsal, it's impossible. There is one player with the ball, but the others are moving continuously. There are differences between the surfaces of contact with the ball. The sole and the toe. But sometimes in football I saw some players using the toe, not the main surface but it is used. The movement without the ball is a big difference.' Carmona asks Conor his view on the biggest distinction. 'The fast pace,' Conor replies. 'The speed of the game.' Carmona nods in agreement. 'It's correct.' I turn to Conor, sitting to my right. 'See, see ... that's what I've been saying to you guys ... You'll need to be like that next week at the national finals.' I look to Carmona for back-up. Teenagers don't listen to their dads, after all. 'It's true,' he nods. The head of coach education at FC Barcelona and its most successful ever futsal coach is suddenly delivering a team talk for my Woodley United Toffees under-16s in the heart of La Masia.

As much as futsal is central to the Barcelona ethos, whether as a standalone sport or as the recognised early *entrenador* (coach) of young footballers, it is totally dependent on the lucrative football section of the club. 'We could not survive without football,' says Carmona. 'That is the truth.' The other four professional sections of the club exist on an estimated budget of about €45m a year,

Carmona says, which includes significant sponsorship funding, usually from a deal with a single company covering all four non-football sections. The nine amateur sections survive on more meagre finances. Revenue from futsal matchdays is dwarfed by football. Even in the top tier of Spain's LNFS, the average attendances in 2019 were between 2,500 and 3,000.[30] The Barcelona first team's venue, Palau Blaugrana, boasts a 7,500 capacity. Football is clearly the club's number one priority, but futsal struggles to compete with basketball for second place. Founded in 1926, the Barça men's basketball team ranks second only to Real Madrid in the list of the most successful clubs in the history of the fully professional national Liga ACB. The make-up of the current La Masia residents, the 10 per cent of the total number of academy recruits who take up the option to eat, sleep and breathe at the training ground, reflects the club's priorities: Carmona reveals that of the sixty-nine young athletes there in 2018, forty-four are footballers, fifteen basketballers, five handball players, three futsal and two roller hockey. Most are from Spain, some from elsewhere in Europe and a handful from other continents. There are no young Argentinians in the house looking to follow in the svelte footsteps of Lionel Messi.

Making the most of scarce resources is a common theme in futsal. The enforced creativity among players skilled in the art of deception is born out of a stark deficit of time and space on court. When I first met Carmona at St George's Park in England a year or so earlier, he was delivering a masterclass coaching session working with England under-19 players, on the same afternoon Portugal's Jorge Braz put on a session. After setting players up in a two-v-two game, with a fifth player feeding balls in, Carmona intervened to urge the attacking duo to rotate positions to escape and score. 'Futsal is for the liars,' he

---

30. Pivotfutsal.com, 'Inside the World's Most Powerful Professional Futsal League: Liga Nacional de Fútbol Sala', 7 May 2019.

declared – a memorably pithy summary of the need for deception to steal precious space. He laughs loudly at La Masia when I remind him of his words. 'Yeah, futsal is for the liars. In a good way, of course.'

Acknowledging the game's inextricable links to Barcelona's identity, Carmona tells me they are working on defining a DNA to apply across all sections. In the meantime, Carmona says the principles of the 'three Ps' Guardiola adhered to are just as apparent in futsal. 'We say that we have to win by respecting the opponent, the referee and rules of the play,' he explains. 'But also by respecting our three big treasures in football, the three Ps: possession of the ball, position of the ball and pressing after losing the ball. This is our way to understand football. This is clear from watching any Barcelona game.' The difference in futsal is the heightened pressure of time and space. Carmona flags up another symbolic link between the speed and intensity of futsal and Guardiola's vision. 'The four seconds. The great goal of Guardiola was to convince players that if when we lose the ball we go five metres towards it, we don't go ten, twenty or thirty metres back behind us. I think it's a similar model in Manchester City now.'

Although a different 'four-second rule' to the one that defines futsal – the time limit on goalkeeper possession and the taking of set plays – it sums up the same devotion to reactions in transition. 'For me, futsal is clearly a very good practice for both football and futsal,' Carmona continues. His keenness during his coaching days to have his teams show inventiveness on court was noted by fellow Catalan Roberto Martínez. The Belgium manager admits to soaking up Carmona's expertise while a player and a novice coach watching the Barcelona futsal team: 'I always found Marc Carmona very interesting to watch. He's the most successful futsal coach in modern times. What he achieved in eleven seasons at Barcelona . . . he was incredible.' The detailed and creative intensity of futsal set plays stood out. 'It's a four-v-four situation at a corner,' Martínez told me. 'So to find a move or an opportunity to score is down to very

specific detail.' These incremental yet crucial details align neatly with the modern eleven-a-side game, in the same way the Brazilian and Spanish futsal goalkeeping techniques are increasingly relevant on grass. The Technical Study Group after Russia 2018, which noted the rise of the 'X-block' save, recognised set plays as another big tactical trend: one in every thirty-one corners led to a goal; and 50 per cent of the 169 goals scored – just two fewer than the record for a thirty-two team tournament, set at France 1998 – came from either set pieces or counter-attacks. Chief technical officer Marco van Basten attributed the phenomenon to greater time spent honing set plays in training than in his day.

Martínez also sees the bigger picture when it comes to futsal, noting the centrality of the game to the Spanish and Catalan culture. 'There's a big influence in Spain,' he told me. 'When you grow up you don't play eleven-a-side in school, it's always futsal. Every school has futsal courts, some of them are outdoors because the weather allows. Some of them are different surfaces on which the ball always reacts in a different way. So the first introduction to football for any kid in Spain is through futsal. When it is just four players and the keeper you touch the ball a lot more in a twenty-minute game than in any bigger sizes.' Once Carmona escorts us up the steps away from La Masia at the rear of the building, the sheer scale of the Ciutat Esportiva Joan Gamper training complex becomes visible. After unlocking a gate to one of the eight full-size football pitches (five grass, three artificial), he points out the futsal, basketball and hand-ball pavilions back across the complex on the other side of La Masia. That's where we're heading next.

Jordi Torras stands tall as a monument to Barcelona's devotion to mastery on the futsal court – with and without the ball – as he greets us at the entrance to the *fútbol sala* pavilion with a beaming smile. Having just graduated from La Masia under the tutelage of

our teacher for the day, Marc Carmona, it's time for us to sneak a glance at where the magic happens. Torras is Barcelona's director of youth futsal coaching. A garlanded former star for club and country, the local boy who departed as a teenager to pursue a professional career (when Barça were amateur in futsal) only to return a seasoned international and World Cup winner ready to captain the club to greatness under Carmona in 2010. 'An amazing player,' Carmona told me a few minutes earlier. 'We finally got him when he was thirty, we convinced him to sign once we reached the first division.' Torras takes us inside the pavilion, pointing out the immaculate changing areas, complete with physio room and ice baths for aching limbs given a pounding on the unforgiving court. With precious little seating – the capacity is 400 – it's a temple of energy, hard work and training, a cavernous sanctuary for practice and honing Carmona's 'game for the liars'. Barça B play LNFS division two matches here, whereas the first team uses the sumptuous Palau Blaugrana arena in the shadow of the Camp Nou.

The futsal pavilion is the only place where any action is taking place today at Joan Gamper. The footballers are on an end-of-season break. It's mid-June and the 2018 World Cup in Russia kicked off a few days ago. Torras tells me the futsal cadets (the under-14s) are about to start a session in preparation for the crucial national championships, a last-minute rehearsal of tactics and set plays, in and out of possession. The links to the DNA of football are clear, says Torras. 'At this stage of the season, we will work a lot on real situations that you can find with the rival and the match,' he explains. Unfortunately, a change in the training schedule means the session is delayed by an hour; we wanted to watch it all, but stay only for the warm-up before heading back to Barcelona to watch England's opening World Cup match against Tunisia on television. It's just three days after Spain kicked off their football World Cup campaign with a 3–3 draw against Portugal and their hat-trick hero Cristiano Ronaldo.

Before we head off I'm keen to discover how Torras views the two codes. First, he says, at Barcelona it's about adapting the 'three Ps' Carmona speaks about. 'It is not easy because of the smaller space and the speed and pressure of the game,' he says. 'We always want to dominate the ball more than the rival, and if we do not have it, we press to make it ours. But you have to know how to manage when you do not have it, and hurt the opponent in one of the situations that most occur in the futsal, which are counter-attacks.' It seems to be working for Barcelona. Since Torras returned to the club in 2010, the futsal first team have not once failed to finish in the top three of the Liga Nacional Fútbol Sala, sharing all nine titles up to 2020 with Ricardinho's rampant Inter Movistar. In the absence of a team from Real Madrid FC, who flirted with establishing a futsal team in the mid-1980s, this rivalry is the equivalent of the Madrid v Barça duopoly in football. In 2019, Barcelona recaptured the title from Inter after five years, with Barça's Brazilian pivot Ferrão leading the way. Although Torras excelled for both teams, his heart is in his hometown club. Just as his affection is plainly for futsal, rather than the eleven-a-side game.

'When I was twelve years old I competed in futsal and soccer,' he recalls. These days the RFEF decrees that kids aged eleven and over cannot play both sports. Torras says the decision to pursue futsal alone was easy for him. 'I could see that I had a better time in futsal, more dynamic, tactical and being in a reduced field you had to think before others. That made me continue in futsal, simply for these reasons. To this day, I think the same.'

* * *

The cultural significance of the sport that won Torras's affections merits locating in a wider historical context. The author Jimmy Burns explains how the militaristic fervour imposed by General

Franco between 1939 and the 1970s ensured Spain's footballing culture was defined by aggression, fight and nationalistic pride. In his excellent book *La Roja: How Soccer Conquered Spain and how Spanish Soccer Conquered the World*, Burns quotes the Falangist newspaper *Arriba* in 1939, a few months after the Spanish Civil War:

> The *furia española* is present in all aspects of Spanish life, to a greater extent than ever. In sport, the *furia* best manifests itself in soccer, a game in which the virility of the Spanish race can find full expression, usually imposing itself, in international contests, over the more technical but less aggressive foreign teams.

'Neither skill nor creativity, let alone fair play, was part of the armoury,' affirms Burns. It was all about the fury. In the mid-1970s, this potent yet futile aggression began to give way to finesse – or at least a craving for more subtlety – at a time when Spain was seeking a different route.

The very first incarnation of *fútbol sala* in Spain emerged in the early 1970s. In keeping with the origins of the sport in Uruguay and Brazil, the Spanish birthplace was Club YMCA in Madrid, the experiment inspired by a proselytiser from South America, an expert Chilean coach called Eduardo Tapia. One of the Spaniards instantly hooked in was António Alberca, who went on to lead the Federación Española de Fútbol Sala (FEFS), which was eventually ousted as a controller of the governance of the game at the inception of the LNFS in 1989. In the first official competitive *fútbol sala* in Spain – a four-team tournament in 1974 – Club YMCA, coached by Tapia, competed against Atlético Peñarol from Montevideo – the original birthplace of the game – and veteran footballers from Madrid's big two, Atlético and Real. Unsurprisingly, a Real Madrid select squad comprising Alfredo Di Stefano and Ferenc Puskás, among others,

stormed to victory as a crowd reportedly 12,000-strong looked on in wonder at the new arrival on the footballing scene, in the dying days of the Franco dictatorship. Like the nation's political order – 'transitioning' to democracy from 1975 onwards after Franco's death – so Spanish football culture entered the throes of realignment, with the small, beguiling *fútbol sala* about to play a much bigger role.

By the turn of the decade, the first nationwide tournament had been won by Interviú Hora XXV, a club founded in 1977 by a journalist, José María García, who named it after the two places he worked, *Interviú* weekly magazine and *Hora XXV*, a nightly news series on the radio station Cadena SER. The roll call of impeccably connected players guaranteed the club and the sport precious airtime and column inches. García recruited fellow journalists to play alongside garlanded former professional footballers, most notably Portugal's majestic Eusébio and Amancio Amaro, the recently retired Real Madrid and Spain winger nicknamed *El Brujo* (The Wizard). But it was García himself who stole the show most games. A strong and predatory goalscorer, he wore the number nine shirt and added to the rich tapestry of talent on show. Other media organisations, including the newspapers *Marca*, *ABC* and *El País*, formed teams to compete against Interviú and Club YMCA.

The victory that sealed the first national league title came on 28 June 1980, in the Antonio Magariños pavilion in Madrid. Interviú-Hora XXV defeated Valencia Disco 5–4, an extra-time goal by the former Real Madrid defender José Luis López Peinado capping a stirring comeback. The Spanish newspaper *Marca*'s match report declared that the 'crowded stands of Magariños' proved *fútbol sala* was a sport that 'every day has more followers'. The club's name subsequently changed to Interviú Lloyd's, and then Interviú Boomerang. Former Caja Segovia coach Jesús Candelas oversaw an era of prolonged success under the latter name, collecting more than twenty trophies, including four consecutive LNFS titles and two UEFA Futsal

Cups, between 2001 and 2006. Under Candelas, *La Máquina Verde* (The Green Machine) blended homegrown talent, notably goalkeeper Luis Amado and inspirational captain Julio, with imported flair in the form of fearsome pivot Marquinho, revered *universal* Schumacher – born Flávio Sérgio Viana in São Paulo but later renamed after the German football keeper Harald Schumacher due to his similar mop of curly hair – and Spain's naturalised Brazilian goalscoring winger, Daniel. Refashioned as Inter Movistar in 2008, the club enjoyed another era of success under Jesús Velasco, who built a team around his own Portuguese-speaking import, Ricardinho.

Nearly 400 miles east of Madrid, the other big outpost at the heart of this quest for a new direction in the 1980s was Barcelona. Just as in Italy, where tennis served to propel *calcio a 5*'s rapid rise, another unlikely source proved instrumental here: hockey. Specifically, a pioneering German coach called Horst Wein, who had published a groundbreaking book, *The Science of Hockey*, a decade or so earlier. In 1986, the studious Hannover-born Wein, holder of a degree in physical education, delivered a talk to Barcelona coaches keen to explore his theories about the importance of game intelligence and learning through realistic small-sided games. A fascinated Carles Rexach, the renowned Barça youth coach who went on to become Johan Cruyff's first-team assistant, encouraged Wein to extend his influence. The RFEF embraced the games-based approach to coaching, allied with its acceptance of futsal as a viable game to enthuse primary-school age children, and published Wein's seminal youth coaching manual *Fútbol a la Medida del Niño* (Football to the Measure of the Child) under its own banner in 1993. The term *funiño* – an amalgamation of fun and *niño* (child) – became a byword for Spanish youth football culture around the same time *fútbol* and *sala* were being merged to form 'futsal'. Wein's bold approach – he later described children's eleven-a-side football as 'a cancer' – has since been largely adopted by most football associations around the

world, though some much sooner than others. The stipulation that children under six should simply play with a ball at home and from seven to nine should only play three-v-three was revolutionary. After progressing to five-, seven- and eight-a-side games, only at the age of fourteen are children thrust on to the giant spaces of an eleven-a-side pitch. 'The soccer children play should fit them perfectly like their shoes,' he once said. 'Kids of eight years are very different from ten, twelve or fourteen year-olds, they should play different, age-appropriate games.'[31]

At the same time Wein was making waves in Barcelona, *fútbol sala* was growing more conspicuous in the towns and cities of newly democratic Spain. The transformation in the late 1980s manifested itself as a euphoric end to the messy divisions in the small-sided game's governance structures, a landmark rapprochement between two competing leagues triggering the formation of the Liga Nacional Fútbol Sala in 1989. The resistance in Catalonia of FIFUSA die-hards to the FIFA league did not disappear. In 2019, the sight of the Catalan national futsal team proudly bellowing out their anthem, *Els Segadors* (The Reapers), before a game against Colombia in the AMF world championship third-place play-off in Misiones, Argentina, is testimony to this fact. Catalonia's 8–0 defeat marked a high point for the team as their opponents, *Los Cafeteros*, bid farewell to the AMF game's best ever player, Jhon Jairo Pinilla. The left-footed wizard of the non-FIFA game known variously as *El Maestro* (Teacher), *Zorro* (the Fox) or simply 'the Messi of futsal', and who had a high-earning stint in the Italian FIFA-affiliated Serie A in the mid-2000s, notched a hat-trick aged thirty-eight in his retirement match. Along with Paraguay, the longtime base of the AMF, Colombia is perhaps the country most associated with this minor version of the game. While

---

31. Interview with *Success in Soccer*, found on Wein's website: http://www.horstwein.net/articles-in-english/

Pinilla is its most famous *hijo* (son), Jaime Arroyave is the man known widely as *El Papá* (the father) for his role in creating what is called *microfútbol* in Colombia. A youth football guru, who later coached Bogotá football giants Millionarios Fútbol Club, Arroyave imported *futebol de salão* to Colombia after witnessing it first-hand in São Paulo in 1966. A long-time critic of FIFA's role in the game, the eighty eight year-old Arroyave – whose 1928 birthday pre-dates the game itself – continued his condemnation of the federation's '*un plagio indebido*' (improper plagiarism) of *microfútbol* in an interview with *El Espectador* newspaper in 2016, when they held the World Cup in his homeland. Despite the consternation off the court, on it the FIFA brand of *Los Cafeteros* – led by the mesmeric number ten known as the 'James Rodríguez of futsal', Angellot Caro – progressed to the last sixteen before being eliminated by Paraguay.

It's little surprise that an AMF presence remains strong in the long-restive autonomous province in north-east Spain: the organisation's fiercely held independence from football's world governing body echoes Catalonia's historic and passionate desire to defy and separate from ruling Spain. Catalonia is not just about men's futsal, of course. In fact, the women's team affiliated to the AMF was founded a few months earlier than the men's in 2004. In football, the Catalan men's team began playing fixtures in 1905, attracting the biggest eleven-a-side stars to wear the symbolic red and yellow stripes in occasional fixtures ever since. Among the willing Catalan recruits are the Barcelona midfield metronomes Xavi and Iniesta, and even Pep Guardiola – who was famously fined £20,000 by the English FA in 2018 for wearing a yellow ribbon on his sweater in solidarity with the Catalan independence movement while on the touchline as Manchester City manager.

In FIFA futsal, the resounding success of the LNFS after it kicked off in 1989 inspired the grassroots. By 1992, 150,000 players and 5,000 teams were registered, 60 per cent of them adults and

40 per cent youths. A women's national league followed in 1994 and a women's national team three years later. By the time Jordi Torras established himself in the Fútbol Sala Martorell first team in 2003, the LNFS was one of three hugely successful national leagues operating independently of the national football association. (Brazil and Russia were the others.) In 2000, the Spanish men's team finally smashed Brazil's monopoly of the world championship by defeating the *seleção* 4–3 in a dramatic final in Guatemala. The repeat victory in 2004 confirmed the pre-eminence of the Spanish way, with a thriving, professional independent *fútbol sala* league at the top, and a dedication to *funiño* and futsal with the youths. No longer a country obsessed with fury, Spain set out on the path to tiki-taka greatness – and world glory in the eleven-a-side game. The man leading the futsal team, Javier Lozano, spoke at the time of the 'collective virtues' of the men's squad. 'The team performance is always higher than the sum of its component parts,' he said in the first edition of the *UEFA Technician* coaching magazine, which was devoted solely to futsal. 'That's how we've managed to beat sides who are better than us.'

The magazine also carried an editorial from Andy Roxburgh, the Scottish technical director of UEFA at the time, lauding the 'remarkable creativity' in futsal as a game in its own right as well as 'developing players for eleven-a-side'. Flagging up Spain's bespoke approach, Lozano told the magazine children in Spain played both sports until their teens, when a choice was made. 'They just go into different rooms in the same building,' he said. The futsal 'room' has continued to attract players. A 2018 study found that nearly two million people – of a population of 46.6 million – played the game, a total of 9.6 per cent of the twenty million participating in sport of any kind. It was the second most popular sport, after football, among children aged six to eighteen. The sweet spot was fifteen to twenty-four, the age group playing it most often. In 2015, 14.2 per cent of all people in Spain who played sport participated in futsal, with just

under 7.6 per cent at least once a week. Lozano's roving, versatile coaching nous ensured he grew well acquainted with the furnishings and layout of the different rooms. In 2002, as futsal world champion coach he was drafted in to assist Spain's football team head coach, José Antonio Camacho, at the football World Cup. And in 2007, after leading Spain to the second futsal world title, the small-sided specialist answered Real Madrid's call, taking on a senior first-team football role along with duties overseeing the youth section. He returned to the futsal 'room' in 2009 as president of the LNFS.

Since the 2018 study, the layout of the figurative house suddenly changed when the league, led with aplomb by Lozano, was seized unceremoniously by the RFEF. In a coup mired in legal wrangles, the LNFS lost control of the national leagues and cup competitions. The federation's claim that no legally binding agreement between the clubs and the league had been signed since 2013 met fierce resistance from the LNFS, with rival names in the game lining up on opposing sides. It was a crisis for the league that Jordi Torras credits with growing the global game while churning out stars such as Spain's double World Cup-winning *fixo* Kike Boned and goalkeeper Luis Amado, plus Portugal's Ricardinho ('the one who has evolved the most', according to Torras). Kike, the 180-cap stalwart of Spain's two World Cup victories, stood up in defence of LNFS independence. Speaking as executive vice-president of ElPozo Murcia, the club he captained and played for over 500 times, Kike told Marca.com he was 'sad, disappointed and outraged' by the RFEF's incursion. He was joined in defence of the league's independence by Lozano.

The upheaval was all the more marked because it came weeks after the league celebrated its thirtieth anniversary by asking fans to select the strongest five players in its history. Kike was named the best *fixo*, edging out the man who succeeded him as most-capped player in Spain's history in 2020, Inter Movistar's Carlos Ortiz. Javi Rodríguez (Barcelona) and Ortiz's teammate Ricardinho were granted the

accolade of best *alas* of all time. The pivot role went to the Spanish-Brazilian *Maravilla*, Paulo Roberto. Although named as Kike's teammate in the putative all-time best quintet, the goalkeeper Luis Amado stood very much in opposition to the ElPozo legend in the off-court battle for control of the Spanish game. The RFEF's takeover 'coming out' party in early 2020 was led by Pedro Rocha, president of the Comité Nacional de Fútbol Sala (CNFS), with Amado and his successor as Spain's goalkeeping supremo, Paco Sedano, in support alongside José Venancio López Hierro, CNFS technical director. Outlining grand ambitions to upgrade the women's league, backed by €1m of funding, and to overhaul the Copa de España, long seen as the pinnacle of the men's game, they also vowed to plough more resources into youth talent identification.

The final declaration, an abiding mission of futsal for a generation, made gaining Olympic status for the sport an urgent priority. Venancio López, the man who led the RFEF's games-based approach to coaching, committed to hosting a global congress to finally gain full recognition from the International Olympic Committee. Nonetheless, the traumatic bout of infighting, after thirty years of independent navigation, left the good ship LNFS suddenly entering choppy and uncharted waters, with plenty of talk about the exciting journey ahead, but precious few guarantees.

CHAPTER 15
IRAN, ASIA, AFRICA AND THE FUTSAL 'REVOLUTION'

SHAHRZAD MOZAFAR IS a young girl sitting in her bedroom, dreaming. Sheltering from the sun that beats down on her parched neighbourhood in Khuzestan province, south-western Iran, she's in full escapism mode, doing what she loves. Outside the four walls of her suburban home, the revolution that dethroned the Shah has also thrown the country – and families like Shahrzad's – into a turmoil that will lead to a bloody and prolonged war with neighbouring Iraq. On this particular day, though, Shahrzad is seeking solace in the love of her life: football. It's a love that's forbidden, according to the prohibitive strictures imposed by the newly powerful conservative clerics heading the Islamic Republic. When she's not kicking a ball about with her sisters in her family garden, she's inside watching football on television. Often doing what she's doing this very day: dreaming football dreams, her mind playing games through so she can commentate on the figurative action, her every word of dramatic monologue captured on tape with a small cassette recorder. It's an outlet for a sport-crazy girl who turned eight at the height of the 1978–9 revolution, a secret indulgence in a country where modesty laws preclude millions of females from any sporting activity by insisting on the wearing of the headscarf in public.

To her parents, it was no great surprise. They knew she was obsessed. 'When my father listened, he loved it,' Mozafar recalls, nearly four decades on. 'He asked me how I could do it without watching any game and just by imagining!' Her proud parents kept the tape for years, eagerly playing it for visitors whenever they could. It was their 'fantastic' support that fanned the flames of her clandestine love affair with football – one that eventually led to a transformative career in futsal that elevates Mozafar as a twenty-first century role model for women in the Islamic world. After she blazed a trail coaching the first Iran women's football team – 'being pioneer of anything that didn't exist before is not easy' – she led the nation's futsal team to the 2018 Asian Football Confederation (AFC) women's title, gaining nominations above esteemed male tacticians for best coach in the world along the way. Mozafar then moved on to lead Kuwait's national women's futsal team and sat proudly in 2019 as the only female coaching instructor in FIFA and the AFC, championing the cause of the women's game from within.

Her life charts the course of sporting history in a country synonymous with clashes between faith and culture. Her back story intertwines with the roots of women's football and futsal, and the growth of the sports in areas of the world where passion flowered too vibrantly to be suppressed. Her journey also highlights futsal's specific role in the stubborn rise of women's sport in Iran, the Middle East and the wider Muslim world. For Mozafar, the resistance she symbolises started early. 'The passion of football was born with me,' she explains. 'I loved football. From the beginning. I have been looking for a ball my whole life. I can remember watching the World Cup in 1982 in Spain. I cried all night when Brazil lost against Italy.'

Mozafar was not alone. A more collective form of female resistance dismantled a huge and significant barrier in 1993, a little over a decade after the political earthquake had deposed the Shah and imposed faith-led restrictions on female sporting activity. The

game-changers were the sport-mad students at Alzahra University in Tehran, the only all-women university in the country. They decided enough was enough. Amid soaring numbers of women becoming educated in the Islamic Republic, the students brought more than a decade of forced abstinence to a halt by compelling the university's administrators to allow a groundbreaking unofficial futsal tournament that attracted nine other college teams. It was nothing short of a cultural revolution that revived female sport. Just like Mozafar, many of the women desperate to play had seen the game snatched away from them as children. The early 1970s had brought girls on to the streets playing alongside boys, with the female game gaining formal acceptance when one of Tehran's biggest clubs, Taj Football Club, started officially training women. The abrupt end to this momentum post-revolution was reflected in the decision by the new government's Physical Education Organisation to take control of the club and change its name from the monarchist Taj, which means 'crown' in Persian, to Esteghlal, which translates as 'independence'. The club's first-team success continued on the pitch, but the women's game was relegated to the periphery. The downturn continued until the Alzahra women intervened.

By 1997, the powerful Physical Education Organisation had formed a futsal committee that eventually sanctioned an official female universities futsal competition involving more than a hundred students in twelve teams. 'For authorities, futsal was a palatable solution for women,' writes Timothy F. Grainey in his book *Beyond Bend it Like Beckham: The Global Phenomenon of Women's Soccer*. 'They could play in an indoor facility where men could easily be locked out. In this way university officials and players were not contravening sharia law.'

For Mozafar, it's been a lifetime of overcoming obstacles in a nation where football and futsal were forbidden for her from the age of eight to twenty-eight. She pursued the game wherever she could. 'When I was a kid and watching the football games on television, I wasn't just a viewer,' she recalls. 'I liked to discuss the games after they finished with my friends and cousins for many hours. I loved to be a coach since I was a kid.' Her experience of Iran's national pastime of street football, *gol koochik*, which means 'small goal' in Persian, brought despair and hope in equal measure. The revolution might have stopped her playing, but it did not halt *gol koochik*. Nor did the subsequent war with Saddam Hussein's US-backed Iraqi regime, a conflict estimated to have killed at least one million people.[32] Mozafar describes the scene on the dusty streets of cities such as the capital, Tehran, not too dissimilar to the one I lived out in north Liverpool at the time, almost 3,000 miles away. 'Many boys were playing,' she remembers. 'In that time the big cities in Iran were not too crowded and you could find some calm streets. They made a goal with bricks or stones and sometimes used parked cars as a goal. If the ball went under the car, it was a goal. The plastic ball they used to play with was made for children . . . it was a toy, actually. So because it was very light, they cut it with a knife to make a slot then they put another one inside to make it heavy and call it two-layers ball. If they were so professional, they made three-layers ball!

'They would play two-v-two, three-v-three, four-v-four, etc. In some neighbourhoods, this was more serious and they painted the street to indicate the dimensions and also made small goals with metal. They also held tournaments in their neighborhoods and would invite teams from other areas to play. They had lots of spectators, including me.' Watching wasn't enough though. She craved playing, and once her family relocated to Tehran for safety when she was a teenager at the height of the war, she found an outlet – and a further safe haven – in an alternative sport: volleyball. She

---

32. https://www.theguardian.com/world/2010/sep/23/iran-iraq-war-anniversary

represented the national team for a decade from the age of eighteen until futsal started in earnest, quitting volleyball for her first love – while fully aware that, at twenty-nine, she was too old to start a new life as a player. Coaching offered the solution. In the early 2000s – 'we had no football yet, just futsal' – she immersed herself in tactics and learning as head coach with various clubs while assisting the coach for the national women's futsal team, which played its first match in October 2001.

In 2005, she received a shock offer to drop futsal and lead the newly formed Iran national football team, which had been invited to the West Asian Football Games by Jordan – which was also initiating a women's team. Although the Tehran club Taj had run a club side as a de facto national team in the mid-1970s, this would be Iran's first truly national team. Daunted at first, Mozafar was soon persuaded by Khadejeh Sepanji, the head of women's football in the Iran Football Federation. It was a rollercoaster ride. 'I was thirty-five, with no football coaching background, and there was no football league or any other football activities. In other words, we didn't have any football players.' With just weeks to put together a squad, she followed her instincts and recruited the futsal players she knew. 'They couldn't even make long and high passes because they had never played on grass before,' she admits. But after a few intensive training sessions, the first Iranian women's football team made it to the Games, clinching the runners-up spot behind the hosts, Jordan, after beating Syria, Bahrain and Palestine. 'This was the beginning of the road of football in my country,' she says. During the next five years, she combined club futsal with her national football duties, winning five titles with various futsal teams in the popular new national league.

The successful 2010 mission to the Youth Olympic Games in Singapore proved to be her last footballing foray. After leading the national team to fourth place, and earning a nomination from AFC for the best coach in Asia, she was lured into the national futsal team set-up, a decision forced upon her when the Iranian Football Federation ordered her to choose between the two sports. It was not the most difficult decision, she says. 'Iran was pioneer in futsal in Asia,' she says, whereas in football it was lagging way behind its Asian rivals. 'So I decided to focus on futsal and let my dreams come true through it.'

Mozafar's driving passion to further the cause of Muslim sportswomen in Iran is shared by Faezeh Hashemi, the daughter of one of the founding fathers of the republic, Akbar Rafsanjani. In the same year that the students at Alzhara University made their futsal breakthrough, Hashemi confirmed her reputation as a strident champion of women's rights by initiating the Women's Islamic Games. While her father, seen as a pragmatist among the throng of hardline Islamic conservatives vying for power, was running the country as fourth president of the republic, the outspoken Hashemi was busy pitching for women's rights, increasing access for women keen to swim, play tennis and golf. One of her early successes was helping create female bike paths in the capital's parks. The Games came about once Hashemi widened her gaze, seeking to allow athletes in Muslim countries to sample the international competition forbidden due to the strict dress codes. As head of the Islamic Women's Sports Federation, and a prominent member of the Iranian parliament, she founded a women's newspaper (it was closed down after a year) and initiated a more sustained era of female sporting participation in the Muslim world. Futsal played a significant part in the breakthrough. Introduced for the 2001 Islamic Games – the same year the first female university league kicked off – futsal was included in the schedule once again in 2005, the last time the Games were held. In 2018, the Iranian minister of sports and youth affairs, Masoud Soltanifar, announced his desire to restart the Games. For Hashemi, the dogged activism continued: the perpetual thorn in the side of the conservative hardliners was jailed for six months in 2012, after being found guilty of spreading anti-regime propaganda.

* * *

Rimla Akhtar is another Muslim woman responsible for pushing back boundaries in the Islamic world. Unlike Mozafar and Hashemi, she is not a daughter of the Islamic Republic. Born to Pakistani parents in west London, Akhtar was a nineteen-year-old Imperial College London chemistry student in 2001 when she donned her futsal shoes to play for Great Britain, the first non-Muslim nation to compete in the Hashemi-inspired Women's Islamic Games. She was one of a nineteen British athletes out in Iran competing in futsal and badminton. Organised by *Muslim News*, a London-based publication catering for the British Muslim community, the players were given £2,000 by the UK Foreign Office towards the cost of the kit. Britain was one of twenty-five countries taking part, the original total of forty nations having dwindled in the weeks before the tournament due to security concerns in the region, in the aftermath of the September 11 terrorist attacks in the United States. Against a backdrop of violent conflict and angst fuelled by religious fundamentalism, the British team embarked on a mission to bust stereotypes about Muslim women and sport.

Akhtar spoke at the time of her pride at representing Britain. 'It's great that Muslim women can get together like this. It's against all the stereotypes that everyone has about us.' Shaheen Mohammed, another British player, had to take time off from her role as an analyst with a London law firm to play. 'We are very lucky to be here,' she told the *Guardian* at the time. 'It's all about participation. Many Muslims don't have access to this kind of event.' Nearly a decade later, Akhtar would play an instrumental part in another historic moment for Muslim women in sport.

On this occasion the groundswell of dissent from the grassroots was matched by convulsions of outrage at the top of the Islamic government. The object of the collective derision? FIFA. Specifically, its decision in 2007 to ban the hijab – a potent symbol of Islamic life for women that was worn while playing sport to meet the strict Islamic dress code laws meaning they must have all their skin covered. Tracksuit bottoms, long-sleeved shirts and the hijab, or headscarf, allowed girls and women to submit to the lawmakers while indulging their passion for the game. FIFA's hugely controversial order came about after Asmahan Mansour, an eleven-year-old Canadian girl from Ontario, was told by a referee at a tournament in the Québécois city of Laval that the covering was not allowed on the pitch. FIFA upheld the impromptu ruling as an official ban on the grounds that 'religious symbolism' was outlawed in sport. Once the justification was smashed by citing the widespread display of religious tattoos and crucifixes on football fields in both the men's and women's game, FIFA rowed back – but maintained the ruling, recalibrating its reasoning as a health and safety concern instead. The ban killed off many footballing dreams, including those of the Iran female football team, who forfeited their chance to make the 2012 London Olympics by pulling out of a qualification match after they were stopped from wearing Islamic headgear. Meanwhile, the Iranian president, Mahmoud Ahmadinejad, voiced the growing frustration with FIFA by branding the federation's decision-makers 'dictators and colonialists' for their actions.

By then chair of the UK's Muslim Women's Sport Foundation, Rimla Akhtar fought hard to overturn the ban, calling it 'one of my proudest moments', and proceeded to gain a place on the English FA's influential council, where she can bang the drum for Muslim male and female participation in football and futsal while rejoicing, as a Liverpool FC fan, in the presence of Mo Salah as a Muslim role model at the top of the Premier League. The pressure brought to bear over the hijab ban by Akhtar and many other campaigners over several years eventually told, with FIFA finally relenting in 2014. Three years later the journey from outlawed garb to fully customisable fashionable kit accessory was complete when Nike launched its own range of hijab complete with fetching trademark swoosh.

* * *

Shahrzad Mozafar recognises the role Iranian women have played in the massive geopolitical shift in attitudes towards the status of females over two decades. 'The FIFA decision was a very big success, not only for Iranian women but also for Muslim women all over the world,' she says proudly. 'The main reason Iran was very firm about this matter was that all members of the team should have the hijab, and if FIFA didn't accept that, Iran would be out of all tournaments for ever.' Iran's players simply needed to be seen, their presence in tournaments giving 'the other Muslim girls self-confidence and courage to come out and play with no shame'. Any 'shame' turned to raucous celebration when Iran's futsal team, led by Mozafar's predecessor as head coach, Forouzan Soleimani, secured the first ever Asian Football Confederation women's futsal title in 2015, a feat repeated in 2018, thrusting Mozafar and Iranian women to the pinnacle of the sport in Asia. While the 2015 success in Malaysia was a historic achievement, it was also marred by a controversy that rocked the sporting world – and exposed the distance still to travel on the road to equality for women.

Iran's inspirational captain Niloufar Ardalan missed the tournament after her husband refused to allow her to travel, insisting she stayed at home to accompany their seven-year-old son on his first day at school. Nicknamed 'Lady Goal' for her predatory left-footed prowess, the thirty year-old star player's case swiftly became a *cause célèbre* in a nation where husbands can legitimately deny their wives permission to leave the country. Ardalan's distraught teammates rallied in her honour, triumphing in adversity as the outstanding Fereshteh Karimi shone in Ardalan's number seven shirt, sealing the historic title (and the tournament's most valuable player accolade) with the only goal in the final against Japan. The national team's defiance intensified. Ardalan's right to travel with the squad to Guatemala for the women's unofficial world championships later that year was secured after a dramatic eleventh-hour intervention by President Hassan Rouhani to uphold her high-profile challenge to the law.[33]

For Mozafar, who was promoted to national team head coach after the 2015 victory, the historic nature of her role in the futsal team's stark achievements didn't really sink in until minutes after the emphatic repeat victory in the 2018 final, a 5–2 defeat of Japan in Bangkok. 'I was like a marathon runner that crosses the finish line. I had been waiting for that moment for many years and had seen it in my dreams several times. I had a very light feeling and I wish my father were alive to see it.' It was a huge victory in the quest for equality of treatment in Iran for the women's game, and put the team at the forefront of the global sport, ready to compete whenever FIFA finally launches a women's World Cup. The prospect of Mozafar's young stars competing with the likes of Brazil, led by the best player in the world, Amandinha, and Europe's strongest teams, Spain and Portugal, was an enticing one for Asia's strongest nation. 'Nobody could ignore the champion any more,' recalls Mozafar. Or so she thought.

---

33. The Niloufar Ardalan case is believed to be the inspiration for Sohail Beiraghi's evocative 'fact-based' film *Cold Sweat*, which charts the fictitious Iranian futsal captain Afrooz's fight for justice after being banned from attending AFC finals by her husband, and caused a stir among Iran's hardline clerics, who accused the director of undermining family values after its release in 2018.

Donald Trump's residency at the White House changed the state of play. Iran's 2018 AFC victory came just over a year after the new US president's tenure began. Within a year, Trump had imposed harsh economic sanctions on Tehran after abruptly abandoning the 2015 nuclear deal. Described by Iran's President Rouhani as an act of 'economic war', the sanctions devastated the country's economy, taking a wrecking ball to the fragile structure of women's futsal and imposing the sort of neglect Mozafar had hoped that the double AFC crown would safeguard against. Beset by stasis and sanctions in Iran, Mozafar departed for Kuwait, where she sought to replicate the success in her homeland, by developing a culture of female futsal from the youngest girls to the adult national team. Without a head coach, the Iranian team laboured on the court in the Victory Day Women Cup tournament, held annually by Russia to mark the anniversary of the end of the Second World War, when they lost heavily to all three opponents: Spain, Portugal and the hosts. 'Women's sports have always suffered from lack of money and budget,' Mozafar tells me. 'This is a global issue. I always wanted to put my full time and energy on futsal, but I couldn't because coaching never would provide me enough money itself.' Women's futsal – and football – should be professional, she says, so players and coaches can devote all their energy to the game. Hossein Shams, the former men's national team coach seen as the 'grandfather' of Iranian futsal, is much more forthright on the impact of futsal's status as the poor relation to football, the relative poverty of the women's game and the dire impact of sanctions. Speaking to me in 2019, shortly after Mozafar's move to Kuwait the previous year, he says the women's game is suffering most as the sponsors desert futsal and devote precious resources to football, volleyball and basketball.

It's not just the women's game that's being left behind. The men's futsal league is now 'very weak', he warns. 'The players and coaches are very angry and they left the country.' About a hundred players fled Iran after the sanctions hit. 'The money in Iran is very weak. The players have left for Tajikistan, Azerbaijan, Uzbekistan, China, Lebanon, Iraq and other countries.' It's a clear example of the Iranian players' similarity to the Brazilians – as Marquinhos Xavier pointed out – ready, willing and able to transport their huge futsal talents abroad. Shams cites one of Iran's greatest players ever, the national futsal team captain Ali Asghar Hassanzadeh. In 2018 he left Iran's Mes Sungun, where he had just won the AFC Futsal Club Championship, to join Shenzhen Nanling Tielang in China. 'It's a very good salary,' explains Shams. 'More than $10,000 for one month . . . with bonus, it will be $15,000 a month. It's much more than in Iran.' The exodus – starting in 2016 with winger Hossein Tayyebi's switch from Tasisat Daryaei in Tehran to Leo Higuita's Kazakh champions Kairat Almaty – reflects badly on the federation's priorities, insists Shams. 'In all countries, the big money goes to football. It is the same in the Iranian federation. All the money goes to the men's football team, and very little to the women's game and futsal.'

A few weeks after Shams spoke to me, the former Manchester United and Portugal coach Carlos Queiroz left his post as head coach of Iran's national football team after guiding Team Melli to two consecutive World Cup tournaments. His replacement, the former Belgium national team coach Marc Wilmots, quit acrimoniously just seven months later. It's clear that sport in Iran was in a state of flux at the end of the second decade of the twenty-first century. The pressure exerted by FIFA on Iran to lift its longstanding ban on women attending most male sporting events also intensified in late 2019, when twenty-nine year-old Sahar Khodayari died after setting herself alight in fear of a long jail sentence while awaiting trial for attending a football match at the Azadi stadium in Tehran dressed as a man. The death of the so-called 'blue girl' – named after the colours of her beloved Esteghlal team – incited an outpouring of anger against gender inequality in Iran. A month later, a glimmer of hope came when women were allowed into a stadium to watch a men's football match for the first time since 1981. A few thousand female fans packed a segregated section of the Azadi Stadium, celebrating as Iran beat Cambodia 14–0 in a qualifier for the 2022 World Cup.

This sliver of progress cannot disguise the threat to the fragile women's game, brought on by the sanctions. The men's game, with the national team long known as the 'kings of Asian futsal', stands higher, with arguably much further to fall. Shams orchestrated the team's ascent to prominence in the early days, after accepting the call from the Iranian federation to switch from football to futsal in 1997 – just as Mozafar did a few years later. His first stint as national team coach set the ball rolling on Iran's dominance of the AFC futsal championships, the victory in the inaugural 1999 tournament swiftly followed by six consecutive titles. Shams returned to national team duty in 2006 to thrust Team Melli on to the world stage, clinching fifth place at the 2008 World Cup in Brazil, with the iconic pivot and record goalscorer, Vahid Shamsaei, captaining the side. 'It surprised the futsal world,' Shams says.

The figurative high point for the men's game came after Shams had returned to club coaching. And it was accompanied by the literal elevation of the Brazilian futsal superstar Falcão. The date was 20 September 2016, the location Coliseo Bicentenario, in Bucaramanga, Colombia, and it was the victorious Team Melli futsal squad who held the Brazilian star aloft on court, cheering and celebrating, in a show of respect for the retiring giant of the game after Iran had stunned Brazil by knocking them out of the World Cup on penalties, a triumph that preceded a third-place play-off victory over Ricardinho's Portugal. In the shadow of the towering Andes mountains, Iran's long, arduous trek had reached a new pinnacle. They were the third strongest team in the world. Shams laughs loudly with pride. 'It was amazing for Iran. Amazing,' he roars. 'People were very surprised around the world. But it was a great result for us. It was a victory against the best team in world. All the Iranian people were very happy.'

The popularity of the game in Iran is staggering. About sixteen million people – men, women and children – play futsal regularly, according to Shams, a figure that eclipses the other huge futsal-playing nations, Brazil and Spain. 'They have together only twelve million,' he says. It's clear that Iran has a long-established and passionate futsal culture, from the streets to the schools and universities. Shams says that of the fourteen million students in schools and universities, 8.7 million males and females play futsal. Despite the uncertainty since Mozafar's departure, Shams insists the advances made by the women's game will not be lost. 'The Iranian girls will be at the front of the female game around the world,' he says.

The most successful coach in Iranian futsal history is quick to identify the roots of the success as being 'without coaches, of course': it's the *gol koochik* culture dominant in Iranian cities for decades, on the streets where Shahrzad Mozafar was forced to stand and watch as a young girl. 'Futsal came from street football,' he says. 'It is very famous here. All players before going to grass, they play in the street. This is the football foundation of futsal. People go to the street, then to futsal. Then afterwards they select football or futsal.' It's the same three-stage journey so successful in Brazil – first the street, then the futsal courts, before a pathway is selected at the football/futsal crossroads. Despite the tragic fate of the 'blue girl' and the continued financial upheaval reflecting an Islamic Republic hobbled by geopolitical and socio-cultural issues, the revolutionary game of futsal – backed by its own vocal and adaptable advocates – seems too deeply entrenched in the culture for its continued growth to be thwarted.

* * *

'Iran in the west and Japan in the east was where it all started,' Steve Harris tells me, adding a layer of context to the massive growth of futsal in Asia. Japan's rise in the game runs parallel with the life of its biggest male star, Benfica's gifted *ala* Rafael Katsutoshi Henmi. Born in 1992, the year the football J League kicked off, the young Rafael moved to Brazil with his family aged two, in the year the Japanese Futsal Federation was formed once Harris, the long-time Japanese futsal administrator, and his mentor, Takao Sakae, officially severed ties with the remnants of FIFUSA. When Henmi returned to Japan in 2008 as a teenager imbued with *sendo livre* flair, Japan's prominence in the game was established. While shining less brightly than the Asian continent's most luminous star, Hossein Shams's Iran, the Samurai Blue ascended quickly in the firmament having broken Iran's stranglehold in Asia by winning the AFC championship in 2006. On the world stage, the Japanese reached the last sixteen in the 2012 World Cup, their prominence confirmed by the arrival of Ricardinho for his lucrative stint at Nagoya Oceans in 2010.

If Henmi became Japanese futsal's most famous offspring, the forebears of the game can be traced back to 1974, when an anthropologist from Sapporo University, Professor Shibata, returned from a trip to Brazil – the source of Henmi's inspiration – after witnessing *futebol de salão* in person. With a rule book in hand, the professor embarked on a mission to spread the game, his legacy Hokkaido's status as a hive of futsal activity nearly five decades on. Harris sees the passion for futsal in Japan as a neat cultural fit. 'When you think about traditional Japanese culture, you think about the architecture, how refined and aesthetics things are. Mastery is a Japanese thing. Whether it's football or futsal, they recognise straight away. This is mastery. This is magic. Futsal taps into that mentality.'

Among the forty-seven nations affiliated to federations within the AFC, dozens play yet none are approaching saturation point. Alongside Iran in the Central zone are five of the seven 'stans', along with India and Nepal. Kazakhstan moved to UEFA in 2002, while Pakistan sits in the AFC's South region. In the West, Kuwait, Saudi Arabia and Lebanon lead the way. Japan dominates the East, where the massive untapped futsal promise among China's millions of football-loving youngsters stands out. Finally, in the ASEAN federation, to which Australia has been affiliated since 2006, Thailand, Malaysia and Vietnam head the pile of nascent futsal-playing nations. An indication of the continent's growing clout came in 2013, when Vietnam, led by the globetrotting Italian coach Sergio Gargelli, registered the first victory over Brazil by an Asian nation, edging out the *seleção* 3–2 in a four-team tournament in Ho Chi Minh City. Gargelli had earlier assisted Miguel Rodrigo, the Spanish coach cited by Argentina's Diego Giustozzi as a big influence, in charge of the Japan national team, and in 2018 he took the reins in China. By this time, Rodrigo had moved on to Vietnam, both men further extending the influence of European coaches at the heart of the game in Asia. But in 2020, it's Indonesia, with a population of 260 million, that typifies the potent growth yet to be achieved in the biggest continent on Earth, home to 4.5 billion people. The country's biggest futsal icons – Bayu Saptaji and Ardiansyah Runtuboy – boast 1.2 million Instagram followers between them.

'Futsal is a kind of a hack,' explains Harris. 'It's bringing an end to the limitations of a country and its geography and allowing countries to formalise and give organisation and structure to what is essentially people enjoying football in the most casual possible way.' Asian nations see futsal as 'a vehicle to plug into football culture globally', he says. India gave it a go in 2016. The glitzy Premier Futsal tournament attracted a curious combination of futsal and football superstars, past and present, alongside Indian small-sided players and up-and-coming talents hand-picked by the Brazilian Falcão. With the former Portugal winger Luis Figo as figurehead, the competition proved a hit, orchestrated by Indian entrepreneurs with futsal experts such as England's Doug Reed drafted in as consultants. Former Manchester United stars Ryan Giggs and Paul Scholes joined Falcão and his Brazilian eleven-a-side compatriots Ronaldinho and Cafu on court alongside the former Argentina striker Hernán Crespo. For two years, the tournaments proved freakishly entertaining – but the first nation to truly join the established Asian big hitters of Iran and Japan was Thailand.

In the decade after the Thai men's national team appeared in its first World Cup, Guatemala 2000, the game's popularity and professionalism grew as rapidly as the population, which soared to just under seventy million by 2020. 'The game in Thailand is all about *dern sai*,' says Tachapat 'Ben' Benjasiriwan, the chairman of the biggest futsal team in the country, PTT Chonburi Bluewave. The literal translation of *dern sai* is a walking journey, 'a bit like a musician's road tour', Ben tells me, where players are lured from town to town to play in high-profile tournaments attracting crowds of paying spectators. The game and the tournaments emerged from a street culture. 'It used to be like Brazil here with lots of street futsal on concrete,' explains Ben, the public face of the nine-times champions of the Thai professional league. Aged twenty-seven, he is the son of the timber magnate Adisak Benjasiriwan, who is known nationwide as the guiding figure of futsal in Thailand after bankrolling the formation of the men's national league in 2006, stumping up his own cash to buy the TV rights to secure crucial airtime. The next stage on the pathway to professionalism of the small-sided game – called 'Toh Lek' (small table) in Thailand – was victory in the bid to host the 2012 futsal world championship. It came just four years after another coup: in his other role at the Thai FA, Adisak managed to lure the esteemed Spanish coach of the Galician Santiago Futsal Club, José María Pazos Méndez, aka Pulpis, to lead the national team.

By the time of the World Cup in 2012, the Dutch star of the 1989 FIFA world championship, Vic Hermans, had replaced Pulpis as coach and led the team to the last-sixteen knockout stage. Hermans's vast experience as a national team coach – he led Hong Kong to the second FIFA world championships in 1992 and Malaysia in 1996 – proved invaluable, while he also continued his predecessor's progress in enhancing the quality of the national league. The Thai impact on court was confirmed when the goal of the tournament in 2012 was credited to the man soaking up all this imported coaching expertise and fast becoming an icon of the small-sided game in Asia: the Chonburi Bluewave and Thailand pivot Suphawut Thueanklang.

By 2020, just as the coronavirus pandemic derailed global sport, Thai futsal appeared in rude health, with Panat 'Ter' Kittipanuwong leading the new generation as Chonburi's rising star. Ben tells me the average salary in the largely professional men's league is about $1,500 a month. (The figure for Thai football is about five times higher, he admits.) In 2018, Ben and his father secured a three-year deal to host the annual Intercontinental Cup, bringing the world's biggest club sides to the capital to play before packed crowds in the 12,000-capacity Bangkok Futsal Arena. At the base of the game, Bangkok is also the hotbed, with every school boasting its own futsal court. Elsewhere in the country, Ben tells me it's played in an estimated 60 per cent of schools, usually indoors, but outdoors too, on one of the 1,000-plus concrete courts nationwide. About 3.5 million play regularly – 5 per cent of the population. Ben says the attraction for Thai people is simple: 'It's the feeling that anything can happen. This is the highlight and the charm of futsal. It's why we like Toh Lek.'

* * *

While Asia is fast making the world game a viable tussle between four confederations – the AFC, UEFA, CONMEBOL (South America) and CONCACAF (North and Central America) – the two outliers in terms of participation are Oceania and Africa. In the former, the Solomon Islands rule supreme as the long-dominant force at national team level in the men's game, despite holding the unwanted record of the heaviest defeat in World Cup history – a thumping 31–2 loss to Russia at Brazil 2008. At the grassroots, it's different. The coming nation is New Zealand, where there's an ambitious plan to make futsal the indoor sport of choice in a country where the oval ball dominates every aspect of the cultural landscape. With a sports-mad population of nearly five million, New Zealand's potential dwarfs its Oceania rival. In 2018, with 25,000 registered futsal players in New Zealand, futsal was one of the fastest-growing team sports in the country – especially in secondary schools.

In Africa, the paucity of indoor facilities and infrastructure has stunted progress in all bar the most advanced North African nations. Egypt, Libya and Morocco slug it out as the strongest men's teams. Egypt's youngsters represented the continent in the inaugural futsal tournament at the Youth Olympic Games in 2018. Cameroon made it to the Games to compete in the historic women's event, a sure sign of commitment from a nation with a long history in football. In the men's game, while North African countries dominate, exceptions prevail further south. In 1989, Zimbabwe and Algeria competed in FIFA's inaugural world championships. Despite early promise, the Confederation of African Football (CAF) nations proved resistant to a nascent futsal culture taking root. CAF's late arrival to the futsal party, following the other FIFA confederations by introducing a national team championship for the men's game in 2000, signalled an overdue rise in participation. Between 2006 and the World Cup in 2012, the number of African nations officially playing the game doubled, taking its total to over half of the continent. CAF's decision to intensify its commitment came after only five nations bothered to enter the qualifiers for the 1996 World Cup: Somalia, Ghana, Zimbabwe, Zaire and Egypt, who won the qualifiers to reach their first tournament proper. This success established the Pharaohs as the unofficial kings of Africa, displaying an individualistic one-v-one flair to win the subsequent two African futsal championships and reach the quarter-finals of the 2000 world championship. Since 2008, when Libya stole the Africa Cup of Nations crown, Morocco has emerged as a force, securing the title in 2016 and 2020, and thereby clinching one of the three berths allocated for CAF teams in the 2020 Lithuania World Cup postponed due to Covid-19. The defeated finalists, Egypt, and third-place play-off winners, Angola, took the other two spots. This tournament painted a true picture of the fragile yet bewitching potential in a continent with a bigger population – 1.2 billion – than the futsal powerhouses of Europe and South America combined.

Chaos reigned before a ball had been kicked. South Africa, a nation with teams in both FIFA and AMF codes, sensationally pulled out days before the first match, citing concerns over the venue chosen by the hosts, Morocco. The games were played in Laayoune, a city in the disputed territory of Western Sahara. Partially occupied by Morocco, the area is also claimed by the Sahrawi people as their homeland since it ceased to be a Spanish colony in 1975. Under pressure from the South African government, its FA pulled out and the team was replaced by Mauritius. After the first game, a 4–2 loss to Equatorial Guinea, Mauritius also backed out, citing similar pressure from their government – a sudden exit that left the team administrators in dispute with the CAF over unpaid hotel bills.

Although diminished by the unseemly political futsal off the court, the spectacular action in the arena caught the eye. The two rising lusophone nations, Angola and Mozambique, served up an early exhibition of outstanding individual play and team cohesion. Favito dazzled in the all-yellow kit of Mozambique, performing tricks galore – including an audacious *chapeau/sombrero* (hat) flick that bemused his Angolan opponent. Not to be outdone, the outrageously talented Magno Felipe Gomes, known as Manocele, clinched goal of the tournament in the same match, with an overhead rainbow flick and stunning volley to put Angola 5–2 ahead on their way to a 7–4 victory. The clip went viral on social media, prompting Brazilian news site *O Globo* to pronounce Manocele 'The Angolan Falcáo'. The fleet-footed number ten's exploits set pulses racing in the big leagues of Europe and South America, where clubs remain ever vigilant for the brightest talents from hitherto untapped markets such as Africa. Although halted by Covid-19, the momentum embodied by Manocele returned with conviction when the south-west African nation was announced as the home of Africa's first ever professional futsal league, scheduled to kick off in early 2021. The Angolan Futsal Federation cited the Brazilian LNF as its inspiration, a hugely successful franchise system itself modelled on the most coveted court-sport league set-up in history: US basketball's NBA. This curious cascade of influence raises the question of whether the birthplace of indoor court sports, some 8,000 miles north-west of Africa, could yet enter the fray and recreate what it did for basketball by monetising the passion, desire and rich potential in the indoor small-sided game.

CHAPTER 16

THE UNITED STATES AND FRANCE: THE COMING NATIONS

'IT'S ABOUT THE excitement, the speed, the sound. It's about the style of play, the compactness of the field. All the characteristics of an ideal sport for the American sports fan.' Bob Bell got it. The owner of the famously successful San Diego Sockers was speaking in a television documentary aired at the dawn of the 1980s, eulogising about the hugely popular Major Indoor Soccer League (MISL). Lauded by the narrator as a 'vision of the future', indoor football was big business, rivalling the North American Soccer League (NASL) for glamour despite the presence of Pelé and other world-renowned footballers in the US outdoor game.

The greatest court-sport nation in the world, which would be indirectly influencing African futsal almost half a century later, took instantly to the latest iteration of indoor 'soccer'. Slaviša Žungul, a free-scoring striker for Hajduk Split in Yugoslavia until he defected to the US in 1978 – the year the MISL kicked off – became the face of the indoor game. After Americanising his name, trading Slaviša for 'Steve', Žungul also earned the moniker 'the Nureyev of soccer' as he dominated the MISL goalscoring charts; this despite only signing up to play indoors because of a ban on participating in the FIFA-affiliated outdoor game, having fled his homeland while still under contract at

Hajduk Split due to fears he would be conscripted to the military. By the time he retired in 1990, at the age of thirty-five, Žungul had racked up eight MISL titles – four with the San Diego Sockers and four with the New York Arrows – and finished with a record 652 goals, nearly 200 clear of his nearest rival Branko Segota, another fellow Yugoslav who grew up in Canada. In a memorable eulogy to Žungul in *Sports Illustrated* headlined 'He's The Lord of All Indoors', the author J.D. Reed called him 'the Pelé of the indoor game' and noted how the game was fast becoming the sport of choice for US soccer fans. The analysis, written in 1981, charted the rapid evolution of a game that just three years earlier had 'resembled human pinball'. Having lost 'its penny-arcade look', the indoor six-a-side game had 'developed its own tactics, strategies, set plays and theory', declared Reed.

It was not the first time indoor football had flourished in the United States. About thirty miles west of the Nassau Coliseum where Žungul shot the New York Arrows to glory, the famous Madison Square Garden had flirted with the game shortly after the third iteration of the venue opened to much fanfare in 1925. The interest was short-lived. But the second coming of the outdoor eleven-a-side American Soccer League in 1933 eventually led to experimental indoor contests among its teams. There was a brief bout of matches in the Garden in 1939. Then in February 1941, just ten months before the invasion of Pearl Harbor triggered US entry into the Second World War, the Garden played host to a fractious and violent night of the sporting variety, offering an early eleven-a-side cameo of the small-sided MISL 'human pinball' – with its notorious hockey-style side boards for rebounds – which Žungul would revel in four decades later. In the opening game, St Mary's Celtics lost 2–0 to Brookhattan Truckers, a blood-and-thunder encounter described by the *New York Daily News* as a 'riotous debut' for the watching 8,000 spectators. Several players retired injured due to the treacherous surface – an unsubtle concrete and cork combination – and the random violence that punctuated the affair. These indoor clashes continued to flourish in the US in the 1950s and 1960s. But while certainly entertaining, they were simply not futsal. Just like the MISL 'human pinball' that was to follow, they were merely the latest in a long line of indoor, small-sided iterations of the eleven-a-side game, offering precious little of *futebol de salão*'s carefully controlled creativity.

* * *

It was only a matter of time: the delighted spectators had got what they craved. The Falcon had swooped. Falcão, four-times best player in the world, opened his goal-scoring account on his North American futsal debut with a rudimentary strike by the Brazilian's majestically high standards – but it was one that announced the arrival of the Intercontinental Futsal Cup on the US mainland for the first time. In Greensboro, North Carolina, to be precise. Falcão had registered the fourth goal for Intelli Orlandia, from São Paulo state, in a 7–2 hammering of the Guatemala City team FSC Glucosoral, in a four-day extravaganza of futsal.

It was 2013, and for the first time since FIFA had taken control of the Intercontinental Futsal Cup it was being held outside South America or Europe. Only Brazil, Spain and Portugal (once) had been handed the pleasure. In the pre-FIFA years, from 1997 onwards, it had been held most years in Moscow. The homogeneity at organisational level was matched by a cast-iron duopoly on the court. In the seven tournaments since FIFA's takeover in 2004, only two teams had won the thing: Carlos Barbosa of Brazil and Madrid's Inter Movistar. Inter's name had changed more times in the past nine years than the event had different winners.[34] The watching

---

34. Since the Greensboro breakthrough, the cup has moved to Kazakhstan, Doha in Qatar and Bangkok, Thailand, where it was run for a second time by the Benjasiriwans for

thousands in the Coliseum arena knew how lucky they were. This was not a reincarnation of the blood and thunder of traditional US indoor football. This was the art of futsal. Over the four days in June 2013, nearly 7,000 people marvelled as the world's big guns, a line-up including Orlandia, with a young Guitta stalking the goal to back up Falcão's brilliance, their Brazilian rivals Carlos Barbosa, the Miguelin-inspired Spanish giants ElPozo Murcia (who once tried to recruit Argentina's Diego Maradona), the eventual winners, Dinamo Moscow, and the late-entry homegrown team, World United (who replaced Argentina's Boca Juniors at the eleventh hour).

Rob Andrews is an ideas man. He doesn't wait around for things to happen. Speaking at length from his home in Raleigh, North Carolina, the football and futsal coach with an enormous passion for the small-sided game is describing in vivid detail his seminal year in southern Spain in 2006 as a callow undergraduate from Emory and Henry College, Virginia. 'It was my awakening,' he says; it fuelled an intense love affair with futsal, a sport he says 'simply has to be *the* version of soccer' for the United States.

'I'd landed in Granada in southern Spain for my senior year,' he recalls. 'We went to school from 8 a.m. until 12 p.m. We came home for lunch and then went back in the afternoon. Or sometimes we went into the city, or took a siesta. Whatever we wanted, we did. So what I would do is eat my lunch really quickly and go down to the "pistas", or the courts. There were eight concrete courts, side by side and it was one euro to rent them for an hour. We never paid the one euro. There were about thirty people who would wait until one court opened and would go on when it opened. And the winner would stay on. That's what I wanted to do.' At this point, Andrews feels compelled to explain how he was the captain of his university

Chonburi in late 2019.

team, a 'really strong player', armed with crisp white Puma football trainers and a swanky new Adidas ball from that year's Euros. He looked the part. He felt the part. He was about to play 'soccer' for a bit of fun. The sun was shining. He was on top of the world. What could possibly go wrong?

The Greensboro Coliseum gig hosting Falcão and co. was no accident. It was the culmination of months of dedication on the part of two futsal game-changers: Andrews, the fast-talking, globetrotting American, and his Spanish amigo Miguel Andrés Moreno, a former professional player who went on to coach at Inter Movistar and Dinamo Moscow. The forensically detailed organisation paid off. The biggest teams were all there, apart from the European champions Barcelona, and the crowds had responded. The ambitious plan to use a proper court paid off: no mean feat given the task involved shipping in the panels used in that year's Copa del Rey in the Spanish LNFS. This was serious. Andrews and Andrés Moreno meant business.

'The first night it was mayhem for Falcão,' Andrews later told the futsalonline website. The fans also came to realise that futsal was more than a game of individual brilliance. As well as the myriad stars on show, the team game ethos came through loud and clear when Dinamo Moscow, a cohesive, tactically astute Russian outfit, triumphed in the final. The US fans now understood that it was 'a real, professional sport'. Andrews knew he wanted more futsal in the US. He knew why and he knew how. He just had to make it happen.

The seminal day, back in Granada, is on instant recall in Andrews' memory bank. 'It was in one of the games at the courts. There was a guy there. He was wearing jeans, his shoes were untied, he was wearing a tank top. It was a hot day. He was probably pushing, like, 225 pounds, he wasn't any more than five foot ten. About my height.

But he was smoking. Smoking before, during and after the game. You get the idea. Everything wrong, right. Everything wrong. And I can't get the ball off of this guy. I can't get near him . . . I'm running around and he's making me dance like a puppet.'

In the mid-afternoon heat, Andrews' puffed-out chest deflated and the gloss of his varnished ego melted away, rapidly reducing the college team captain to a personification of the cruel aphorism 'all the gear, no idea'. It was a landmark moment, an epiphany as the searing sun glared brightly on the dusty, packed outdoor courts of Granada. He was about 4,000 miles from the Carolinas – but it might as well have been four million, given the intensity of the culture shock. 'And I thought,' he recalls. 'I thought, I've had a coach since I was five years old! . . . I've never played unorganised soccer before. Yet this guy's never, ever had a coach. He's never played for a team. He's from the streets! I can't get the ball from him because he understands the game in a fundamentally different way than I do. It was so frustrating . . . I've had private coaches, I've played at university. I'm in the top 1 per cent of the country among players who played soccer at university.

'So I wondered. I thought: What's the problem here?'

Dinamo Moscow were not the only winners in that showpiece Greensboro event. In his burgeoning role as the president of a new organisation called USA Futsal, Andrews hit the jackpot too. He was a futsal novice no longer. Two years after transforming a vacant retail space in Raleigh into a futsal hub for thousands of players, Andrews could offer leagues and pick-up games – just like he'd experienced in Granada. His daring venture – 'I just found the vision – it pulls you' – profited from two pieces of good fortune: the right time and the right place. He approached the development company behind a 'decrepit shopping centre with 20 per cent occupancy rate' with a plan to redevelop vacant space to bring tenants, customers and dollars flooding in. His well-timed boldness, rewarded with a deal on a low rent for the site, also came in the right location.

The US soccer and futsal hierarchy is famously horizontal. US Soccer, the country's nominal equivalent of a national football association, rarely gets involved in parochial matters. 'It's left to the clubs,' Andrews says. That was the big picture. At a local level, conditions were equally benign: North Carolina is one of only eleven states to sanction year-round schooling. In Raleigh, the public (state) schools operate on a six weeks on, three weeks off basis, with groups of schools alternating. For fifty-two weeks of the year at least one-third of school-age children are kicking their heels in any given week, creating a market in paid-for childcare. The McGregor Village futsal centre succeeded instantly, attracting thousands of kids to play, with many teams formed as the centre became a hotbed of futsal talent. Success brought a problem though. 'We were the best teams,' he recalls. 'We were beating everyone. We needed some real futsal opposition.' Yet again, he didn't wait. Again, he turned to Spain for a solution.

The World Futsal Championships is an annual event held in Barcelona between Christmas and New Year attracting dozens of the strongest youth teams from around the world. In late 2019 it reached its seventh year, orchestrated by Andrews and the thriving futsal organisation he founded, now renamed United Futsal. On court, Barcelona and Brazilian teams such as Corinthians tend to dominate what has become the biggest youth futsal attraction in the world. The sole English success came in 2016, when Olé Futsal Academy from London edged out Barcelona to the Alevin (under-12) title. Bringing the Intercontinental Cup to North Carolina a year after starting the Barcelona tournament threw up yet another stroke of fortune allowing Andrews to be 'pulled along' by futsal. A chance meeting in the VIP room in Greensboro with a journalist from soccer.com, Derwin Williams, started the ball rolling on the third element in Andrews' futsal strategy. While chatting to Andrews, Williams took a call from a contact at Disney and began eulogising about the game that was unfolding before his eyes. Andrews joined the conversation, noted the contact and within months had signed a five-year deal to put on a festival of youth futsal at Disney's ESPN Wide World of Sports arena in Orlando, starting in 2014. The month chosen was August, when many of the estimated one million-plus annual Brazilian visitors to Orlando are in town (only Canada and the UK have more annual tourists heading to Florida).[35] Yet again, Lady Luck and keen judgment had combined sweetly in futsal's favour.

Andrews shuffled home a changed man after his encounter in Granada, showering himself down and vowing to immerse himself in this culture of unstructured, unregulated artistry he'd fallen victim to. 'It's where we went every day. It was a beautiful thing. Sometimes you'd get on once, sometimes you stayed on for five hours. Once you start winning, you won't relinquish the court until you have to.' It reminded him of YMCA pick-up basketball in the US. He lived like a Spanish street player, immersed in the unvarnished, untainted game, in context, without adornment, uncoached, free of outside interference. 'It became the social fabric of everything we did there. It's where my friends went, it's where my friends were.' It was the real deal. Like a vibrant sunny day, compared with the dark night of the sterilised, over-organised (and often over-priced) 'soccer clinics' he'd been exposed to in his youth. 'It was part of the culture in Spain,' he adds. 'Futsal was a subculture more than it was a sport.'

Upon returning to the US, it became clear he'd smuggled back a truly life-changing experience. 'Although I didn't know much about futsal then, I knew this game we'd been playing out there was guaranteed to make players better.' The tournaments he has put on since – from

---

35. From Florida Review and Travel Guide 2019: https://floridareview.co.uk/useful-resources/florida-tourism-numbers

the Barcelona youth 'Worlds' to the Greensboro showcase and Disney festival – are simply the recreation of his own Spanish experiences. 'I've brought back the spectacle I saw in Granada. What I felt. I played. I touched.' That nicotine-fuelled, overweight puppet-master from the dusty courts is clearly still pulling the futsal strings from afar.

When Falcão returned to the United States in 2016, the clamour for futsal was tangible. Again, the Brazilian scored. This time he was in Disney's ESPN arena, the same Orlando venue where Andrews' United Futsal youth tournament was held. Although only an exhibition game, the match was seen as history in the making. 'The marketability is really unique,' Donnie Nelson, president of basketball operations at the Dallas Mavericks NBA team, said afterwards. The 3,000-plus crowd gasped as Falcão traded wow moments with the heir to his throne of world's best player, Ricardinho, the galácticos engaged in a pulsating contest, intended to inspire a growing US audience, that ended 9–8 for the Brazilian's team. Nelson's declaration was not a non sequitur. He was speaking in his capacity as executive director of the Professional Futsal League (PFL), which had been burrowing into the minds of futsal fans worldwide since its inauguration was announced months earlier. Amid supercharged hype (and with the public support of the billionaire tycoon, actor, philanthropist and owner of the Dallas Mavericks, Mark Cuban), the PFL vowed to create the biggest and best professional league on the globe. Within weeks the marketing push had begun, with Cuban adding cachet as a household name due to his long stint as a 'shark' investor on the hit ABC show *Shark Tank* – and a fortune estimated by *Forbes* to be just shy of $4bn in 2018. Nelson's ambitions for the sport with 'unique marketability' were outlined to *FourFourTwo* magazine:

> 'I think we can become the urban solution for US Soccer. Because a lot of kids in inner-cities don't have access to fields,

and they've got a lot of natural talent, but they don't have the infrastructure to really get in involved with soccer. We think the timing is right. We in the NBA know a little something about urban marketing, and so the sport itself was soccer born on a basketball court — or soccer and basketball combined.'

Fast-forward five years, and the league is yet to kick off. More hype, promises – and gilt-edged goalscoring opportunities – have given way to silence, yielding rumours and confusion as the momentum ebbs away. So, what's the hold-up? Why is the league with con-firmed interest from some of the biggest clubs in Europe (including Barcelona and Benfica) and South America (Corinthians and Boca Juniors), as well as some of the biggest professional sporting behemoths in the US, struggling to get out of the starting blocks? It's about quality, declares Andrews, whose futsal remit extends to sitting on the small team of chief strategists behind the league. Speaking on the phone one spring morning from his home in Raleigh, North Carolina, he sounds as unapologetic as he is unequivocal. 'It's the only aim. To be the best. If it was about just making money, or ticket sales, why wouldn't we have launched by now? Why didn't we launch and jump at the first TV deal we were offered? It's because we're waiting for it to be perfect. You only get one chance to make a first impression.' But the firm interest is there, he says. So is the backing. As well as Cuban and Nelson, the strongest voice of US futsal, Keith Tozer, is the PFL commissioner and remains convinced the league holds the key to futsal's breakthrough into mainstream US culture. Speaking on the World of Futsal podcast in 2019 to Alexander Para, the man who trademarked the word 'futsal' in the mid-1980s, Tozer said the PFL was vital to boost the sport's profile, enhance its flourishing grassroots development and arrest the decline of the US national futsal men's team in the world game.

In the CONCACAF region, the US has been eclipsed since the mid-1990s by Guatemala and Costa Rica, who boast their own sustainable professional leagues. 'We're in no rush to get to the marketplace,' Tozer tells me. 'When we do launch, we need to have everything in order: the referees programme, the courts – hopefully some of the best in the world – the coaches, the teams. Everything.' He understands that 'everyone's been waiting for us to start' but he repeats Andrews' line that everything has to be right. They're committed to the FIFA rules, but are considering modifications to suit US sporting tastes and the associated television audience. It's important that sporting events last at least two hours in the US, he explains, 'for the TV rights and advertising revenue'. Basketball and hockey games exceed two hours, while NFL and baseball take up three and a half hours of advertisement-rich airtime. The PFL is looking for games to edge over the 120-minute threshold by having four quarters instead of two halves, and wants to modify the tackling rule (to avoid costly injuries due to crippling insurance fees in the States) and tinker with the fly-goalkeeper rules – a change that will excite critics of Leo Higuita's 'powerplay' exploits for Kazakhstan and AFC Kairat.

'In the meantime, the grassroots is booming,' says Tozer, who is also a FIFA futsal coach instructor. 'This is the opposite of the MISL in 1978. It was like an upside-down mortgage back then. They had a professional league but zero grassroots game. No indoor soccer. Within fifteen years there were 5,000 indoor centres built in the United States . . . The Major League Soccer is getting involved in futsal, Adidas, Nike and Walmart are building outdoor courts. The US Soccer foundation is building mini-pitches. It's booming everywhere.' This may be so, but the governance and structures are where it gets messy in the United States, inviting an analogy with a distinct period of flux in US history: the Wild West era.

Just as the romanticised age of relentless nineteenth-century westward expansion was defined by conquest, survival and pioneering persistence, so too is the world of futsal in a land where the national US Soccer Federation largely stands aside from parochial developments in individual states. Alongside US Soccer and its various affiliated organisations, the non-FIFA AMF began a viable professional league in the US in 2015. Although 'more like a third division level' according to Alexander Para, Major League Futsal proved sustainable, running men's and women's competitions for four months a year. The grandly named National Futsal Premier League – playing to FIFA rules – also kicked off in the Great Lakes region in January 2019, initially with just seven teams. Both these leagues, however lacking in glamour and reach, therefore boast a clear one-goal lead over the putative PFL despite its glitzy promotional matches and heavyweight backers. At the flourishing youth level, US Youth Futsal (USYF), with Keith Tozer as technical director, runs hundreds of leagues, operates ID talent centres and competes with Para's US Futsal to take teams overseas to represent the US. In 2018, USYF alone had an estimated 50,000 boys and girls playing the game. Other organisations run their own shows, such as Andrews' United Futsal. The positive effects of a free-for-all are clear to see. That's not the only thing visible about futsal in the US.

The former LA Galaxy and Everton winger Landon Donovan admits to having had his 'eyes opened' to futsal's development potential early in 2019. The prolific goalscorer in Major League Soccer (MLS) – with 145 goals – and joint top scorer in the history of the national team caused a minor tremor when he signed up to play in the six-a-side astroturf Major Arena Soccer League in February for the San Diego Sockers, the club where MISL king Steve Žungul made his name. The three-month gig earned Donovan north of a quarter of a million dollars, about five times as much as the highest-paid player in the professional indoor game there. Describing his experience to Tozer on the World of Futsal podcast, Donovan remarked how many of his teammates – 'some of the best technical players I've ever played with' – spoke of futsal as the game that formed their skills, offering an 'incomparable' format for developing youth players. 'I think it should be mandatory across the board,' said Donovan. The coaching guru behind the rise of women's football in the US, Anson Dorrance, has long used futsal sessions to add creative flair to his players. Like Donovan, he sees futsal as a 'game changer' for the type of footballer the US system develops.

The big MLS clubs are getting the message too. Orlando City FC's foundation built six outdoor futsal courts to cater for the city's football-crazy Latino population. When I visited one such court in 2019, a twenty-six metre by sixteen metre caged rectangle bearing the club's purple colours and totemic lion's head, I found it nestled near the car park of the Engelwood Neighborhood Center in east Orlando, the court sandwiched between a swimming pool and two basketball courts, with an adjacent school's softball pitch, and soccer fields looming large. This assembly of rival sports facilities paints a vivid picture of the difficulties confronting any bid to promote futsal as the future sport of choice for American children. It's a similar level of competition indoor football faced to secure a stage at the in-demand Madison Square Garden nearly a century earlier. Orlando City are not alone in their quest. Nearly 2,000 miles away, LA Galaxy are busy funding futsal pitches for public use and to aid the game's development in the biggest urban sprawl in the States. It's all supported by US Soccer as part of its mini-pitch initiative. Perhaps more meaningful than the outdoor courts for pick-up games is the move by DC United, fresh from the coup of signing the 'last of the true street footballers', Wayne Rooney, in 2018, to create a futsal academy to run alongside its football youth programme. The rumble of change signifies a shift in the tectonic plates beneath the US, threatening to alter the landscape when it comes to futsal – and its potential to gain a new mass audience.

* * *

For Ricardinho it was simple. A sliver of space, a chance, a glance, the shot. Goal. Not an ounce of energy wasted. The thrift and prudence in *O Mágico*'s debut goal triggered a markedly more lavish reaction from joyous teammates and fans alike. Ricardinho's artistry was a hefty first repayment on the big investment incurred by his new Paris-based paymasters, ACCS. Two more debut goals for the six-times best player on the planet sealed a 6–0 victory away at Nantes Métropole in France's futsal Ligue 1. The most talked-about club in world futsal had arrived.

It was 'an amazing moment' for the French game, the ACCS president, Sami Sellami, tells me a few weeks into the 2020–21 season. Ricardinho's signature represents the club's biggest coup in an audacious nine-month recruitment drive that began in late 2019. Following swiftly in the Portuguese superstar's svelte footsteps were two Inter Movistar teammates – the celebrated Spain *fixo* and captain Carlos *El Espartano* (the Spartan) Ortiz and the veteran Brazilian pivot Humberto. Their revered coach, Jesús Velasco, came next. Then Ricardinho's Portuguese ally Bruno Coelho swapped Lisbon and Benfica for the apparently brighter lights of the Paris suburbs.

While big names such as the established French international Kevin Ramirez departed for Mouvaux Lille Métropole, the new boys bolstered a squad already brimming with talent, including the two standout stars of African champions Morocco, Bilal Bakkali and Soufiane El Mesrar, and the giant Serbian shot-stopper Miodrag Aksentijević. The goalkeeper of the tournament in the 2016 Euros in Belgrade, Aksentijević was also the man beaten in a group match by his now teammate Ricardinho's famous 'Akka 3000' wonder strike. With the Portuguese icon heading the bill on a contract reportedly worth a basic minimum of €1m over three seasons, suddenly France was seen as the coming nation of the sport. The ACCS recruitment spree unleashed a burst of Gallic stardust on the global game just as the brash talk emanating from the United States over its coming PFL had fallen silent. France had stolen a march on the PFL's billionaire-backed glitzy promises.

The rise of ACCS is meteoric. Founded as a multi-sports club in 2008 for 'social and educational purposes', it was originally called ACCES, an acronym for Citizen, Cultural, Educational and Sports Association. Fast forward to 2020 and the adult futsal section, set up just six years earlier, boasts a collection of futsal *galácticos* unlike any the sport has known. After a merger in 2019 with another club, Paris Métropole, it settled on a new name – ACCS Asnières Villeneuve 92 – to reflect the club's strong links with the two partner cities, or communes, whose local authorities help fund it. The number 92 is taken from the statistical code attached to another of its backers, the Hauts-de-Seine department authority.

In the eyes of some of its critics, in France and elsewhere, ACCS is dismissed as an arriviste, an attention-seeking upstart, bulldozing its way through the established order of the sport. For the club's beguiling president, Sellami, the truth of the matter is explained by another French word synonymous with quality. 'It's champagne,' he explains eagerly. 'We want to create champagne futsal.'

An engaging entrepreneur in his mid-thirties, Sellami tells me the first game simply confirmed the validity of their plan. 'The players are not here just to take a salary,' he insists. 'Ricardinho came to ACCS to show his project, which is to invite French futsal to be exceptional. To change its mentality, its mindset, and the way to play.' Sellami's theatrical background – as an actor, comedian and playwright – infuses his sense of ambition. 'It's important we make an amazing game, with lots of show,' he insists. 'If futsal wants to be famous it needs to be spectacular. And this is what we have started.' Although the 'project' is just beginning – 'ACCS is only an adolescent,' he says – Sellami states boldly that ACCS will win the Champions League within two years. 'It's my dream,' he vows. 'The second dream is that a lot of people know about how we win. Our history. This is more important than becoming champions. How we started from nothing. Without a euro in the bank.'

A curious mix of public and private funding, the club's annual budget soared from €700,000 in 2019–20 to €2m the next season. But this is no futsal equivalent of their Qatar-backed footballing neighbours Paris Saint-Germain. 'ACCS is a social project that opens doors,' says Sellami. 'It's a new way to put start-up projects in poor parts of the city. Politicians like it a lot.' Local authorities contribute 40 per cent of the club's income. The other 60 per cent is split equally between private sponsors and the club's own funds. It's the sort of business venture that would no doubt go down well on *Shark Tank*, the hit US investor show synonymous with the billionaire tycoon and backer of the putative PFL, Mark Cuban. 'Of course there is a risk,' admits Sellami, speaking as the economic meltdown caused by the 2020 coronavirus pandemic plays out. 'But I'm not afraid. We are ambitious and professional. We are not just about winning. We want to build and create something.'

A couple of miles north-east of ACCS's 1,300-seat Arena Teddy Riner in Asnières-sur-Seine, the suburb of Sarcelles boasts a proud reputation for breeding young players on its unforgiving streets and courts. The French international striker Wissam Ben Yedder is a famous product, emerging there as one of the so-called 'boys from the banlieues' – along with his childhood friend, the Manchester City and Algeria winger Riyad Mahrez. In 2017, shortly before joining Monaco as a €40m recruit from Sevilla in Spain, the striker spoke about his 'happy memories' growing up immersed in the culture of *ballon sur bitume* (street football on concrete), pitting his wits against bigger, older kids. His subsequent emergence in futsal aged sixteen, where he earned the nickname 'Romário' at his club Garges

Djibson and went on to represent France, burnished his predatory skills before a switch to football.

In 2019, the legendary France international striker Jean-Pierre Papin hailed Ben Yedder's 'perfect' technique, formed on the forty metre by twenty metre court. 'He's a real finisher, a killer in the penalty box,' Papin told beIN SPORTS, as Ben Yedder slugged it out with PSG's Kylian Mbappé at the top of the Ligue 1 goalscoring charts. The timeline of Ben Yedder's emergence runs parallel with the shift in the Fédération Française de Football's approach to the small-sided game, a growing recognition that futsal offers youngsters a natural next step from the chaotic streets and cages of the banlieues to the more tactically refined indoor court.

The concrete and cage culture offers greater freedom and access to playing than the more formal version of small-sided football, Le Five, which has long been embedded in the nation's infrastructure. France is not alone. A growing legion of south London boys strutting their stuff at the top of European football – from Crystal Palace's Wilfried Zaha to Borussia Dortmund's Jadon Sancho and Liverpool's Joe Gomez – bear testimony to the rise of casual gladiatorial contests on similar terrain in boroughs such as Croydon, described in the *Guardian* by Barney Ronay in 2016 as 'a concrete Catalonia'. The futsal court provides the same breathless opportunity to play. But as a separate FIFA-sanctioned sport it goes further, the tactical grammar of the game eliciting in older youth players the necessary essential game nous to thrive under pressure. As a bona fide professional option, it also offers a second route to the top for players outside eleven-a-side football.

Unlike the English FA, the FFF means business in finally building France into a FIFA futsal powerhouse to offer these playing options at the grassroots and challenge the traditional European giants of Spain, Portugal, Russia and Italy at the elite level. In 2018 the federation's mission gained new impetus. The men's national team, founded in 1997, reached its first major tournament, the UEFA European Championships. At the youth level, the FFF made an even bigger statement. Its first group of fifteen-year-old boys were recruited for French futsal's version of the famously productive Clairefontaine football *pôle*, or elite academy, started in 1988 and still unleashing high-end game changers on world football decades later. Long after Thierry Henry went through the boarding-school hothouse for teenage stars, Kylian Mbappé – another boy from the *banlieues* – emerged as a new prototype of the modern footballer. Clairefontaine opened an equivalent for female footballers in 1998. The launch of the futsal *pôle* in 2018 injected sharp focus onto a sport the French men's national team coach, Pierre Jacky, describes as 'basketball for the feet'. The FFF president, Noël Le Graët, spoke ominously at the launch: 'We were a little late [to futsal] but we are working to make up for it. The sixteen residents of this *pôle* are pioneers.' Sami Sellami praises the FFF's commitment, particularly its decision to screen Ligue 1 matches on its streaming channel. A women's national team and greater youth participation are on the agenda too. 'But we need more,' he warns. 'We don't have five years to wait.' In 2019, Olympique Lyonnais entered the fray as the first high-profile football club in France to sanction a futsal section. Sharing the facilities at Lycée Saint-Louis-Saint-Bruno, in the 1st arrondissement of Lyon, with the FFF's *pôle* youngsters, they kicked off the regional third tier. Sellami believes the FFF's stake in futsal will intensify once more football clubs follow Lyon's lead.

Whatever the football clubs do, French futsal is the priority, he says. Acknowledging the friction in many nations between futsal and the football associations, he dismisses AMF's 'conflict with FIFA' as counter-productive. 'Even if we don't like the national federation, we have to admit that FIFA makes things good for futsal. It is the best way to go.' The battle worth pursuing is the quest for more urgency in the federations and greater control over the FIFA game: 'We need people of futsal managing futsal. This is the good fight.' France's futsal clubs can lead the way; once this happens, football clubs will flock to the game, he predicts.

Sellami's voice ticks up a notch when I enquire about the rich potential in France. 'Our goal is to develop the French futsal players and train a new generation,' he declares. Along with Ricardinho et al., the left-footed French winger Landry N'Gala – another Sarcelles boy – also arrived in 2020 from rivals Garges Djibson. 'Our players lack visibility [in the global game],' Sellami continues. 'But N'Gala is very strong. Great skills. And Nelson Lutin and Souheil Mouhoudine, both young boys, they are amazing. They are the best potential in Europe. All the players here, the coaches, Ricardinho, they are all very impressed . . . they are the future of European futsal.' The excitement surrounding Lutin, aged twenty-three, is palpable. Labelled 'the Mbappé of futsal', the baby-faced winger grew up playing handball and only turned to futsal aged sixteen after a three-year spell in football. The French contingent are headed by the veteran of the club, thirty-year-old Abdessamad Mohammed. On top of this, Ricardinho's friendship with PSG's futsal-formed Brazilian superstar Neymar is expected to see him join the French international winger Franck Ribéry as a public supporter of the ACCS mission. Sellami says talk of the Brazilian attending ACCS matches is no fantasy. 'It will happen,' he insists. France, and its young players, can become a showcase for the sport all too often rudely dismissed as 'a false soccer'. 'Futsal is a hybrid,' he explains. 'It's a bit of basketball, a bit of handball . . . it is a beautiful discipline. Futsal needs to be proud of its identity. It is a show, like the NBA, like soccer . . . all these things make it unique. This is what I want to promote here.'

It is an enchanting script, and one that confirms Sellami and France as new characters in the long and protracted drama of the futsal story, running from the dusty YMCAs of 1930s Montevideo to the sumptuous Arena Teddy Riner on the left bank of the Seine some ninety years on. It's an energetic plot twist. And the self-confessed futsal impresario with a mission to put on a spectacular 'champagne show' seems determined to remain centre stage.

EPILOGUE
THE FUTURE GAME

I'M ON COURT playing with my eldest son again. He has just turned eighteen, as have his friends and teammates, Harjot Singh Brar and Stephen Walker Boyd, our goalkeeper, or goal attacker (he loves doing 'a Higuita'). The boys I coached have joined us oldies. It seems like a major staging post on a journey into the world of proper futsal, seen, played and coached through my own prism of street football.

There is a stillness in the hall. Conor locks the ball tightly beneath his left sole, his shoe caressing it like a cooling hand strokes an overheated brow. As the ball rolls back and forth, side to side, his eyes survey the scene, as three green-shirted opponents lurk. But he's totally at ease, staying on the ball, looking for gaps in the wall of bodies protecting the opposition's goal. A swift pass sideways shifts the burden, forcing the gang of four opponents to reconfigure their collective pose. Chris Ryman picks it up, again with the sole, feigns to attack the area where Harjot is marked closely, but instead calmly rolls the ball back to me. He shifts wide as I adopt the sole-roll dance stance, a micro-pause followed by a faux pass to ward off the potential advances of my nearest opponent. I'm still learning from my mistakes – even in my late forties. Previous errors, and Ricardinho's tears of laughter out in Portugal, have left a deep but motivational scar.

We're in total control: collective composure under concerted, relentless pressure. And it competes with the best feeling I've had on a futsal court or football pitch. We keep the ball for another few moves, each of us passing, cutting forward and rotating into space to maintain the intensity and probing zeal that's grown over the past fifteen minutes. It's our very own version of Zego's 4-0 formation, and autopilot kicks in as the components of our futsal flying machine crank into action without thought. We're 2–1 down to Aylesbury Futsal Club – who have a strong contingent of savvy Portuguese players on court in this school hall near Reading – but we're on top, pressing for an equaliser in the semi-final of the Berks and Bucks county qualifier for the FA Futsal Cup 2019–20.

It's fitting we're in a school. Futsal has just been accepted on the GCSE and A-level PE curriculum in England from 2020, the news coming as the English FA struck a three-year deal with the Japanese gaming giant Pokémon to sponsor all its youth futsal, including a Pokémon national schools futsal cup. The FA's PE and coaching in education specialists, one of whom is our teammate Lawrence Lok, have added futsal guidance to the expert advice they offer teachers all over the country. There is unanimous agreement around the world that schools hold the key to a vibrant futsal culture. Now that futsal's place in the Premier League academy games programme is also firmly established, youth futsal can finally take off in England. The big 'if', of course, is whether the English FA seizes the moment. On a grander scale, the Olympic dream is also a step closer to reality. The day before our match, it was confirmed that men's and women's futsal would remain in the Youth Olympics in Dakar in 2022 after the success of its debut in Buenos Aires in 2018. With Spain's RFEF vowing to lead the push, hopes are high that futsal will finally adorn the full Olympic Games.

The pleasure of playing on court matches the global mood music. The exhilaration is intense and the physical load immense in a frenetic first half that leaves us 2–0 down at the break. The winner of our match will kick off the final against Reading Royals immediately afterwards, and the winner of *that* match will progress to the next stage of the FA Cup. Royals confirmed their status as a rising force in English futsal when the adult first team playing today clinched the National Futsal League Premiership South months later in the season curtailed by the coronavirus shutdown. Shortly afterwards, in mid-2020, the club guided selflessly by Fernando Silva struck up a global partnership with ACCS. Silva told me the link-up would raise the profile of futsal in England and France, two nations playing catch-up to his home nation, Portugal. Sami Sellami, the ACCS president, said he wanted to help Reading Royals become the biggest club in England.

Back in the here and now, once we've pulled a goal back, it's game on – and a couple of minutes later, our equaliser comes. Aylesbury break quickly, but Conor and I combine to wrestle back possession. Chris latches on to the ball and skips away down the right. Sizing up the keeper, he fires the ball goalwards, beyond a despairing David de Gea-style split save, and straight into the advancing Harjot's path. The youngster rams the ball into the net, the bulge swiftly followed by a huge crash, as a lunging Aylesbury defender skid-lands into the net, like a giant hooked carp. Our bench explodes with joy, and a ripple of appreciative applause rises from the watching crowd in recognition of a textbook counter-attack and second-post finish. Just like the ones counted carefully by André Rodrigues and the other talent whisperers at Benfica's academy. We can win this. We know we can.

When the game restarts, we resume controlled precision. Every aspect of the futsal I've watched, learned about and tried to play and coach over a decade or so is on display, as my own team of boys and old men comes of age in unison. Conor and Harjot continue as inverted wingers – right-footed Harjot on the left and Conor, a lefty, on the right – enabling them to deceive markers with the oriented sole control Mićo Martić explained in great depth. It's a tactical and technical awareness that they've learned on court. This is a collision between futsal and street football cultures to produce a new generation of players. A generation skilled in the art of daring one-v-one combat, but equally ready to submit to the overriding need of the collective. Wrongly labelled as a game of individual tricks and wizardry, futsal clearly infuses in players a powerful ethos of responsibility and team solidarity.

We pursue a winner with conviction. A flowing move begins with Matt McFrederick pinning their *fixo* to receive a pinpoint long throw from our keeper, Stephen. Matt secures the ball, plays it back to Chris, who fires it first time to Conor wide left. He scoops the ball over his pressing opponent, its flight evading the near-post goalkeeper's grasp as Lawrence darts in at the far post to make a volleyed connection with his right foot. The ball glances off the crossbar and dips down forlornly on the other side. Agony. With just twenty seconds remaining, Chris narrowly misses too with a towering header – a rarity in futsal – from a diagonal pass by me into the tiny chasm between their *fixo* and the keeper. It's a harbinger of more torture to come. The referee blows the whistle. The forty minutes is up. It's penalties.

Even at this lowly amateur level, futsal is a spectacle. It also brings the slings and arrows of often outrageous fortune that define competitive sport. And just as our team was unable to clinch victory in a stirring finish to normal time, the game of futsal somehow struggles to convert gilt-edged opportunities into solid results, as a global and marketable product to be bought, sold and screened more widely. In a twenty-first century age of social media, digital disruption and celebrity stars, futsal seems laden with obvious viral potential.

It's not as though there are no precedents. The twenty-first century is the age of shrunken sports with gigabyte-size potency. Whether it's cricket (first T20, then The Hundred), rugby (the renegade five-a-side 'rock 'n' roll' of RugbyX) or netball (Fast5), long-established team sports are seeking to unleash a fresh zeal for a shorter, snappier version among their target audience: Generation Z, the legion of youngsters born almost pre-wired into a world of high-speed internet-fuelled social media, who crave more bang for their buck. Even individual sports are getting in on the act: tennis has many shorter, more exciting versions (Fast4 Tennis, Tie Break Tens and Thirty30); GolfSixes offers big cash prizes to professionals playing against a 'shot clock'; even the sedate world of indoor bowls has a new format in Australia, where the Ultimate Bowls Championship is sold as 'fun, fast and fresh – revolutionising the game'. In late 2019, swimming dipped its toe in the water, so to speak, when the International Swimming League was launched. Bankrolled by the Ukrainian energy tycoon Konstantin Grigorishin, it features teams of swimmers up against each other in a shorter (twenty-five metre) pool with a backdrop of poolside disco beats from a live DJ and an atmosphere geared towards fan engagement, big viewing audiences, merchandising and sponsorship deals. The sport's biggest names all signed up. This is where futsal has an advantage: not only is it a long-established professional game in its own right, it has ready-made world stars, such as Ricardinho and the Brazilian Barcelona pivot Ferrão in the men's game; and the Brazilian superstar Amandinha and Portuguese prodigy Fifó in the women's. Futsal is ready to roll.

In Europe, UEFA is very much on the ball. With a self-appointed futsal fan as president, the Slovenian Aleksander Čeferin, UEFA broke new ground in September 2019 by running its first under-19 men's European Championships. This came a few months after another historic futsal first: a UEFA Women's European Championships. The sudden presence of traditional footballing giants France and Germany hands the game a further shot of European adrenaline. The Deutscher Fussball-Bund (German

Football Association) committed to starting a 'professionally ran' futsal Bundesliga in the 2021–22 season, just six years after forming its national men's team. In Spain, the Brazilian Ronaldo vowed to upgrade futsal's role in the academy at Real Valladolid, the La Liga club he bought control of in 2018.

Futsal has also evolved from the subject of soundbites voiced by eleven-a-side luminaries to a game demanding scientific attention. Luca Oppici, an Italian academic with a year in Inter Milan reserves on his CV, was funded by UEFA to study the futsal landscape. His work added weight to two studies by researchers at Liverpool John Moores University undertaken around the time of the Manchester United four-v-four experiment Paul McGuinness was involved in. Researchers found players touched the ball up to six times more often in small-pitch games than in eleven-a-side. Not rocket science, of course, but a second Liverpool study concluded it was the denser futsal ball probably contributing to greater time on the ball per player when compared with five-a-side football. Oppici delved deeper. Analysing the gaze of Barcelona youth futsal players compared with Australian eleven-a-side footballers, he discovered futsal players simply looked up more often. They also had significantly 'higher technical intensity', with 23 per cent more passes a minute, quicker execution of passes (by about half a second) and greater accuracy. Crucially, when they switched codes, the passing performance of the futsal players improved, whereas with the footballers it remained static. He put the futsal ball under the microscope too. As well as its velocity and power exceeding a standard football's for the first 75 per cent of the 'impact duration' – which may explain why the shooting prowess of futsal players appears so powerful – the denser, less bouncy feel appeared to enhance passing and decision-making.

But this being futsal, the organisational storm clouds all too often loom large. Shortly after the men's under-19 Euros, the regard with which the world governing body holds the small-sided game came under scrutiny again. The two strongest teams in the world, Brazil and Argentina, were all ready to fly out to the United States for a four-team tournament; hopes were high this might prove the occasion to finally get the US league off the ground. However, just two weeks before the first scheduled game in Miami, the event was called off without explanation. On Twitter, the *Verde-Amarela* head coach, Marquinhos, said the cancellation showed FIFA's 'disrespect to the world of futsal' – a feeling only compounded when Tite's Brazil football team then played a friendly against Colombia – also in Miami. The conclusion that FIFA cares only about football was difficult to avoid. It was also a jolt for the stuttering US national team, denied the opportunity of competitive action. But then, as is customary in futsal – where two steps forward invariably follow a big lurch back – within weeks the US announced a new dawn in the men's game with the appointment of head coach, the former Serbian footballer and futsal player Dušan Jakica. FIFA also seemed to react by lengthening from four days to ten the annual windows for international matches, raising the prospect that the farce of Brazil and Argentina's aborted US trip will never be repeated. The chances of a FIFA Women's World Cup arriving some day soon also increased at a stroke. These events might hopefully shock the English FA into action, the lack of a women's team to enter the qualifiers for the 2021 UEFA European Championships its most notable failure to adhere to the bold plans spelled out in its Fast Forward with Futsal strategy. Only time will tell whether the English FA truly practises what it preaches.

But back to the game. And the penalties. 'Who wants to take one?' I look around and sense a vacuum of desire. 'I'll take the first.' I hope this will do the trick. Chris raises his hand, as does Conor. 'Who else?' Lawrence volunteers. Then Harjot. That's our five. Aylesbury win the toss and score first. I score. It's 1–1. They continue to convert despite Stephen getting a hand, thigh or midriff to every shot. He's got a knack for saving penalties. And he's confident after his crucial save in a shoot-out in the regional under-16 finals about eighteen months ago. Chris, Conor, Lawrence and Harjot put away their kicks in turn – all taken from the six-metre mark, every one dispatched low, hard and unstoppable into the corner of the net – to make it 5–5. Pedro Barroso, a new Portuguese signing with thirty years of futsal nous under his belt, calmly converts our sixth kick to keep us in the tie as we enter sudden death. Then they miss. Matt steps up to clinch the victory, the goal that will send us beyond our national league rivals and into the final. Unfortunately, their keeper guesses correctly, down to his left, and deflects the ball to safety. They score again, and now it's Ricardo's turn. He jokes, laughs and asks Stephen if he wants to go next. Ricardo is recovering from injury and hasn't played a minute today. Nor has our youngest player, Matt Costello, seventeen, who looks on nervously. Ricardo steps up. After a huge, almost tragicomic run-up that betrays his trepidation, his shot is too central, too straight. Simply too predictable. And it's the result of a slip as he strikes the ball. He's down in agony, clutching his reinjured thigh as the Aylesbury players leap about in celebrations that contrast with our own desolation. Ricardo is still down. And we're out. But it's been a blast. And given that it came thirty-six hours after I'd worked all night at the *Guardian* to help finesse their coverage of the 2019 UK general election, I was not entirely distraught that I didn't have to play another forty minutes right away.

For me, the day meant more than just winning and losing. It was a satisfying culmination of my playing and coaching career, offering further confirmation of my view that, as well as a professional sport of rich commercial potential, it is a clear way forward in any country denuded of inner-city street football. While coaching my sons' teams over the years – and more recently playing on the same court as my eldest – it's clear that futsal can provide twenty-first century children with a modern version of the freedom I found as a boy: spoilt for choice between breathless street contests on the oller, or in the car-less car park; fiercely competitive indoor and outdoor five-a-side matches; and those marathon duels with my brother on rain-sodden Liverpool streets, pursuing my dad on his unending quest for work.

Put simply, futsal enriches the culture, nature and intensity of the ball-playing experience – from the grassroots to the top of the footballing tree. In England, and especially at youth level, it offers a blank canvas on which a new sporting image can be painted. The game hailed in Brazil as a 'laboratory of improvisation' is one in which experimentation should be compulsory. Just as it is in Shahrzad Mozafar's Iran, Falcão's Brazil, Roberto Martínez's Spain and Ricardinho's Portugal. Futsal is undoubtedly a sport on the move. And despite the constant turbulence, the only way has to be up.

DIAGRAMS

BASIC POSITIONS IN FUTSAL
Pitch Size: 40m x 20m

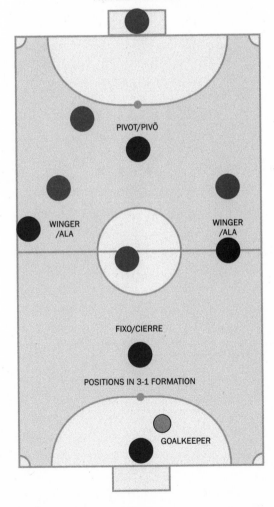

PIVOT/PIVÔ

WINGER
/ALA

WINGER
/ALA

FIXO/CIERRE

POSITIONS IN 3-1 FORMATION

GOALKEEPER

Y-FORMATION HIGH-PRESSING DEFENCE

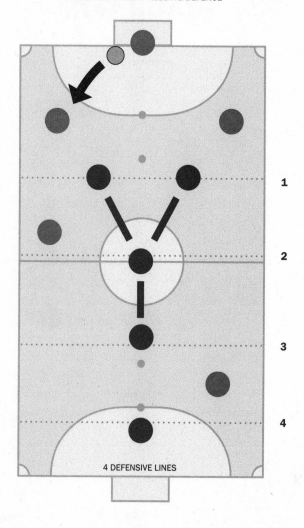

1

2

3

4

4 DEFENSIVE LINES

FUTSAL

Y-FORMATION WHOLE-COURT HIGH-PRESSING TRAP

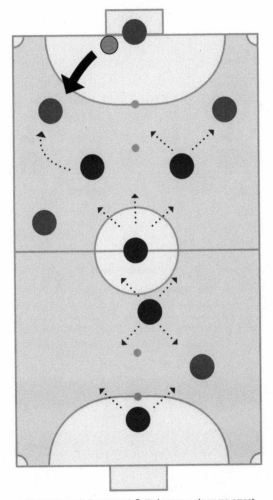

Black arrows = ball movement. Dotted arrows = player movement

BUTTERFLY ROTATION*

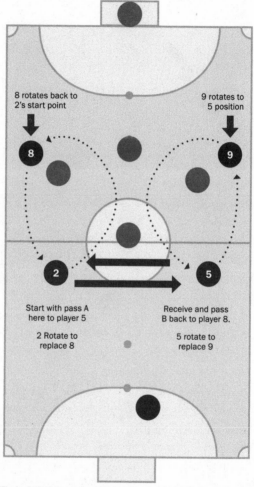

8 rotates back to
2's start point

9 rotates to
5 position

Start with pass A
here to player 5

Receive and pass
B back to player 8.

2 Rotate to
replace 8

5 rotate to
replace 9

*The synchronised movements are simply default principles. Futsal players must react to
events on court. But the idea is to create three options for the player on the ball at all times,
with a view to exploiting space to play forward whenever the chance arises.

BIBLIOGRAPHY

Balagué, Guillem *Messi* (Orion, 2013)

Bayle, Emmanuel and Clastres, Patrick *Global Sport Leaders: A Biographical Analysis of International Sport Management* (Palgrave Macmillan, 2018)

Belchem, John *Merseypride: Essays in Liverpool Exceptionalism* (Liverpool University Press, 2006)

Bellos, Alex *Eyewitness Travel Guide: Brazil* (DK, 2012)

Bellos, Alex *Futebol: The Brazilian Way of Life* (Bloomsbury, 2014)

Brachet, Jérôme *The Amazing Story of Futsal from 1930 to Today* (L'Union Nationale Clubs de Futsal, 2009): https://www.academia.edu/20997576/LUnion_Nationale_des_Clubs_de_Futsal_Present_The_Amazing_Story_of_FUTSAL_from_1930_to_today_Teacher_Tribute_Juan_Carlos_CERIANI_GRAVIER_1903_1996_

Burkett, Seth *The Boy in Brazil: Living, Loving and Learning in the Land of Football* (Floodlit Dreams Ltd., 2014)

Burns, Jimmy *La Roja: A Journey Through Spanish Football* (Simon & Schuster, 2012)

Caioli, Luca *Neymar: The Making of the World's Greatest New Number 10* (Icon, 2014)

Caioli, Luca *Neymar: The Unstoppable Rise of Barcelona's Brazilian Superstar* (Icon, 2017)

Calvin, Michael *No Hunger in Paradise: The Players. The Journey. The Dream.* (Arrow, 2017)

Cartwright, John *Football for the Brave* (M Press, 2008)

Cox, Michael *The Mixer: The Story of Premier League Tactics, from Route One to False Nines* (HarperCollins, 2017)

Cox, Michael *Zonal Marking: The Making of Modern European Football* (HarperCollins, 2019)

Coyle, Daniel *The Talent Code* (Arrow, 2009)

Cruyff, Johan *My Turn: The Autobiography* (Macmillan, 2016)

De Andrade, Marcos Xavier *Futsal: From Basics to High Performance* (S2C & Secco Editora, 2018)

Elliott, Tony and Woodage, Adam *A Modern Approach to Goalkeeping: Findings From Five Formats of the Beautiful Game* (Grassroots Goalkeeping, 2017)

Figueiredo, Vicente *A História do Futebol de Salão: Origem, Evolução e Estatística* (Não Disponível, 1996 [Portuguese])

Foot, John *Calcio: A History of Italian Football* (Harper Perennial, 2007)

Frost, Diane and North, Peter *Militant Liverpool: A City on the Edge* (Liverpool University Press, 2013)

Galeano, Eduardo *Football in Sun and Shadow* (Penguin, 2018)

Goldblatt, David *The Ball Is Round* (Penguin, 2006)

Goldblatt, David *The Game of Our Lives* (Penguin, 2014)

Grainey, Timothy F. *Beyond Bend It Like Beckham: The Global Phenomenon of Women's Soccer* (University of Nebraska Press, 2012)

Harris, Harry and Fullbrook, Danny *Wayne Rooney: The Story of Football's Wonder Kid* (Robson Books, 2003)

Hermans, Vic and Engler, Rainer *Futsal: Technique, Tactics, Training* (Meyer & Meyer Sport, 2010)

Hughes, Charles *The Football Association Coaching Book of Soccer Tactics and Skills* (Queen Anne Press, 1991 ed.)

Hughes, Simon *On the Brink: A Journey Through English Football's North West* (deCoubertin Books, 2017)

Hughes, Simon *There She Goes: Liverpool, a City on its Own – The Long Decade: 1979–1993* (deCoubertin Books, 2019)

Jankowski, Timo *Coaching Soccer Like Guardiola and Mourinho: The Concept of Tactical Periodisation* (Meyer & Meyer Sport, 2016)

Kittleson, Roger *The Country of Football: Soccer and the Making of Modern Brazil* (University of California Press, 2014)

Maestri, Anderson *Coaching Futsal: Understanding, Improving and Perfecting* (CreateSpace Independent Publishing Platform, 2012)

Martiño, Adri *Futsal from the Basics* (2018)

McTear, Euan *Hijacking La Liga: How Atlético Madrid Broke Barcelona and Real Madrid's Duopoloy on Spanish Football* (Pitch Publishing, 2017)

Pelé *The Autobiography* (Pocket Books, 2007)

Perarnau, Marti *Pep Confidential: The Inside Story of Pep Guardiola's First Season at Bayern Munich* (Arena Sport, 2014)

Physick, Ray *Played in Liverpool: Charting the Heritage of a City at Play* (English Heritage, 2006)

Ricardinho *Ricardinho: La magia acontece donde hay dedicación* (Córner, 2019 [Spanish])

Ronay, Barney *How Football (Nearly) Came Home: Adventures in Putin's World Cup* (HarperCollins, 2018)

Skubala, Michael and Burkett, Seth *Developing the Modern Footballer Through Futsal* (Bennion Kearny Ltd., 2015)

Sturgess, Peter *Futsal: Training, Technique and Tactics* (Bloomsbury Sport, 2017)

Syed, Matthew *Bounce: The Myth of Talent and the Power of Practice* (Fourth Estate, 2011)

Vialli, Gianluca and Marcotti, Gabriele *The Italian Job: A Journey to the Heart of Two Great Footballing Cultures* (Bantam, 2006)

Wahl, Grant, *Football 2.0: How the World's Best Play the Modern Game* (BackPage Press, 2018)

Williams, Richard *The Perfect 10: Football's Dreamers, Schemers, Playmakers and Playboys – The Men Who Wore Football's Magic Number* (Faber & Faber, 2007)

Williams, Tom *Do You Speak Football?* (Bloomsbury Sport, 2018)

Wilson, Jonathan *Inverting the Pyramid: The History of Football Tactics* (Wiedenfeld & Nicolson, 2018)

Wilson, Jonathan *The Outsider: A History of the Goalkeeper* (Orion, 2012)

WEBSITES

abc.net.au

as.com

bbc.co.uk

beinsports.com

bleacherreport.com

blog.seur.com/deporte

broganrogantrevinoandhogan.wordpress.com

bundesliga.com

coachesvoice.com

copa90.com

dw.com

elitesoccercoaching.net

fifa.com

footballqatar.com

france-futsal.com

futsal-times.com

futsalcorner.es

futsalfeed.com

futsalfocus.net
futsalplanet.com
futsalonline.com
gazetaesportiva.com
inbedwithmaradona.com
mappemonde.mgm.fr
maslsoccer.com
nlpfutsal.com
pasionfutsal.com.ar
pivotfutsal.com
soccertoday.com
skysports.com
theathletic.com
thefa.com
theplayerstribune.com
thesefootballtimes.co
uefa.com
usyouthfutsal.com
veja.abril.com.br

NEWSPAPERS/MAGAZINES/PODCASTS

Buenos Aires Herald (Argentina)
Blizzard (UK)
Daily Mail (UK)
Daily Mirror (UK)
Diario AS (Spain)
Diário de Notícias (Portugal)
Corriere della serra (Italy)
El Espectador (Colombia)
Forbes (United States)
FourFourTwo (UK)
The Guardian (UK)

The Independent (UK)
Lancashire Telegraph (UK)
La Voz de Tajo (Spain)
L'Equipe (France)
Liverpool Echo (UK)
Los Angeles Times (United States)
Mundial (UK)
New York Times (United States)
O Globo (Brazil)
Publico (Portugal)
Record (Portugal)
Sydney Morning Herald (Australia)
Tehran Times (Iran)
The Daily Telegraph (UK)
The Times (UK)
Veja (Brazil)
When Saturday Comes (UK)
World of Futsal podcast

ACKNOWLEDGEMENTS

THANKS FIRSTLY TO the book's editor, Tom Clayton, for the idea, persistence and judicious pruning of the manuscript; to all at Melville House for patient professionalism during the coronavirus pandemic, and the eagle-eyed subeditor/copyeditor Steve Gove. Thank you also to Oliver Munson, my agent, for the encouragement; to Mark Burns and Seth Burkett; and a nod to *Guardian* journalists past (Ian Cobain and Daniel Taylor) and present (particularly Miles Brignall and Adharanand Finn), for authorly advice, plus Andy Hunter, Marcus Christensen and Jon Brodkin for steers, and the *Guardian*'s archive supremo, Richard Nelsson.

Handily for a book on futsal, the other people who assisted me fit neatly into five categories.

Firstly, the world of futsal: I owe the *Guardian*'s own England international, Calvin Dickson, a debt of gratitude for many enlightening conversations – and putting theory into practice in our competitive *Guardian* futsal kickabouts. Doug Reed and Graeme Dell gave up time to help me cast the interview net widely. I learned much from dozens of interviewees, especially Mićo Martić, Marquinhos Xavier, Shahrzad Mozafar, Leo Higuita, Tachapat Benjasiriwan, Valerio Scalabrelli, Steve Harris and Keith Tozer. Special appreciation is due to Marc Carmona and Jordi Torras for hosting me at Barcelona; in Portugal, the same goes to Jorge Braz, Ricardinho, Rui Da Cruz, Bruno Henrique and the Benfica coaches. At the 2021 World Cup, Kris Fernandes, Miguel Rodrigo and Oscar García. In England, thank you to coaches at Helvécia Futsal Club and Escolla Futsal Club's Rodrigo Sousa, Gilberto Damiano and Cristiano Coelho (my first proper futsal coach), plus Escolla's guest coaches from the Brazilian Minas Tênis Clube, Diogo and Alisson. Sadly, not every conversation made the cut but all helped deepen my understanding. For helping me overcome the language barrier, *muchas gracias* to Doug Reed in England and *muito obrigado* to Leandro Afonso and the England futsal captain, Raoni Medina, at Helvécia, Leozinho Cruz, the goalkeeper coach at AFC Kairat in Kazakhstan, and of course, my teammate, Ricardo Medeiros.

Branching out to football: thanks to Alan Irvine and Roberto Martínez for their invaluable insight. I'm grateful for Roberto's generosity – and the help of Grant Best – in formulating the foreword. Likewise Maximilian Kilman's thoughts proved illuminating.

Thirdly, at the FA in England: as well as Graeme Dell, many players, coaches, educators and mentors deserve a mention, particularly Ian Bateman, Pete Sturgess and Mike Skubala (who opened my eyes to the grammar of the game, along with Daniel Berdejo-del-Fresno, on my Level Two course at St George's Park); thanks to Luís Mendonça and Pete Vallance for letting me sit in on Uefa B sessions; and to Peter Glynn, Lawrence Lok, Danny Fenner, Ian Parkes, Paul McGuinness, Tony McCallum, Tina Reed, Andy Ritchie, Luis Melville, Kevin England, Marc Forrest, James Barlow, Steve Punshon, Matt Fejos, Marc Birkett, Tony Elliott, Andy Reading and Matt Reveley. At a county FA level, Simon Wears at the Berks and Bucks deserves a medal. At Liverpool FA, thanks to Anthony Smith and Stuart Carrington for stirring reminiscences. I'm also grateful to scouse contemporaries of the 1970s and 80s for their thoughts, notably Sonny Phillips, Tony Ungi, John Connor, Joe Murray, Paddy O'Brien, Michael Doyle, John

Hennigan and the sage of amateur football on Twitter, Anthony Williamson.

The 'futsal family' in Reading is the fourth name on the appreciation team sheet: thank you to Simon Griffiths, Chris Ryman, Matt McFrederick, Dave Horkan, Antonio 'Carlos' Tavares, Sergio Cortés and Pedro Barroso. Fernando Silva and Rich Oxley at Reading Royals continue their influence. As a coach, I'm grateful to Sean Dirkin, Graham Coates and Paul Whitty for always getting youth matches on; and to my first mentor, Richard Tyndall, co-coach Stephen Moody, and the children I coached at grassroots clubs Whiteknights, Laurel Park and Woodley United – plus parents (especially Satwant Singh Brar, Andy Dykes, Steve Pearse, Laurence and Pietro Spanu, Elaine Boyd, Margaret Obonyo, Karen Arkwright, Ted O'Callaghan, Kevin Harrington and Chris Hartnell) for trusting there is a different way to go.

The fifth and most important 'player' in my starting five is my own family: snippets of healthy feedback were forthcoming from my sons, particularly Dominic, when discussing futsal. As well as playing in my team aged eighteen, my eldest son, Conor, also put a shift in transcribing hours of interviews. Thank you, boys. And to my brother, Tony, for toughening me up in street tussles over a ball. To Christopher West, my father-in-law, for reading draft chapters. Finally, there's the women in my life. Firstly, my mum, Kathleen, who actually played a bigger part in my obsession with football than my dad did. I owe my mum a lot. As I do my long-suffering wife, Emily, who inspired me to get the job done, challenging my thoughts with a history professor's insight and brutally honest questioning. Furthermore, her stoicism was remarkable once futsal emerged as a second sport in my life, on top of football. These words act as both my apology and an ode to her forbearance after futsal stomped rudely into our busy family life, leaving a footprint that forced her to adapt a stock refrain when I go on a bit. 'It's only football, no one cares,' she used to say. Now it's no longer 'only' football. There's futsal too. Thank you very much, Em.

ABOUT THE AUTHOR

JAMIE FAHEY is a *Guardian* journalist and production editor with more than twenty years' experience on several national newspapers and six years in regional journalism. Consumed by football – and later futsal – since childhood, he graduated from street football in Liverpool to play semi-professionally in the north of England and Wales as an adult, and is an award-winning grassroots football and futsal coach with a coach mentor role at the FA. He is the *Guardian*'s primary reporter on futsal and considered a leading voice on the sport. His website is futsalstreetspot.com. *Futsal: The Indoor Game That Is Revolutioning World Soccer* is his first book.